TENNIS LIFE

Player Stories, Insights and Lessons Learned,
From Junior to Pro Player to Coach

Ward Snyder

Copyright © 2022 Ward Snyder

No part of this book may be reproduced, or stored in a retrieval system, or transmitted in any form, or by any means electronic, mechanical, photocopying, recording, or otherwise, without express consent of the author.

All rights reserved

ISBN: 9798449104335

Cover Design by Robin Elder

For Daniel Kraft, my mother's brother. One of the kindest, gentlest, and warmest people that I have ever known. His incredible passion for tennis manifested itself whenever he stepped onto the court.

And for my lifelong friend and sidekick, Rick (Dick) Quinby. You had an amazing passion for life, adventure, and tennis, my dear friend. Taken from this world way too early, you will forever be in my thoughts.

CONTENTS

Introduction v

Rob Castorri 1
Taylor Dent 11
Lawson Duncan 18
Larry Gottfried 26
Geoff Grant 35
Dave Grant 41
George Hardie 47
Andy Johnston 56
Noah Johnston 65
Chuck Kriese 71
Steve Krulevitz 83
Billy Martin 93
Fernando Maynetto 103
Ricky Meyer 112
Evan Phillips 119
Keith Richardson 131
Laurie Fleming Rowley 141

Bunner Smith 147

Harold Solomon 155

Mike Sprengelmeyer.....................................173

Chris Sylvan 184

Trey Waltke 194

Robbie Weiss...202

Sophie Woorons, Ph.D. 209

The Author's Story 216

Tennis Life in Pictures..................................232

One More Thing...246

Acknowledgements.......................................248

About the Author 250

INTRODUCTION

Tennis. Once you get hooked on this wonderful sport, there is no denying the adrenaline of stepping onto the court, day in and day out. It can happen to anyone at any age and when it does, you have engaged yourself in the addiction that I call what else? Tennis life. The physical, social, competitive, and mental aspects of the game are hard to beat, certainly why many call it the sport of a lifetime. Whether you're a recreational player, junior player, tour player, tennis pro, or coach, you know exactly what I'm talking about.

At an early age, I knew it was the sport for me over any other. When I was just twelve years old, I was interviewed by a reporter for the Baltimore Sun after winning my first Middle Atlantic Boys Singles Championship in the 12 and Under division. I googled the article online recently, a grin spreading across my face upon reading the opening paragraph again for the first time in over 54 years:

To a nine-year-old boy who is the shortstop on a little league team, as well as a tennis player, having to make the decision to do one and drop the other is a dilemma tantamount to picking one friend over another. Ward Snyder picked tennis as his "best" friend and the selection of three years ago paid off yesterday as the Silver Spring, Maryland youth captured his first Middle Atlantic Boys Singles title in the 12 and Under division.

That win marked the beginning of a successful junior career, making it to Nationals numerous times by the time I was fourteen. To get that far, I had to be blessed with three things: athleticism, parents that supported my mission and great coaching—and I am thankful that I had all three. However, my later teen and college years would prove to be deeply disappointing. Looking back at my failures and what went wrong, I realize I could have benefited by getting advice from others like myself who came before me, who had failed along the way, even as journeymen and tour players. As the saying goes, hindsight is 20/20—that is one of the premises for this book and why I wanted to write it. To that end, and in the following chapters, you will receive seasoned advice and intimate looks back from many of the great players I came up with my junior and college years. Any player that has worked through the arduous process of climbing up the junior rankings, competed among the top divisions of the NCAA, and made it to the tour gets my vote as a talented player, even though most of them aren't household names. How were many of them able to crack the world's top ten, top twenty, top 100, or top 150? Their unique and valuable perspectives could provide beneficial advice and encouragement to the up-and-coming junior player in his or her quest to achieve future greatness. My contributors have been so kind and selfless to share their stories, whether successful or not, and with this vulnerability and honesty comes insight into what it takes to make or break it on the tour. Therefore, and without further ado, THIS is *Tennis Life*.

ROB CASTORRI

I was late to the junior tennis party so to speak and didn't start playing until I was 11 years old. Living in Ft. Lauderdale, not far from famed Holiday Park, my mom decided she wanted her kids to learn how to play. Our father wasn't so inclined, so my mom had to skim out of the tight weekly grocery budget to fund instruction from Jimmy Evert. Along with my brother, Rick, and my sisters, Alexis and Peggy, we alternated taking lessons with him. As I blossomed into a decent player, I also had lessons with Fred Fleming, father of junior prodigies, Laurie and Carrie Fleming. He taught a slightly more aggressive style than Mr. Evert's and equally productive. As was typical at the time, I learned to hit with an Eastern forehand grip, a slice one-handed backhand, and the conventional serve and volley. At such a ripe old age, my game was behind the others, but the good news is that I caught up quickly to my peers due to my added strength and maturity. They all had more experience, both in practicing and competitive competition, but it didn't take long for me to compete successfully. Although I began playing tournaments in the 12's and more in the

14's and 16's, I shared my time on the court with basketball once I got to high school. I played on the Cardinal Gibbons basketball team for most of the year and then a few months of tennis in the spring. With my mom coaching the girls' team, I had a natural reason to stay with my tennis, although basketball was more my preference back then. In fact, I earned All County Honors, my basketball prowess obviously much better at the time than my tennis prowess. But since I was only 6'3", it limited my future in hoops, and once I graduated from high school, tennis took front and center.

Post high school, I was offered a dual scholarship at Biscayne College, but chose to accept a full tennis scholarship to the University of Tennessee at Chattanooga. The big draw from me was Coach Bill Tym. Bill was a former tour player and knew the game as well as anyone I had ever met. Playing under his tutelage transformed my game. He emphasized statistics, strategy, three hard practices a day (which the NCAA allowed back then), discipline and toughness. We started each day with a workout before class, followed by an after-school session, then another one later that evening! He also advocated playing with an offensive attitude. That meant you played your game while looking for every opportunity to attack. In other words, play a defensive game with an offensive attitude. I excelled in his program, moving from the number four player to the number one player. I lost to several good players along the way, such as Charlie Ellis, John Sadri, and Fernando Maynetto, but recall taking them to three sets. Perhaps the most memorable college defeat came against Tim Davis in the NCAA Division II Championships' round of 16. There was a lot riding on the match, as the winner would make All-American status. Coach Tym even flew out for the important event. I hate to admit it, but the pressure and my worthy opponent got the better of me in a match that I really should have won.

My college career ended with a loss, earlier than expected, in my fourth NCAA tournament appearance. Because I had devoted so much of my energies over four years to win that event, I had every reason to be depressed. Instead, I remember getting up early the next morning to practice with Coach Tym, who'd had such a dramatic impact in my life, thinking this was the first day of the rest of my tennis career and hopeful about what it held for me. That attitude is what I'm very proud of and what earned me collegiate wins over players like Bruce Foxworth, being a four-time team MVP, and a two-time Division II All-American. After college, I began my teaching career back in my old hometown of Ft. Lauderdale, but I wasn't finished competing. I continued to improve my game, feeling that there was still a better tennis version of Rob Castorri, who just needed more time to learn and compete. Persisting until I succeeded was my motto and I was the captain of my own destiny. I began competing on weekends in different tournaments, especially a new amateur circuit called the Youth Tennis Federation circuit, as well as local USTA satellite events. Another factor that spurred my continual improvement were the many opportunities I had to practice with a touring pros when they'd come to town. Practicing with players like Brian Gottfried, Chris Evert, and Billie Jean King, was a common event for me while living in South Florida at that time. I remember going on an incredible 12 month run of winning 12 of 17 events I entered, earning the #1 men's ranking in the state. Having never been ranked higher than 24 in the state of Florida, this was a great achievement for me.

It was during an arranged session with a visiting touring pro that I had the most significant result for my career at that time. The year was 1980 and I would be practicing against the world number nine player, Harold Solomon. I was teaching tennis and running my tennis academy at The Gate, a racquet club in Ft. Lauderdale, while simultaneously coaching the tennis team at my high school alma mater. Harold contacted me about practicing and it was a great chance to work on my game with one of the world's best, who also just happened to be a good acquaintance. He came to The Gate, and there were a handful of interested spectators who gathered to watch, in what started out as a practice match but turned into a three-set battle. The pressure of playing someone with such talent was foremost in my mind—the thought of embarrassing myself in front of club members absolutely nerve wracking. Amazingly, not only did I give him a good battle, but I won! My serve and volley were on that day, and the confidence I gained from the victory, even if just a practice match, was huge. So much so, that shortly thereafter, it empowered me to give up teaching to pursue my dream of playing on the tour. Long story short, I went to Europe to play in the ATP satellites and after seven months, ended up ranked 660 in the world in singles and 420 in doubles—not good enough to pursue the tour dream, but validation that I was a decent player.

My less-than-optimal results during the pro circuit brings me to the subject of losses. I had way too many of them to dwell on any one in particular. But since the author asked me to, it seems I must pull a few out of the hat. I recall playing world number 49, Francisco Gonzalez, in the Hunger Project event in Ft. Lauderdale, losing to him in three sets. I also lost to very tough Spanish Davis Cupper, Sergio Casale, in three sets. Yet, with many tough three-set losses, there were also several victories, and all of them combined to help me become a better player and that's a positive that I will take.

One possible cause of such poor results? My occasional lack of self-control, and I'll give the reader some examples. I was playing the Italian Pro Circuit against a tough Romanian in the familiar third set. My opponent made a bad call, and I was pissed. I retorted, "If you're going to call that out, then you can have the match." Next thing you know, the chair umpire declared me in default and awarded the match to the Romanian. I argued in vain, the verdict continuing to be "you said it" from the umpire's lips. Wish I could say that was my only default, but my McEnroe-like bad boy temper continued to get the better of me.

It was in another first round match in Germany (in a state championship that I had a great shot of winning), that I played someone I had defeated soundly in the previous year's team finals. I hit two first serve aces in the first game. Both were called out. Upon the changeover, I showed my opponent the two marks and circled them, as there was no doubt in my mind that he had cheated me. I promptly took my racquet and threw it into the net in disgust. Wouldn't you know the tournament referee just happened to be nearby and defaulted me. It cost me a good chance at winning 10K—though ultimately it was my fault.

Last but certainly not least, is a story involving a good friend. At a tournament in Holland, I played doubles with native and buddy, Michael Shapers throughout the 4-week circuit. We both qualified for the Masters' event that was being played in Michael's hometown. Naturally, I got to stay with Michael during the event, and ironically, we had to play each other in the first round. In the first set of the match, I felt Michael had made some bad calls and I lost it yet once again. I left my racquet on the court to go in search of the tournament referee. The result was another default. Needless to say, I wasn't invited to stay with Michael ever again but thankfully, managed to repair our friendship years later.

Looking back at those unfortunate meltdowns, I think I was caught up in the pressure of supporting myself—poorly managing the challenges that lower ranked players such as myself faced. Earning the vital ranking points from wins would have eased the cash burden of expenses and entry fees. The pressure to do so boiled over in dramatic frustration, leading to costly defaults. Anger simply got the best of me. Here's an ironic side note. It was during those seven years of playing German league tennis, that I came up against a 16-year-old Boris Becker, the ninth ranked junior in the world. In winning that match, I recall a most interesting moment that came afterwards, when we were both in the locker room. I walked up to the dejected young junior, who had acted up a bit on the court, and remember telling him he was a great player who would be a champion one day, urging him to act more like a champion and not a punk. A year later, he was crowned Wimbledon champion.

Once off the tour, I had an intervention in my life that was nothing short of the hand of God, reaching down and taking hold of me. After the birth of our first child, Emily Brooke, I had the strongest urge to leave Florida to work as an assistant pro for the next most influential man of my life, Bob Mapes, at the HEB tennis center in Corpus Christi, Texas. To this day, that move made no sense for who I was and where my roots were in Florida. But it was there, under Bob's tutelage and God's timing, that I became the man I've been these past 40 plus years. My spiritual life changed in such a dramatic way, that I never looked at anyone and anything the same as I did prior. Thinking back on those early days of my young adult career, the achievements I had in rankings and wins were special for me, considering I played very few tournaments as a junior. However, they all paled in comparison to what had become important to me. I still had a strong competitive spirit that continued to drive my ambition and competitiveness, but the feeling of contentment had now entered my life—as a player, coach, husband, and father. I recall when playing in German league matches, the sudden realization that God had taken the bitterness of losing in competition away from me and replaced it with a peace about who I really was and what really satisfied me. Although tennis had become a huge part of my life, it no longer defined me. Nor did my successes or failures. During this time, my wife and I had our second child, Christian Castorri, and life couldn't have been any better.

By the late 1980s, I was living in Atlanta and proud co-owner/general manager of the Northside Athletic Club. It became the host facility for the inaugural event called the Atlanta Senior Invitational, a national tournament that's been running strong for 30 plus years. I was both the tournament director as well as a participant for several years. I soon found out that being preoccupied with the duties of running such a big tourna inadvertently helped to relieve my nerves, and it was here that I had a succession of wins over some high-quality opponents on three separate occasions—Horace Reid, Pat Dupre, Sal Castillo, Mark Vines, Toby Crabel. Pat Dupre reached the semifinals of Wimbledon and was the world's number 14 in 1980, while Mark Vines reached a career high ranking of 110 in 1982. Once again, these wins were confidence boosters, as they meant I could compete with these guys, and afterwards, I went on to win several significant senior tournaments around the U.S.

Now to the subject of junior tennis. If my adult-self could go back and give advice to my junior-self, this is what I would tell that hot headed kid. Develop toughness in all sorts of ways. I worked construction during two of my four high school summers, and this gave me a bit of a tougher side. For today's juniors, I feel they should work a job of some kind, preferably in a tennis related capacity, but even if at a fast-food restaurant—and make the best of it even if you don't like it. I believe in learning to become comfortable being uncomfortable. It's something you'll need to come to terms with if your goal is to be the best tennis player you can be. Develop your focus by using methods and techniques that will strengthen your mental abilities. I'm sure there are techniques you can find on YouTube that will help with that, like what my sister, Alexis, discusses in her book, *Mental Aerobics*. Since attitude is the only thing we control in life, and especially in competition, learning to have a positive attitude towards the things that happen to you is vital for success.

Whether you learned the game of tennis through a personal coach, an academy, or just plain competing, the two above mentioned concepts are of vital importance. For sure, a coach can help you develop skill sets that are necessary. Nevertheless, it's up to you to make them your strengths. Take Federer. Although he had good coaching early on, it's my opinion that his positive attitude towards the game and his desire to become the best made him the legend he is today. But if you find that you can't model your attitude after the great Swiss Maestro, find a way to be comfortable with your own unique personality and make the best of it. Don't misunderstand me. It doesn't give you the green light to be a jerk or antisocial. It just means that you're human like all the rest of us.

As far as nerves and how to handle them, it's something every athlete must tangle with, as it's part of the job. Although I must say the great ones rarely show them. Interestingly, I found that if I was preoccupied before a match, I would often perform at my best. So, I recommend that you find the state of mind that you need to perform at your best.

Finally, I suggest that anyone striving to be great at something conduct themselves with responsibility and humility, and that includes tennis. A junior who is fortunate enough to become a pro should always do just that. An example? Two legendary players that handled themselves differently in front of the public eye—Federer and Connors. I believe Roger understands that tennis is bigger than himself, and thus, the game deserves respect, especially while on court. In contrast, it appeared that Jimmy was more important to "Jimmy" (at least in his own mind), considering how he conducted himself on the court. Bottom line, always remember you are on a public stage, and do your best to earn respect for the sport and yourself—no matter how great you are.

Sad to say, my playing days are now over. As of this writing, I live in McLean, Virginia where I'm general manager of the Tuckahoe Recreation Club, and any hopes of competing nationally in the 65's hinge on my balky knee—the wear and tear it's suffered over the last five decades an issue. Looking back, I enjoyed competing against so many incredible players and regret that I couldn't close the deal in those close contests. I knew that I could compete physically, but the mental side of the game was my downfall in many ways. Thank goodness my wife, Ann, was always by my side to soften the blows. She accompanied me on the circuit, and the joy of traveling the world with the person I love made it that much more special. After the circuit, there were a few sweet gigs along the way, which included working for Ivan Lendl, Harold Solomon, and Stan Smith in differing capacities. So, I must say, reflecting on the good, the bad, the successes and the failures, and everything in between, it's been a truly amazing journey.

WARD'S SKINNY ON ROB

I've known Rob since we were in our early teens. Our lives have gone their separate ways, but when they intersect, and they often do, it's always great to see him. However, there's a side of Rob that was newly revealed to me in his chapter. Hearing him discuss his temper tantrums and resulting defaults on the circuit was a surprise, something that I've never personally witnessed. I've watched him navigate through the toughest senior field in the country to win the Atlanta Senior Invitational on more than one occasion. Never did I see Rob show any outward emotion or hear him say anything in disgust, which tells me he really did learn to reign in his temper.

Rob was certainly late to the tennis party, whether it was starting to play at an older age than most, or growing into a much better player through his college years. I have little doubt that he would have succeeded more on the pro circuit and would have made it to the tour, had he started earlier and had more advanced instruction. Jimmy Evert and the others at Holiday Park were exceptionally good, but possibly better suited instructors for the women's game.

I had the pleasure of playing Rob once while competing in Pompano Beach at the Broward County District Championships. It was the doubles finals, and a lot was at stake, as the winning team would earn direct entry into the state championships. Yours truly and my partner, Daniel Tauber managed to beat the higher ranked team of Rob and his partner, Craig Campbell. We ended up the second seed in the state championship, only to lose too early in the tournament.

Rob's practice match with Harold Solomon was quite interesting to me. If the reader remembers, I too practiced with Harold, but the outcome was much different. While Rob served and volleyed his way to victory, I got pinned at the baseline by Harold's phenomenal ground strokes. His technique of hitting the ball on the rise took time away from me and I pretty much got creamed. Guess one might say different strokes for different folks—Rob's outcome was a real positive while mine was a real letdown.

When it comes down to the quality of a human being, great father, husband and teacher, Rob is number one in my book. His advice to juniors comes from the heart and his strong beliefs. He has a sincere desire to help others and to see him instructing a student is inspiring—his passion and knowledge for our sport second to none. I hope you've enjoyed his story as I have. He may not have been a household name on the junior or pro circuit, but he's among the best in the country at his mature young age of 66. Provided his knee can rebound in the near future, it's a safe bet that you will see him at the top of the senior rankings yet once again.

TAYLOR DENT

There was no denying the game of tennis for me, my pedigree saw to that. My mother, Betty Ann Grub, is a former professional tennis player. Much of her success came on the doubles courts, to include reaching the final of the 1977 U.S. Open with partner, Renee Richards. She also played World Team Tennis for the Florida Flamingos. My father is former tour player, Phil Dent. In 1977, he reached a career singles high ranking of 12 in the world, was a finalist in the 1977 Australian Open (losing to Jimmy Connors) and won 25 doubles titles. He even had stints coaching Maria Sharapova and Michael Chang. Speaking of Michael Chang, it was around the age of ten that I watched him train with my father at our California home, motivating me to start taking my DNA seriously. A few years later, I decided my goal was to hold up the winner's trophy at a grand slam and that's when my father began coaching me in earnest. He said I was a natural, even with my serve. In 1996, when I turned 17, the decision was looming as to whether I should go to college or skip it to turn pro. I had numerous scholarship offers since I had finished my junior career reaching the semi-finals of Nationals at Kalamazoo. But I had other ideas. Keep in mind, that back in my day, one's career barely lasted past the age of 30. Thus, I felt the urgency to go out at once and make a living—and that's what I did. I started out playing the satellite circuit, eventually making my way into the main draw of major tournaments. In 2002, I won my first tour title in Newport. The following year, I would win three more titles to include the Memphis Indoors, beating future world number one, Andy Roddick. It appeared that I had finally made it and thought my teenage dream might come to fruition. For the next two years, I gave it my all at the four majors but never made it past the fourth round. I did however reach my singles career high of 21 in the world. Approximately six months after reaching that milestone, I looked across the court for the first time at a young Novak Djokovic, the meeting occurring at the Hopman Cup in Australia. If I'd only known at the time the greatness he would achieve and the icon he would become in the tennis world. I beat him handily in singles during that first meeting, as well as in mixed doubles a few days later—in hindsight, a pretty darn sweet career highlight. My partner, Lisa Raymond, and I went on to win the tournament and lift the Hopman Cup trophy.

But by early winter of 2006, back problems I'd been dealing with most of my adult life had become unbearable. I pulled out of a second-round match in Rotterdam that February and soon after, I was diagnosed with a broken bone. I was basically couch/bedridden with pain for the next year, nearly 23 hours a day. A few surgical procedures were tried during that time, but nothing helped. With no other alternative, I underwent a fusion in September of 2007. With support from my parents and my wife, Jennifer, I rehabbed from the surgery and worked on strengthening my core to help protect my back. It was February of 2008 when I realized I could make an official comeback and ironically, the first thing that came back wasn't the forehand, backhand or serve ... but my tenacity. Trust me when I say that competing again was a miracle. By 2009, I started notching some decent wins. Which leads me to what I feel is my most memorable win ever—the second round against Spaniard, Ivan Navarro, in the 2009 U.S. Open. I was fortunate to get a wildcard into the event, and to be battling on a grand slam court after all I had been through was nothing short of amazing. We played a long five sets. The stats showed that combined, we attacked the net a total of 255 times! And we hit so many hard serves into the net, that we tore the net buckle, causing play to stop for a five-minute repair. We both held match points. I remember having a set point in every set, but Navarro was a tough competitor, taking it to 11-9 in the fifth set tiebreaker. The last point? My backhand return of serve passing shot that landed softly in the corner for the winner and the match—the New York crowd went nuts! I'll never forget the joy I felt. In fact, so much so, that after shaking hands with both Navarro and the umpire, I asked the umpire for his microphone and shouted to the crowd, "You guys were so unbelievable, I love it here, let's go!" A few minutes later in the interview with Pam Shriver, she told me she had never seen anyone grab the umpire's microphone before and I replied, "I owed the fans that. They were my third leg and my backbone. The crowd just never stopped. They were there with me the whole time. The U.S. Open is such a unique experience for a tennis player. It's really unbelievable that I have the privilege to experience it." After that interview, I circled the court, touching hands with the crowd—twice. I think the word had gotten out about my back woes and long absence from tennis. And certainly, being an American in New York City didn't quell their enthusiasm.

In late 2010, I retired permanently from the tour so that I could be a full-time husband and father to our newborn son, Declan. However, not before recording open era fastest serve records in three of the four grand slams: 147 mph at the U.S. Open against Navarro, 149 mph at the French, and 148 mph at Wimbledon against Djokovic. The French Open and Wimbledon records are still intact as of this writing. Which reminds me of another fun one for the record books. When I won my first tour title in Newport back in 2002, my father and I became the first father and son to win ATP singles titles. It still holds to this day but watch out—Petr Korda and his son, Sebastian, could be around the corner!

I look back at my ten plus years as a pro and think my perspective on various aspects of the journey are worth sharing to the up and coming junior. The first bit of advice? Learn to play aggressively. And you need 10,000 hours of court time. That translates to four hours per day from the age of 10 to the age of 20—you can't out coach hard work. In general, I don't suggest playing up in age groups. While there may be less pressure to win, damage can occur to your game due to strokes breaking down by doing so. In other words, there tends to be a built-in excuse when there's less pressure to win, but that's not necessarily a good thing. Of course, there are exceptions if a junior is dominant in his/her age division. Then playing up makes sense. And if that's the case, beating your competition boosts your confidence and gives more credibility to your game and style.

When it comes to college—to go or not to go? In my younger years, the money was not there and since most players retired around the age of 30, the better option was not to attend college. Not so today. Due to a multitude of factors, I think everyone should entertain the idea of attending for at least one year. Tennis has grown in popularity and with that comes more lucrative prize money, endorsement opportunities, options to travel, the hiring of coaches, physios, et cetera.

As far as dealing with nerves and pressure, I always focused on what I could control. I suggest being loyal to your game—and do so with confidence. If I was loyal to my process, I was okay with missing shots. I was into rituals, that is sticking to and following my routine between points and then back to only what I could control. Yes, everyone gets nervous but manage it by focusing on some of what I just described. It worked for me.

What was my secret to making it on the tour? Once again, I was loyal to my brand of tennis and expected to be successful as a result. It didn't matter who was on the other side of the net because I always felt that I had puncher's chance by sticking to my game and executing. I didn't want to be a jack of all trades, but rather excel with my attacking game. Winning was not placed ahead of playing my game. My dad told me once, "There's not much sophistication attached to tennis. It's important to be solid but not necessarily with all your strokes. Certainly skilled though."

When it comes to regrets, I have one in particular. I might have adopted a different style of play had I predicted the game would change so drastically due to better racquets, strings, and slower surfaces. My game became difficult to execute because the players in the latter half of my career had far more firepower, thus their ability to hit harder return of serves and passing shots—from virtually anywhere on the court. This made my life tougher at the net and in effect, put more pressure on my ground strokes. Don't get me wrong, my ground strokes were certainly adequate. However, combined with the slower courts, they limited my ability to play the younger guys. When I was coming up, I learned to hit return of serves like my heroes, Becker and Sampras, and that meant relatively conservative shots with minimal topspin. Basically, I played it safe. I never prepared for what was to come ... how was I to know?

Reflecting on my tennis journey, I think my career high ranking of 21 was the best I could achieve considering my game. Although my forehand was a bit stiff, my backhand was steady and efficient, and I had a slice that enabled me to attack the net. My serve was the staple of my game and even so, I could have spent more time on hitting specific targets rather than blasting it in the 140-mph range. About not reaching my childhood goal to win a grand slam. I'd like to blame that on my back problems, as they caused me to lose nearly three years of prime playing time. Nevertheless, coming back for that epic Navarro match at the U.S. Open and the pure joy I felt after winning it, gave me tremendous satisfaction after everything I'd been through.

My tennis playing days are long gone but my passion to teach young up-and-coming juniors is what I now do every day, alongside my dad and wife, Jennifer, a former tour player herself. We run the Dent Tennis Academy, located at the Birch Racquet and Lawn Club in Keller, Texas. We instruct everyone, from beginners to pros on the tour. Our ultimate goal is to help players improve as much as they wish to improve, no matter the level. So, for now, I continue passing on my love of the game, knowledge, and experience to any and all enthusiasts coming through the academy—especially to those juniors with the big dream of making it on the tour. Perhaps one day, I can live vicariously through one of my students when they win a coveted grand slam!

WARD'S SKINNY ON TAYLOR

It was in 2018 when I first met Taylor. The event was a USPTA seminar in Nashville, Tennessee, and he was the featured guest. There were several exhibitors and after viewing their demonstrations, it was time to go court side with Taylor. I'll never forget the moment. He grabbed a few balls and proceeded to chat with the crowd about how to hit various serves. Suddenly, he threw up the perfect toss and hit a 130-mph missile, nearly jumping out of his Sperry Topsiders! The sound on the court was deafening, the perfection of his delivery amazing. He must have just gotten off the plane, as it was quite evident that he hadn't had time to change his clothes. He was wearing long shorts, a collared work shirt and the boat shoes with no socks. I thought it begged the question, what about warming up first? So, I asked him. He looked at me and calmly replied, "I don't need a warmup, it's all in the wrist." Having been the recipient of a torn rotator cuff due to lack of proper warm up myself, I was very sensitive to the damage one might cause this vital body part if not primed. But with Taylor? No worries whatsoever! After the demonstration, I told him that I'd personally witnessed the drama filled match between his father, Phil, and Harold Solomon in Washington D.C. I was surprised that he wasn't familiar with the contest, and I had the pleasure of giving him the interesting details.

It's amazing to think Taylor's longevity on the tour ran the gamut of who's who among the biggest names, from Sampras, Agassi, and Rafter, to the three greatest players of all time, Nadal, Federer, and Djokovic. When interviewing Taylor for this book, I asked him about his nerves before playing those tennis titans. His answer seemed profound. He replied, "I find it impossible to be a spectator and player at the same time. When I played, it didn't matter who was on the other side of the net. Any reputation or ranking that the opponent brought made no difference to me. I intended to play to win, always with the thought that if I could execute my brand, then the victory would happen. That helped to alleviate pre match jitters no matter the celebrity status across from me."

To those players lucky enough to attend the Dent Tennis Academy in Texas, I can't think of a better person, mentor, or coach than Taylor. With his dad and wife by his side, they collectively bring 50 years of experience and love for the game of tennis, to those with the passion for the sport. If I could have a junior do over, I'd seriously consider being taken under the Dent family wing for my coaching! A sincere thanks to Taylor for sharing his impressive story with *Tennis Life*.

LAWSON DUNCAN

I was born in 1964 in the town of Cullowhee, North Carolina. Ten years later, I was introduced to the game of tennis by my dad. I started out hitting on a backboard, then honed the rest of my skills with the help of my dad, even though he wasn't a tennis instructor per se. I was a good athlete even as a kid which helped. Particularly blessed with speed, the attribute ultimately evolved into one of my best assets.

I played junior tournaments, achieving rankings in my home state and nationally as well. My goal was to play on the ATP tour, the desire always foremost in my mind when practicing or competing. College was next on my plate and fortunately, there were some great opportunities for me. I was recruited by several top schools including Clemson, Stanford, Texas, Georgia, UNC, Tennessee, and Illinois. Being a member of the country's Junior Davis Cup team exposed me to some of the previously mentioned colleges and their respective coaches, thus I had a good idea what to expect.

However, it was a no brainer which one to choose—Clemson checked all the boxes. I had already developed a good relationship with Coach Chuck Kriese, as he was one of the coaches I ran into when traveling. After numerous letters, phone calls and visits with him, I signed a letter of intent for a full scholarship at Clemson in 1983. It was a blessing, since Clemson was a prominent school and Chuck happened to be one of the best coaches in the country.

Not every player could handle the workload Coach Kriese gave, but I welcomed every minute of it. He expected hard work both on and off the court, scheduled more matches than one can imagine, and knew the game well. I gained so much out of that first year under his leadership. Nevertheless, I cut the experience short due to my success as a player, and after making the NCAA finals in 1984, I left Clemson to join the ATP tour. The time seemed right for me, having won 70 matches that year. It was an NCAA record that I am still enormously proud of to this day. Interestingly, a year or two after I left Clemson, the NCAA instituted the rule limiting a player's number of practice hours and matches in a single season, and I was told it was because of me. Thus, I have a record that will never be broken—since nobody will ever win 70 matches in a single season again!

I began competing on the ATP tour the summer of 1984, lucky enough to get straight into the main draws since I had a high enough ranking. By spring of 1985, I'd reached the finals of three European tournaments, all within a month, and as a result, had earned my top world ranking of 47 by May. Interestingly, as significant as the wins in those three tournaments were, I can think of other tour victories that have special meaning too. Beating Johan Kriek at the 1989 U.S. Open in four sets. Playing unseeded in the 1989 U.S. Clay Court Championships in Charleston and beating Tim Wilkison in the semifinals (only to lose to fellow Clemson alum, Jay Berger, in the final). Another memorable victory came against Harold Solomon at the 1985 Grand Prix event in Washington D.C., where I defeated him convincingly, 6-3, 6-1.

One iconic player I managed to defeat three times was Guillermo Vilas, albeit late in his career, but still proud to take three from him. An honorable mention— I beat Ivan Lendl in an exhibition in Washington, D.C., and even though it didn't count toward rankings or records, it was personally satisfying to beat such a great champion.

Then there are those pesky losses. The one that stands out the most to me is the NCAA final in Athens, Georgia against Michael Pernfors, UGA's number one. Obviously, it took place in front of a highly partisan crowd. Going into the contest, I was brimming with confidence, since a few weeks before, I'd beat him handily in a dual match in straight sets. I started out too tentatively, unlike the first time I played him. I tried to make up for it by becoming overly aggressive and I paid for it. The NCAA crown eluded me that day, and it would be my only attempt at winning the exclusive title, as the tour was beckoning.

Another frustrating loss came in the semifinals of the 1988 U.S. Clay Courts in Charleston. I was up a set, two service breaks and 40-15 on Andre Agassi. Winning the next point would have provided a comfortable lead of 5-2 in the second. But Andre had something to say about my kick serve when serving up the next point. I thought I'd placed it in a good spot (the backhand corner), but Andre ran around it, standing way outside the doubles lines. He nailed an inside to inside forehand down the line for a winner. I was stunned and suffice to say, it spurred him on to a comeback victory.

The other tough loss came in the 1988 French Open in the round of 16 against Mats Wilander. This was a huge moment in my career as it was a coveted major, on my favorite surface, and an opportunity to go deep into the draw with a victory. It was a hard-fought battle, but Mats prevailed by the score of 7-5, 6-3, 6-2. Oh, how I wanted that one.

Discussing my toughest losses brings to mind the toughest players I ever played. Then again, it seemed everyone I faced on the tour was tough. But there were two players that just had my number. Thomas Muster, the tough Austrian clay court specialist was my biggest nemesis. I played him on four separate occasions and could never defeat him. We played a similar game, but he was just better at it, plain and simple. The guy played every point one hundred percent, never giving up. The other player was Kent Karlson. The reader may not be familiar with him, but this guy hit the ball harder and heavier than anyone I had ever seen. He was known by his peers in this regard, but always seemed to get injured and didn't cover the court as well as others. Nevertheless, he left a profound impression on me and though I played many greats in my journey, he was by far the toughest foe I ever faced.

So, what was my secret to playing on the tour? Being healthy is job one! No matter how great your game is, if your body is ailing, you have no chance for success. The physical stress on the body, coupled with the mental pressure will wear you out. To overcome both is essential and I prided myself on being in excellent shape at all times. Spending the year at Clemson was a significant help since Coach Kriese was a proponent of interval training, and I continued that method of training on the tour.

Of course, I would love to have been as great as Federer—then again who wouldn't? But I was good enough to win a lot of matches. Having a big shot and using my strength was key, the combination translating into my big forehand. I learned with a semi-western grip and an open stance, helping to achieve far more topspin than most. My athletic ability and speed afoot enabled me to patrol the baseline, enhancing my chances on just about any clay surface.

I managed nerves and pressure the way most players do today. My match preparation often took me away from the actual venue. At times, I would hire a taxi to drop me off in a park somewhere, so that I could relax and take my mind off the imminent pressure.

Whether a walk in the woods or a park, or to see the local sights, I liked to get away from it all to relax. And for me to be at my best required a good night's sleep. My strategy worked, keeping my nerves in check before a match. But once play began, a different set of issues would be the challenge. Like most players, a towel would always be nearby and usually hanging on a chair, wall, fence—anywhere near the baseline. Often, I would cover my head, close my eyes, and envision myself back at home in Cullowhee, on my favorite court.

I must share a couple of fun anecdotes from my time on the tour. The first ties back to my school days. I was considered fast and ran track for a time in high school. Kind of crazy, but I didn't even train with the team. I would just show up for the track meet and compete! I got to Clemson, where Coach Kriese would time our runs at the track, standing at the finish line with his stopwatch and clipboard in hand. One day, I set the record for his training program by running 400 meters in 50 seconds flat. My reputation for speed preceded me once I was on the tour, and I had a standing bet with the other players—$10,000 for anyone who thought they could beat me in a two-hundred-yard race, getting a ten-yard head start. I never had one taker but would have welcomed the challenge.

However, the story that comes to mind more than anything was the time I got locked out of my temporary home during the U.S. Open. I had ordered a pizza and salad from Ray's Pizza, and they came to my Manhattan digs much earlier than I expected. Just getting out of the shower, I threw on my underwear, grabbed my wallet and rushed to the front door. I had to go through another door before making it to the front door, and as I did so, I heard it swing shut behind me and lock! I quickly paid the gentleman, grabbed my food, and returned to the locked door. I had a small panic attack trying to find a solution. After doing everything I could to try to unlock it, I abandoned all hope. I placed a small rock between the front door and the sidewalk (so as not to get locked out of the house entirely) and proceeded to walk barefoot up the sidewalk, wallet in hand, wearing only my underwear. I finally got to a pay phone and dialed the police. It took about an hour and a half for them to arrive at the house, and then time to assess the situation and determine that I was for real. Once convinced, they contacted the local fire department. They arrived with a ladder, extending it along the wall and up to the second story window, which fortunately was open. I climbed the ladder, waved goodbye to the firefighters, and prepared my pizza as if nothing had happened. My kind friends, the owners of the house, were away for the week, and when they returned their first question was, "Did you have any problems?" I was reluctant to tell them what happened but inquired if they had ever experienced a problem with the door self-locking. They replied in the affirmative—that it happened all the time. It was then they informed me a key was hidden beneath the flowerpot! I just smiled. I never revealed to them what happened … until now in *Tennis Life*. I'm confident they will find it humorous, just as I continue to after all these years. To this day, I vividly remember the sound of the door locking behind me and later parading around downtown Manhattan in my underwear.

My advice to juniors:

- If you want to be a great player, then focus all your attention on becoming one and make it your obsession.
- Ride your strengths. I had a big forehand and used it as much as possible. Whatever your strength may be, practice it, work it nonstop, and make it your mission to wear your opponents out with it.
- Dedicate yourself at an early age. I committed myself to tennis and devoted my youth to improving and beating all comers. Start young and commit to it.
- Be ahead of the crowd. I like to think ahead of my peer group. Maybe play up in age divisions to expose yourself to bigger and stronger kids.

- Expose yourself to talented players. Always seek out the best competition and strive to overcome the challenges inherent with doing so. You will learn more from better competition. And if you lose to them, that's okay. It will just let you know what you need to work on.
- Tolerance for pressure. Develop this at an early age and get used to it. Playing tournaments, practice matches, high school and college matches all have the element of pressure built in. Embrace it and overcome nerves. Everybody gets nervous but learning how to handle it when young decreases the chances of having issues when you are older. That worked well for me.
- I can't imagine forgoing college. At least give it a try. It's entirely up to each individual when it comes to this very important decision. Picking the right school, with the right coach and in a geographic locale that suits your preference (not too far from home) is key. In my case, I had an incredible freshman year, and thus felt confident in leaving college to join the tour. However, everyone is different, and no one size fits all when it comes to college. If you do go to college, I can't stress enough your choice of coach, because you will spend more time with him than you probably did with your dad when growing up.

I played nine years on the ATP tour, never regretting one moment. It was my dream to play the best in the world —I did that and more. Though I hoped to win a major just like any other tour player, it proved to be a very elusive task. I had my shot at the French Open, but Wilander got the best of me. Sometimes, I just wasn't good enough and I am okay with that—such is life. Bottom line is, I got to play the sport I love and made a decent living at it. Now I have the pleasure of passing that love for the game on to others as a teaching professional. As of this writing, I'm the head teaching professional at the Crowne Plaza Resort in Asheville,

North Carolina, and enjoying every minute of it. It's been an amazing journey.

WARD'S SKINNY ON LAWSON

For Hall of Fame Coach Chuck Kriese to say Lawson is "The best athlete I ever coached" is a special accolade indeed. It speaks volumes since so many amazing players were recruited by Coach Kriese, and to put him on this pedestal –wow! Lawson's work ethic was known to be second to none. After four hours of practice during the day, he would often visit the backboard for another hour of hitting after dinner!

Lawson not only set the all-time singles match record at Clemson by winning 70 matches in one season, but he also set the record off the court for the fastest mile … four minutes, forty-one seconds. He took immense pride in his ability to move on the court, and evidently his movement off the court was quite remarkable as well.

I am especially impressed with Lawson's maturity at such a youthful age. As a freshman at Clemson, he was ahead of the pack in that respect, soaking in all that Coach Kriese had to offer and nearly winning the NCAA Championships at the end of the season in Athens, Georgia. He's a legend around the tennis complex at Clemson University. I've heard stories regarding his powerful forehand. Andy Johnston, another Clemson Hall of Fame Coach, and contributor to this book, said that after hitting with Lawson, "My arm was ready to fall off."

Thanks so much for sharing your story, Lawson. I'm confident aspiring tour players can learn volumes from your advice and experience. Your playing style was certainly ahead of its time. To crack the top fifty in the world and have wins over former top five players—well done.

LARRY GOTTFRIED

It's been a mere 59 years since I fell in love with the sport of tennis, first hitting when I was four. My brother Brian was already hard at work on the courts, showing promising signs of becoming an excellent junior player, while I batted the ball around, trying to emulate his every big brother move and stroke. From the moment I picked up a racquet, I always looked up to him and was ever so proud when he reached a career high world number three in 1977.

I soon started to practice just about every day. Safe to say, and if you happened to be one of the locals hanging out at Ft. Lauderdale's, Holiday Park, I most likely hit with you. Every day after school, my mom would drive me to the courts while I changed clothes in the car, barely missing a beat in the transition from school to tennis. I must admit that school was not my love, and of course I made it through—even earned a college degree at

Trinity. But hitting tennis balls against anyone and everyone would be the highlight of my existence during the first third of my life. Though my time was limited on school days, the weekend would be an all-day affair, starting with the earliest available court time until sunset, thus my routine throughout the junior years.

Holiday Park, being the home of the tennis playing Evert family, drew a lot of talent. I played against so many different gals and guys. The older men, who spent the winter months playing there, included Dick Fell, Bill Chick, Michael Hoffberger, and countless others, while the younger players consisted of a who's who at the legendary facility. I fondly recall playing with Rick Quinby, Al Gutman, Jeanie, Chrissie, John and Drew Evert, Brad Milton, Laurie and Carrie Fleming, and Ward, the author of this book.

I was fortunate to have the occasional lesson with Jimmy Evert, father of Chrissie and patriarch of Holiday Park (now called the Jimmy Evert Tennis Center). Mr. Evert was a proponent of hard work and consistency, and that was right up my alley. I relished the thought of not missing a ball, more than I ever did hitting a winner. Mr. Evert's philosophy obviously translated well to up-and-coming juniors, if one measures his success by the results of his famous world number one daughter. Speaking of world number one Chrissie, I'd like to mention something that happened a few times while I was employed as head tennis pro at the Tennis Club in Ft. Lauderdale in the early 1980's. Her father called me on more than one occasion to hit with his famous daughter. So, I would drive over to Holiday Park to work out with the number one female player in the world. After a few sessions, I received a check in the mail from Mr. Evert. I called him to let him know that I didn't expect a penny for my time, that I was perfectly happy to hit with her. Who wouldn't be? However, he insisted and wouldn't take no for an answer. He was certainly a class act.

In addition to the Holiday Park regimen, I was fortunate to have my big brother's coach, Nick Bollettieri, take me under his wing, inviting me to attend his summer camp in Wisconsin. I think I was around age eleven or twelve at the time. To soak in the knowledge from both Nick and one pro in particular, Andy Brandi, really helped build my game. Nick was the technical guy, and he'd spend many hours with me, especially on Sundays before the next group of campers would come in. I worked with several of his assistants, but it was Andy's tutelage that really resonated with me. During my time there, Nick took me to Amherst College where I was blessed to work with the Australian great, Harry Hopman. Mr. Hopman was the best trainer I'd ever encountered, and together with Nick, he helped me build a solid foundation. I'm especially grateful to Nick for his kindness and generosity in inviting me to spend a few summers with his incredible staff and associate professionals. He made an enormous impact with my tennis, and I'll always have fond memories of my time with him.

I played competitively throughout my junior career and managed to win the national 18 and Under championships at Kalamazoo in both singles and doubles, with John McEnroe as both my singles foe and doubles partner. I beat John in a five set singles final and then we teamed up to defeat the doubles team of Van Winitsky and Jeff Robbins. Winning the singles title gave me a wildcard into the U.S. Open later that summer, along with a wildcard for John and me in doubles as well. He and I earned an interesting statistic by doing so—we were, and still are, the youngest combined age to compete at the U.S. Open in the open era—I was 15 and he was 16.

I accepted a full tennis scholarship to Trinity University in San Antonio, Texas, attending from 1977 to 1979. Outside tournaments would be limited to my freshman and sophomore years. I earned a spot on the U.S. Jr. Davis Cup team, regarded as one of the top juniors in the country, but I wasn't terribly motivated by what most players consider an honor. I liked the practice and preparation much more than competing in the tournaments. During that time, I attained a world ranking of 208, but knew that wasn't good enough. I also wanted to stay in school to pursue my degree and enjoy the college experience. I remember discussing my misgivings with my brother, and the question of when to give up school and join the tour. Brian assured me that I would know when it would be the right time for me. Interestingly, I can't say there was ever a right time for me, as I wanted to play on my own terms and not play full time on the tour. I found that I could never really embrace the travel, hotels, planning, and commitment to a tour lifestyle and consequently, didn't perform well in some of the events.

Now to the tour itself. The author asked me to talk about my most memorable wins. Well, my wins are not really something that I think about since I am more interested in my losses. As crazy as that may seem, it's just the way I'm wired. However, here goes! I would say the best win of my career was in 1977 in South Orange, New Jersey, when I beat world number ten, Wojtek Fibak, in the round of 32. Unfortunately, I couldn't follow up that win, losing a close match to the South African, Ray Moore, in the next round. Another notable victory for me came in the 1976 U.S. Open, when I faced Australia's, Colin Dibley. I was just 17 and Colin was expected to make quick work of me. I won the match, 7-6, 6-3, recording my first win at Forest Hills. The victory earned me the cover and feature article for the May 1977 issue of Boy's Life Magazine. Last but not least, a memorable win for me came in the Rice Invitational event in Houston, Texas. I won the tournament, defeating Dan Valentincic in the final. Even more special was the headline in the sport section of the newspaper which stated something like "Gottfried brothers win two tournaments". Brian had coincidentally won his tour event at River Oaks, and for both of us to win on the same day was a wonderful moment for me.

As I stated earlier, the losses meant more to me than the wins and I know the reader is asking why. Because I'm amazed that I was able to compete with some of the all-time greats, even though I didn't beat any of them. In fact, so much so, that I think it's incredibly cool I was victim number six to Guillermo Vilas, who won 46 consecutive matches in 1977! From my perspective, I was living the dream and to actually play against the greats of the time? Well, it was just incredibly surreal in my mind. Winning wasn't everything to me, and perhaps that was one of the reasons I didn't last long on the tour.

A few of my more interesting tour losses? The first one occurred playing with partner, John McEnroe, in a doubles match at the 1977 Washington D.C. tournament. We faced the number one team in the world, Fred McNair and Sherwood Stewart. I was basically content to be out there competing against this great team, while John on the other hand, was adamant that we could and would beat them. We ended up having a match point but came up short. The loss was heightened for me because we would have faced my brother and Raul Ramirez in the next round. To have faced Brian in a tournament would have been incredibly special indeed.

The other memorable doubles loss occurred again with McEnroe when we earned the wildcard into the U.S. Open after our win at Kalamazoo. We played one of the best doubles teams in the world, the Australian duo of Phil Dent and John Alexander. I remember being really excited about taking one set in the loss, while John was absolutely bummed in defeat. But to witness his focus and determination to win regardless of the pedigree of the opponents, speaks volumes about the great Johnny Mac and what he later achieved on the tour.

Looking back, do I have any regrets? The answer is an emphatic yes, regarding one particular issue. I was too hard on myself and wished that I could have enjoyed the experience more than I did. Take someone like Roger Federer. When I watch him play, he seems to enjoy virtually every aspect of the game. He appears to genuinely embrace the press conferences, the autograph signing, the pressure packed tournament play, the travel, et cetera. I wish I could have been more like that. For example, I never took the time to enjoy the beautiful mountains of North Conway, New

Hampshire when I was there for an event, putting myself through self-inflicted pressure, as if my matches were a win or die scenario. I rarely took time to see the sights that were so accessible, spending most of my time around the tennis venue at any given tournament.

Now to my advice for anyone coming up through juniors. First and foremost is to keep it fun. Enjoy the experience of both winning and losing. I'm a proponent of hard practice and lots of sets and drills, with the primary focus being on consistency. Don't neglect your weaknesses. Dedicated practice with the help of professional guidance breeds success in later years. I had a great coach at my alma mater, in Bobby McKinley at Trinity University. I can't stress enough the importance of having someone like him. Bobby told us to always have a Plan B, a strategy that I didn't employ enough. My comfort zone was the baseline and though it worked fairly well in college, I needed to spend more time working on my weakness—the serve and volley. The emphasis on winning matches can sometimes take away from your ability to grow as a player. Yes, winning is especially important, but one must put that concept in its proper perspective, as developing a Plan B is equally essential when Plan A is not working. Had I heeded Coach McKinley's advice, I'm certain my few years on the tour would have resulted in more victories. All that being said, the successes I did produce prior to and during the brief stint on the tour, were mostly due to my strong backcourt game. I hated to make errors and found it more rewarding to play with consistency rather than going for winners. I developed a better backhand than forehand due largely in part to my on-court sessions with Nick Bollettieri and Andy Brandi. The backhand was my foundation, my very long backswing key in turning it into a weapon. I also have the great Aussie, Ken Rosewall, to thank. He had a phenomenal slice backhand. I would study his stroke from frame to frame using my "flip book" the ingenious use of bound paper before the invention of the video camera. If flipped quickly enough, it would appear as if it were a video rather than the compilation of still shots.

I would be lax if I didn't touch on the player whom I most admired—my brother, Brian. He was and will always be my role model, in both tennis and life in general. He had an amazing career with 25 tournament singles titles and 54 doubles titles. My strokes may have mirrored his, but I couldn't produce them with the same success. Nevertheless, I'm satisfied with that. He even employed me for one year. I traveled with him, organized his schedule, and practiced with him on occasion. We both enjoyed the arrangement, as well as the time spent together, but I felt the need to go out on my own, which I did.

I had a wonderful ride—through juniors, college and beyond. To recap, I didn't have the success on the professional tour like I had in my earlier years. However, I think back fondly to the tournaments I played around the world; the wins, the losses, and all else associated with my journey. My playing days have long been over but teaching as I do at the Boca Raton Resort keeps my tennis alive and well, and I couldn't be more content. Best of all is the enjoyment I get from teaching my students how to become better players.

I hope having shared my experience might in some way benefit the reader, whether you're an up-and-coming junior, league player or recreational player. There is no doubt—tennis has been the sport of my lifetime and I wouldn't have had it any other way.

WARD'S SKINNY ON LARRY

Larry and I go back over fifty years, to those golden days at Holiday Park, where we had the privilege of keeping company with an elite group of up-and-coming players. Even as a young kid, Larry was well mannered, showing amazing sportsmanship beyond his years. He also possessed a very solid backcourt game early on, that only got stronger with age and maturity.

Seems crazy thinking about it now, but surprisingly, we played each other only one time in actual competition. It was at our high school match in Broward County, pitting Ft. Lauderdale High School against Northeast High School. Both of us were playing the number one position and scheduled to play after school on a Tuesday. We played a practice match the day before, with Larry beating me soundly. In the high school contest, I would go on to play one of my best matches, defeating Larry in two sets. I remember him shaking his head, as we both knew he was the much better player. Nevertheless, for some unknown reason, I was able to elevate my inferior game that day to defeat him. At least it was a fun memory for one of us. The day after the match, we played again, and he turned the tables, beating me with relative ease.

Years later, after we had gone our separate ways to college, I ran into him. My team from Clemson journeyed to Texas to compete in a stellar field of top universities from around the nation. I clearly remember the depth of the field, and the guy still standing at the end was none other than Larry. He ran through the gamut of players to the final, defeating a particularly good opponent in Dan Valentincic, by the convincing score of 6-2, 6-2. I recall each point being hard fought, but it was Larry who prevailed with the easy victory.

As previously discussed by Larry, he didn't like dealing with the complexity of tour life and tournament schedules. Having witnessed him in action while working as the head professional at the Tennis Club in Ft. Lauderdale years ago, I can attest to his claim. One day, I had the pleasure as a spectator, to watch Larry and brother Brian, take sets off Harold Solomon and Wojtek Fibak. I remember asking Larry, "Why don't you go out on the tour?" He replied in a very matter-of-fact manner, "I like to play when I like to play, and that would be on my schedule only."

I feel blessed to have known Larry all these years. He has led an exemplary life both on and off the courts. There is little doubt that he could have achieved so much more had he wanted to, but his chosen path did not include the grind that is required for success. He is quite content with his body of work, as he should be. But don't let that fool you for one minute. His passion for the game is evident in his every word, and to hear him speak about his tennis journey with such modesty would impress anyone who has the pleasure of meeting him. Remember, he takes more pride in relishing his losses to the top players, rather than relishing his wins, like when he turned the tables on Fibak, the world number 10!

Larry Gottfried is the epitome of a gentleman player—he is genuine, polite, and salt of the earth. I'm so grateful for his candid contribution to this book and his enduring friendship. Thanks, my friend!

GEOFF GRANT

It seems I was destined to play high level tennis from the womb, since both of my parents were passionately involved with the sport before I was even conceived. When I was four years old, my dad was busy giving tennis lessons in a housing development in Florida. He had also started running a satellite tennis circuit for young pros ranked 150 or greater—to give them a chance to get experience and gain points to compete at the ATP level. It was called W.A.T.CH. (the spelling/punctuation is correct), which stood for World Association of Tennis Champions, the first of its kind in the world. My older brother, Kevin, and I, would help our father pick up balls during W.A.T.CH. tournaments. We were always surrounded by players, several even staying at our house. During his free time, Dad would hit with me, and that's when my interest in tennis really took off. So much so, that I started hitting nonstop against the garage door. There would be times when my parents would have to drag me in for dinner because I'd be self-absorbed in a make-believe match, against either McEnroe or

Borg, in the tiebreaker of the fifth set, determined to remain undefeated against them both. And I did! That's the advantage of being a six-year-old kid, right? Tennis truly brought our family together. At the same early age, my dad and I would play against my mother and brother. The court time together didn't last long as we got older and better, but it was a lot of fun while it did.

My father continued to coach me for the next several years. Before I knew it, I was ranked nationally at age 11. We were living near Pittsburgh, Pennsylvania at the time. My father was working for Penn Athletic Company, so my mother would take me to all our tournaments. There would be occasions when there were limited vacancies at motels, and creative solutions to the problem were the order of the day. I remember this one time when we traveled from Pittsburgh to Ohio for 14 and 16 and Under events. Along with myself, my brother, and my mother, we were accompanied by another mother and her two sons. There was only one room available at the local motel, so of course we had no choice but to crash together. Two double beds and only one rollaway bed would force one person to sleep on the floor. Our mothers wanted us to get the best night's sleep possible, meaning one mother would have to sacrifice her quality of zzz's. Well, not surprisingly, it was determined that the carpet was rather nasty. The other mother, who was much smaller in stature than mine, insisted on sleeping in the bathtub as she had done at another tournament. The things parents will do to give their kids the best chance for success! Mine certainly did throughout the years and I will forever be grateful.

Eventually, we moved to Sudbury, Massachusetts and my time playing at Lincoln-Sudbury High was limited due to constraints caused by my commitment to play in New England, as well as national tournaments. As a result of playing in the sanctioned tournaments, my ranking continued to rise. I reached the number one ranking as a 17 and 18-year-old in New England and the number eight ranking nationally as an 18-year-old. Upon graduation from high school, I accepted a full tennis scholarship to

Duke University. After attaining All-American honors and a degree in political science in 1992, I moved to Tampa, got to train with the likes of Pete Sampras, Andre Agassi, and Jim Courier, and got my first ATP point at the age of 23. I played on the tour from 1994 to 2000. The highlight during those years? When I reached the third round of the U.S. Open in 1998. I beat Javier Sanchez in the first round and then the Russian number one player, Andrei Medvedev, in the second round. In the third round, I was to face German, Oliver Gross on the grandstand court. My nerves were rattled just thinking about playing on grandstand and to make matters worse, my childhood hero and garage door opponent, John McEnroe, was set to call the match for television. It was almost too much for me to handle. But I managed to shake off the demons, long enough to lose the match to Oliver in five sets. Despite exiting after the third round, I believed I had finally made it on the tour and proceeded to reward myself with a pricey Tag Hauer watch. My tour ranking of 109 in 1999 provided my entry into the Australian Open, where I lost in the first round to Australia's best and number one seed at the time, Mark "The Scud" Philippoussis. For you youngsters, he was given the nickname the "scud" due to his go-for-broke style built around his serve, earning him the nickname in homage to the missile by the same name. Though it was satisfying to make it to the big stage against the Scud, playing him in a packed house on opening night was going to be darn intimidating. Having just flown 20 hours, with no coach, no friends to go with me, spending an exorbitant amount of money for the travel, room, and board, I was off to a rocky start. Then I had to wait all day, giving me too much time on my hands and thus the nerves took over. Add a hostile setting with rabid Aussie fans and the stage was set for the unfavorable result. However, I learned a lot from playing Philippoussis and continued to hone my game. Unfortunately, I never won an ATP event. I did however reach the finals of the 1998 Winnetka, Illinois Challenger, beating a young Lleyton Hewitt along the way. But the demanding work required to rise up the ladder was slowly taking its toll on me. I'd spent my life chasing the dream—falling short on the tour and the ever-worsening fatigue reflected in my dwindling bank account.

Enter Mark Keil, an ATP player who decided to film himself and others during the 1999 tour. On a lark, he showed me his footage and I had an idea—to make a behind the scenes documentary of ourselves and fellow journeymen. If I was soon to retire, why not make the last hurrah a memorable one? So, Mark and I teamed up as doubles partners and in January of 2000, I grabbed a camera, and the film, *The Journeymen*, was a go. A Sports Illustrated article described our documentary as "having the feel of a party video being shot by two well-heeled frat boys". We were okay with that since our goal was to entertain with a rawness and honesty not usually seen inside the professional tennis world. We played matches in Hawaii, California, Denmark, and Florida, crossing paths with, and interviewing the likes of Andre Agassi, Goran Ivanisevic, Mark Philippoussis, Boris Becker, Patrick Rafter, and Jim Courier. I did the bulk of the filming, capturing both laughter and bouts of frustration—from Mark mostly, in locker rooms and hotel rooms, at parties and at the stadiums. The tour had not been kind, the losses mounting for us both. By the end of March, we found ourselves in Miami for the Lipton Masters. We literally begged for a wildcard to get into the doubles qualifying and received one. Mark played well, but I struggled immensely. I hadn't been practicing and it showed. Burned out, the 6-0, 6-3 loss was my swan song—Mark turned the camera on me so that I could announce my retirement from the tour. My career earnings totaled $351,932.00. It sounds like a lot for back then, but considering the expenses associated with traveling the world for six years, it was a pittance. After my retirement, I took a job with a prominent hedge fund. A year and a half into the chaos of the financial world, I realized how much I missed a life revolving around tennis. I quit my job and started coaching in New Jersey. I also enjoyed a brief stint as color commentator and host for The Tennis Channel and the U.S. Open. I've spent the last 11 years as Director of Tennis and General Manager of Tenafly Racquet Club in Tenafly, New Jersey, home of the CourtSense Tennis Training Center.

So, if I could go back in time, would I have done anything differently during my tennis heyday? Most certainly. Let's start with my backhand. Rather than the two hander which was most prevalent at the time, I feel that a topspin one hander would have given me more variety and I regret not trying it early on. Then there's the fitness aspect. It's crucial, and though can be costly, is imperative for players today. My biggest regret? Making the choice to go to Duke University. I had college options on the West Coast but chose to be closer to home. Looking back, perhaps the conference, schedule, and coach were not the best for me.

My recommendations for up-and-coming juniors are analogous to my regrets. The two-handed backhand is important even though I personally wish I'd had a topspin one hander. Starting around the age of 12 is the optimum time to develop the one hander (due to lack of developed strength prior to that age, the two hander makes the most sense). I also advocate cross training to improve physical fitness and develop athletic skills. Even though talent can shine through without it, inevitably in a long and hotly contested match, it's the person with the highest fitness level that will most likely end up on top.

In closing, I must say it's been an unforgettable journey for me. Few guys can say they trained with Pete Sampras, Andre Agassi, and Jim Courier, but I can! And considering all the unforgettable characters and adventures I experienced along the journey—it's been an amazing and memorable tennis life.

WARD'S SKINNY ON GEOFF

Upon taking on the shared duties as head tennis professional at Keowee Key in Salem, South Carolina, I became acquainted with avid tennis members, Dave and Suzanne Grant. After getting to know Dave, it didn't take long for him to start talking about his sons, Geoff and Kevin, and their advanced tennis prowess—especially Geoff's. I listened intently out of sheer respect, taking his words with a grain of salt. Before I knew it, the boys were coming to visit their parents, and Dave asked that Brad (the other head pro) and I take them on. Thus, the stage was set, and the match played on a beautiful autumn day. Thankfully, there weren't many spectators in the stands—because it was ugly! I can't recall the score but just holding our serve was an accomplishment. Both Geoff and Kevin showed talent way beyond ours. Yes, I had been forewarned and shame on me for dismissing Dave's familial scouting report. I was certainly left eating humble pie for dessert. I should have done my homework on the internet where Geoff's records could easily have been accessed. The only positive occurrence that afternoon was that post-beat down, Geoff and I teamed up to defeat Kevin and Brad. But to be quite honest, our victory had little to do with my side of the court. I'm proud to say that my friendship with Geoff's parents remains as cordial as ever, and to observe Dave and Suzanne on the courts at Keowee Key gives those watching a glimpse into the reason why their son had so much success during his tennis journey.

Though several years have passed since his days on the ATP tour, Geoff has certainly maintained his game and he continues to do so working with up-and-coming juniors in New Jersey. He came close to becoming a household name, but other than perhaps the notoriety of his cult classic documentary, The Journeymen, he fell short. After witnessing his power, solid stroke production, and speed, I can only imagine what a fierce competitor he must have been in his prime. My sincere appreciation for Geoff "The Journeyman" Grant's contribution to *Tennis Life*!

DAVE GRANT

It just so happens that I'm the father of Geoff Grant, the player you just read about. As he said, his DNA pretty much dictated that he and his older brother, Kevin, pick up a tennis racquet. Their grandfather played and taught me the game when I was growing up in Wisconsin. Throughout my younger years, I never really had a chance to play competitively, mostly just recreationally. That is until I started competing later in life. When Geoff was in college, I was New England's number one ranked player in the 50 and over division. Geoff's mother, Suzanne, is also a lifelong avid tennis player. As one can imagine, our household and dinner conversations pretty much revolved around the sport, and it became a real focal point for us. Tennis brought us together as a family on and off the court.

When Geoff and Kevin were four and seven respectively, the World Association of Tennis Champions, aka W.A.T.CH., was taking off in Florida. It was the forerunner to challengers and futures tournaments. A year after Larry Turville and Armstead Neely set up this new and exciting tennis circuit, I got very involved, becoming the Executive Director. I felt there was need for college players to earn some money before hitting the big stage, and in the process, attain valuable ATP points, giving them a chance to break out onto the tour. A successful player on the W.A.T.CH circuit could earn enough money to get by, while at the same time, developing his skill set in tough competition. Or in other words, aspiring players could simultaneously gain confidence with wins, ATP points, experience, and a little cash. About 800 players ended up competing on W.A.T.CH, which ran between 1971 and 1978. And they weren't all Americans either. There were players from 39 other countries. Each player had to pay a one-time fee of $25 and a $15 fee for each qualifying tournament. The circuit ran every winter/spring for five to ten weeks, offering total prize money of $5000 per event. The winner of each event would take home between $3000 to $4000. Players of note that ultimately graduated from W.A.T.CH were: The founders, Larry Turville and Armistead Neely, Keith Richardson, Tim Gullickson, Rick Fagel, Alvaro Betancur and Joaquim Rasgado. There were other benefits of our circuit as well— those for the spectators. Unlike bigger tournaments, they had easy access to the players. They could also take part in singles and doubles clinics with some of the players, the women one day and the men and kids another day.

After W.A.T.CH was taken over by the USTA, an opportunity presented itself which I couldn't turn down, one that still involved the fuzzy yellow balls—quite literally. I accepted the job as President of the Penn Athletic Company in Pittsburgh, better known as the company that manufactures Penn tennis balls. While there, I made the wise decision to have "Pennsylvania" shortened to just "Penn" on the cans. Penn balls also became the official tennis ball of the French Open while under my watch. And as President of Penn, I was fortunate to take my family to the 1983 French Open, and even more fortunate to be invited to sit in the

President's box. After my stint at the company, we moved to Massachusetts so that I could start my own sports marketing-consulting firm. Once Geoff went off to college in 1988, I started playing in competitive tournaments around New England. That's when I earned the number one ranking in the region's 50 and older division. I even made the round of 16 in a national 50's tournament in New Jersey. During my run for the 50 and over tennis glory, Kevin and I played in several father-son tournaments, making the consolation of a national grass court final, and earning the top five ranking twice in New England.

Speaking of Geoff and Kevin again, it was great that they had each other to practice with growing up. However, as the years went by, it was clear who was the better player and Kevin took it in stride. He knew the national rankings didn't lie and even though he was ranked in the top ten in his section, as well as the U.S., Geoff had the better numbers and was always ranked among the nation's top five players during juniors. I would say I attribute Geoff's success to a few factors. Firstly, he had tremendous hand/eye coordination. Suzanne and I discovered that at the tender age of three, Geoff could catch every ball I threw to him. It was then that we knew he had special talent. Also, in those days, there were less distractions since high tech video games, cell phones and the internet had not yet been born. Even the TV had a finite number of channels. That helped spur on Geoff's numerous imaginary games against Borg and McEnroe against the garage door. I'll never forget the day he finally beat me. It was not a bittersweet moment but a sweet one. The score was 6-4, 6-4 and it was one of the happiest days of my life.

When it comes to college, every talented tennis player has a decision to make—relative to either foregoing college, going to school for a year or two and then joining the tour, or staying in college. In Geoff's days, the option of going for a few years and then returning after playing on the pro tour was not available. Geoff felt compelled to get a good education at Duke while simultaneously playing formidable competition at the number one position. I think he improved a lot in his four years there and he probably wasn't ready to turn pro like so many of his peers. In effect, guys like Sampras and Courier had a head start while my son, at the ripe old age of 28, had pretty much had enough. I can honestly say as his father, that the most enjoyment I ever experienced in tennis was to see Geoff in action on the big stage. Suzanne and I knew he had special talents. Although I'm sure it appears that way, Suzanne and I didn't emphasize his participation in tennis since he excelled in baseball as well. Ultimately, it was his love for tennis that propelled him to success, and boy was he ever so close to winning that fifth set versus Oliver Gross at the U.S. Open. The match on grandstand was the pinnacle moment in his career and to see the sparse crowd grow to standing room only was truly memorable. As Geoff's coach and dad, I knew he should have won the match. Nonetheless, he gave it his all and became a truly great player in my mind.

If I was given a redo with my sons and tennis, what would I do differently? I would encourage them to spend a week or two at a major tennis academy for better training and competition. I firmly believe in different voices and perspectives—that might have made a significant difference in Geoff's career. Though the cost of doing so at the time was expensive, I certainly would have done it had he asked. I did the best I could with my limited financial resources. But I'm still proud of my sons. I've played with them both in the National Father and Son tournaments, winning four silver and five gold balls along the way. In 2019, I won a silver medal with Geoff and a bronze medal with Kevin. Just this year, Geoff and I played the nation's best team in nationals and lost in a third set tiebreaker.

My perspective on the decline of American men's tennis comes down to a couple of reasons. I think due to so many other team sports, our players have more options than foreign players. Team sports begets mediocre talent for the most part while playing an individual sport like tennis requires much more out of an athlete.

Perhaps Americans have gotten lazy. I don't know for sure but there's no doubt that we have a void in the top tier of the world rankings. Case in point, during the W.A.T.CH circuit, 11 of the top 20 players were foreigners. Hopefully, that will change since we have a fine crop of young talent ready to move up the ladder.

Now retired and trying to enjoy life, I volunteer by aiding and developing the tennis team at Daniel High School in Central, South Carolina near Clemson University. I also do a little part time coaching of other student players. Tennis and teaching it, will continue to be my joy and passion as long as it will have me.

WARD'S SKINNY ON DAVE

It was purely by chance in the small world of tennis at Keowee Key, that I got to know Dave and his lovely wife, Suzanne. Both Dave and Suzanne are fine tennis players with classic strokes, and both possess my favorite shot, the one-handed backhand.

When Brad and I took the position as co-head tennis professionals, there were several outstanding, prepaid lessons that were never honored by the previous pro, due to reasons I won't go into. Dave owned a few of them, and when I approached him with the idea of getting together in a doubles format to share the lesson, he emphatically declined. He was tough but honest and insisted on hitting with me privately as he claimed to be a skilled senior player and "just wanted to hit" with no instruction. I obliged and of course was surprised at how solid his game was even though he was nearly 80 at the time. Through the Grants, I had the pleasure of meeting the rest of their family and you know what happened on the tennis courts after meeting their sons.

I'm so thankful to have gotten to know this passionate tennis family and have the utmost respect for their collective achievements. Thanks, Dave, for sharing your interesting journey and congratulations on paving the way for many players, both past and present, toward that elusive dream and goal of playing on the big stage. You certainly made a difference and continue in that vein, as you share your experience and knowledge with high school athletes today. However, please know that I will politely turn down any request for a rematch with your sons, although they are always welcome to talk trash with me anytime!

GEORGE HARDIE

I grew up in Long Beach, California and having sported the 1960's endless summer look with my bleach blond hair, one would think I'd spent my childhood years learning how to surf. Not so. Instead, I hung out at a public park learning how to hit a ball across a net. I went on to play for my high school team, winning the singles championship three times in the Moore League, a seven-school sports league in Southern California. During my junior career, I competed annually at Kalamazoo and always ranked in the top ten in my age division. I was offered a full scholarship at Southern Methodist University in Dallas, Texas. It was the first step in my journey to the pro tour and finally making it seemed like just a formality to me. I knew that I could compete with anyone out there. In fact, I played in the U.S. Open three times during college, and interestingly, each time on a different surface—grass, then clay, then hard. I always felt like a shark, the predator that must keep moving to survive—that was me. But the true defining moment came while a senior at SMU. I reached the finals of the Little Rock pro event and earned 25 ATP points. Getting ATP points was validation that I was qualified and eligible to play on the big stage.

My college experience was a good one. In addition to the leadership of former tour player and coach, John Gardner, playing on a particularly good SMU team was great preparation for me. I needed to mature both mentally and physically, and quite frankly, attending a university is what I consider to be somewhat of a security blanket. It was a hedge in case anything went wrong on the tour, and it gave me a career backup by getting that secondary education. To that end, I am a huge proponent of going to college, particularly playing at one with top players who are all vying for the tour, and under the wing of a coach that knows how to get you there. I played down in the lineup my freshman year, at number three and two, and then held the top position for the next three years. Playing number one in the prestigious Southwest Conference put beneficial pressure on me, and like the tour, assured that I would face extremely difficult opponents each time I stepped out on the court. I embraced the challenge, as most players do, and recommend this invaluable experience to anyone desiring tennis as their career. I'm proud to say I was a four-time All-American as a singles player and one year as a doubles player.

I would be remiss if I didn't mention a particular college match that still sticks in my craw to this day—only a mere 40 years later. It was the 1975 NCAA finals against Billy Martin, the UCLA All-American and top prospect for the tour. Being in the final of that event was truly the biggest match of my life. I won the first two sets by the amazing score of 6-0, 6-1 and it got me thinking (not a good thing), that I could win the huge title. I was playing very well with few unforced errors. But Billy was a great competitor. Would I be able to sustain this crazy one-sided score and win? Of course, I got ahead of myself and thought the NCAA title would be mine. BIG MISTAKE! Billy went on to win the next two sets and we arrived at the final set shootout. Needless to say, and surely as the reader has already concluded, it was to be my demise, but oh so close, with Billy winning four no ad games in the set. Happy to say I got my revenge beating him at the U.S. Open a few years later. It was bittersweet for sure but nice to turn the tables on the guy that took away what would have been the biggest title of my college career. After graduating SMU in 1975, it was time for the pro circuit. One word comes to mind when describing the first several years ... entertaining. An article I wrote for the November 7, 1981, Desert Sun newspaper sums it up best:

I remember back in the dark ages of 1975 when I first came on the circuit. I used to love to listen to the banter and ribaldry of the players as they traded insults and off-color jokes among themselves. While not always up to high standards on an intellectual plane, it invariably was entertaining and fun to listen to. Since the arrival of the Walkman on the scene, I have noticed a definite dropping off in locker room conversation. As a result, the tennis circuit is not nearly as funny a place as it used to be. This is certainly an unfortunate state of affairs because humor is surely one of those aspects of the circuit that keeps me from checking into a rest home.

Traveling on the tour was a bit lonely. I tried to fill up the free hours by writing articles for *Tennis Magazine, International Tennis Weekly,* a French tennis magazine, and Scoreboard, a roundup of the week's news in *Sports Illustrated.* I also ended up inviting my girlfriend of the time, to accompany me on the circuit. In hindsight, it wasn't a good move because I was preoccupied not only with my well-being, but hers too, complicating matters of which I prefer not to get into. Her presence distracted me from managing the ever-constant pressure to perform well and earn the ATP points necessary to qualify for better paying tournaments.

I played as a pro for a modest six years. My most memorable win came in the 1979 U.S. Pro Indoor Championships in Philadelphia. It was in the second round against the number 12 seed and

Romanian number one, Ilie Nastase. To get there, I had to qualify and beat my archrival, Billy Martin, in the process. I beat Nastase 7-5 in the third set, obviously thrilled. However, I had little time to celebrate, as my third-round match was suspiciously scheduled for the early session the next day. I can't prove it, but I think the tournament director was miffed that I beat the number one seed. Thus, without the sufficient rest that I so desperately needed, I didn't make it past the third round.

Another notable win came in January of 1978, when I beat Adriano Panatta in a tough, first round-three setter of the Baltimore Indoor event. I went on to defeat Ross Case and Sherwood Stewart but lost in the finals. 1978 and 1979 would turn out to be my best years, as I reached my career best ATP world ranking of 80. And here is an honorable mention: a chance at victory against Jimmy Connors, the toughest opponent I have ever played. It was at the Washington Star International Championships in 1980. I was up one set and a break, only to lose in three. Jimmy hit the ball so cleanly, early, and precisely, that I felt rushed. The pressure was intense, the time he took away from me effective. That was certainly one that got away.

Speaking of Jimmy, he was the toughest player I ever faced. He put constant pressure on me by hitting the ball on the rise. He was a relentless competitor and fought for every point. He hit very flat, penetrating balls with little spin, thus hitting pinpoint accurate shots with consistent depth and pace, unlike anyone that I ever played. He also possessed one of the best returns of serves ever. The other guy that bothered me was Gene Mayer. He hit with two hands on both sides and could disguise his forehand unlike anyone on the tour, due largely in part to his two-handed technique. He had amazing hands and was one of first players to embrace and utilize the Prince racquet effectively.

Do I have any regrets? Several. The first? My grip. When I was 12 years old and competing in national tournaments, I went from an

Eastern grip to a Continental. Keep in mind, that in those days, it was rare to see grips other than the Continental, and largely due to the fact, that the game was predominantly played on faster surfaces than today (three of the four majors were played on grass). The advantage of the Continental grip was in the handling of lower balls, volleys, overheads and serves. However, it limited my ability to hit a more powerful topspin forehand. With the added power and spin of the stronger Eastern grip, I feel my ranking might have been much better. Having said all this, my Continental grip worked enough, enabling me to win 75 matches on the tour.

I wish that I had been more disciplined in my approach to practice and tennis in general. I loved the sport and relish the great times, to include both the memorable wins and painful losses. After all, the reality is that nobody escapes losses in a tournament except for the ultimate winner. It's easy to look back in the rear-view mirror. With clarity, I can see the talent was clearly there but to make it to the top required more dedication than I gave the sport. I knew when my game was on, it could stand up to some of the best players out there. Unfortunately, it didn't happen with consistency and upon reflection, the buck stopped with me. I left something on the table, but I'm okay with that now.

Not being dedicated enough was also a major issue. I didn't have a full-time coach, and neither did most of my peers. Yet, I am most certain my parents would have hired one for me had I been so inclined. The addition of a coach might have inspired me to play at a higher level, and he probably would have advised against my girlfriend accompanying me on the tour! If I could do it all over again, I would have hired one. The subject of dedication also leads me to some advice for aspiring juniors. Simply—be dedicated! The second, most important piece of advice, is to have fun! If you don't apply these two philosophies, it's doubtful you'll make it on the tour. Assuming the junior player has the talent and love for the game, properly applying the concepts of dedication and fun will likely enhance his or her chances for success.

Lastly, handling nerves and pressure is a constant threat to one's peace when competing on the tour. The pressure can be self-inflicted. And then again, often, the opponent's level of play has a large say so. In 1976, I went through a drought where I lost a considerable number of first round matches. It really had a negative effect on my confidence, self-esteem, ranking, and dwindling bank account. Handling nerves was not my best attribute. However, I worked through the downtimes, and used my experience to build back my concentration and confidence to begin winning again. I learned that eliminating outside distractions was easier by simply focusing on one point at a time.

Notwithstanding the previously mentioned regrets, I will always look back fondly at my time on the tour and playing the peers of my era. Such wonderful memories. I made cherished friendships and enjoyed amazing travels around the world. I would like to think those experiences helped me segue into the world of the wind industry, where over the last 20 years, I've been responsible for the development and acquisition of more than a dozen related projects worldwide. My tennis life ended up being an incredible ride, and I am so pleased that I was able to share highlights of such a sentimental journey.

WARD'S SKINNY ON GEORGE

George has the singular distinction of being the only person in *Tennis Life* whom I have never had the pleasure of meeting. His journey mirrored so many others within these pages—beating some of the best players in the world, to include Jimmy Connors. Though his career high ranking topped out at 81, the fact that he won a set and was up a break over Jimmy is validation of his talent. He readily admits that if he had been more dedicated, and had employed a slight change in his grip, he likely would have achieved even more in his career. He described his path to victories on the tour as analogous to a car. "My game was like an eight-cylinder engine. It had to be running on all cylinders and when it was, I could beat almost anyone."

George also happens to be good friends with another *Tennis Life* contributor, Chris Sylvan, and the rest of my skinny focuses on a very memorable quarterfinal match that took place between the two best buds. It happened in Amarillo, Texas, at the frigid cold Amarillo National Bank Tennis Open during January. There was at least a foot of snow on the ground and thankfully, it was an indoor event.

So, let me set up this drama filled match for the reader. George was the top seed and to his surprise and dismay, they were assigned a less desirable court with no umpire. Obviously, he was ticked and began the contest against his friend with a bit of an attitude. However, he was pretty confident regarding his chances, as his ranking was much better, and he had beaten Chris nearly a hundred times in practice. But he also knew that Chris could be a formidable foe on any given day, especially indoors with fast conditions.

Chris started the match serving non-returnable missile-like bombs, and he won the first set with relative ease. George remained unfazed, turned the tables, and won the second set. In the decisive third set, Chris played brilliantly and with a 5-1 lead, the victory within his reach. However, not so fast, as George had something to say about the outcome. He reeled off eight straight points to break and hold. Once again, Chris was serving for the match at 5-3. The point is still vividly etched in George's mind decades later. Chris served a bomb and rushed the net. George could barely get his racquet on the ball but managed to block it back to Chris's feet, causing his friend to float a weak half volley into the net. Chris promptly tossed his racquet in disgust in the same direction as his errant shot. At 0-15, Chris still had more than a puncher's chance to win with his mighty serve. That is until the tournament director, John Mozola, approached the court, having just witnessed the racquet toss. "Point penalty for racquet abuse and the score is now

0-30," he pronounced. Chris immediately yelled, "You are the worst tournament director in the whole world!" Well, that didn't earn any brownie points from Mozola and the next words out of his mouth were, "That's it! You are defaulted. Game, set and match to George." Chris was beside himself and in the ensuing heated discussion with Mozola, he prefaced his comments to him with, "Listen here, corn oil!" Meanwhile, George told the director to let him be and asked that the point penalty be voided, but his request fell upon deaf ears. Anyone who knows Chris would heartily acknowledge that he had amazing talent, but they also know his temper would sometimes get the better of him. Credit to George that he didn't want to win in such a fashion. However, because Chris had resorted to name calling, Mozola was doubly pissed and both guys were defaulted from the doubles!

It's fitting and rather comical, that the only time they faced one another in an actual tournament, that it would end in such a manner—and Chris only four points away from victory! To hear George give a blow-by-blow recount of the match was quite amusing, especially Chris calling Mozola "corn oil" in honor of the popular brand of cooking oil, Mazola. How funny was that! Knowing Chris as I do, when he reads this, most likely a wry smile and the signature Sylvan chuckle will emanate from his face.

George is an excellent golfer and writer as well. He contributed numerous articles to the International Tennis Federation towards the end of his career. In fact, in 1982, he was given the first-time award for *Contributing Tennis Writer of the Year* at the annual Jack Kramer Tennis Gala, held at the Waldorf Astoria in New York City. In front of a packed house full of tennis royalty, including Arthur Ashe and Ilie Nastase, he walked up to the podium to accept his award from the emcee, comedian Alan King. This was a big moment for a player that seldom made the limelight. George was genuinely pleased and honored, joking with the crowd, "I'm just a happy go lucky journeyman tennis player making a meager 300K per year." His tongue and cheek comment riled a few people and they ridiculed him later, knowing he made much less and was struggling to make ends meet. Amusingly, when George left the podium and approached his seat, Nastase whispered in his ear, "I never lost to you."

After speaking with George for nearly two hours on the phone, I really look forward to shaking his hand in person one day soon. *Tennis Life* is enriched by his inclusion and kudos to this wonderful player and successful entrepreneur. Yes, a journeyman but a fine tennis career nonetheless!

ANDY JOHNSTON

Let's just say I arrived fashionably late to my tennis life, and it was a rather unorthodox arrival at that. I was 15 at the time and my family was living in Summerville, South Carolina, just outside of Charleston. We had two courts in our subdivision and a gentleman named Jim Boswell came to give lessons twice a week. Not sure how the opportunity materialized but he used me as a human ball machine. I would simply hit back to the person he was teaching. I listened to what he told them and became self-taught, never having a tennis lesson from him myself. Soon after, and just in time for my last two years of high school, my father, the base commander at Charleston Air Force Base, was transferred to Scott Air Force Base near Mascoutah, Illinois. I joined the high school tennis team and by my senior year, I was the Mascoutah Indians number one singles player. I played unbeaten my last season, going 14-0.

Upon graduation from high school in 1975, I hopped a bus from Illinois to South Carolina, intent on trying out as a walk-on for the Clemson Tigers tennis team. I chose Clemson over other colleges since my brother and a couple of Summerville friends went there. After settling into my dorm room, I headed to the tennis center to sign up for the tryouts with the new coach, Chuck Kriese. 48 guys signed up for a lone survivor spot. Coach Kriese announced, "And oh by the way, you need to be here at 5:45 tomorrow morning to run." Not surprisingly, some of the guys weren't thrilled with the prospect of getting up so early, resulting in ten no shows the next morning. That one day of running turned into three brutal weeks of 440's and timed miles, all part of Coach's "morning madness" program to weed out the slackers—and boy did he. By the last week, there were only eight of us left. Then he told us "Oh and by the way, now we're going to have a tournament and the guy that wins it will make the team." So, I hacked away with my T2000 racquet, somehow managing to win the contest. Even though I never made the top six players, I got to play some matches and my game improved while on the team. I also soaked in Coach's knowledge and after graduation, he offered me a job as his assistant coach. I'm proud to say, I helped him on the way to producing his first national championship team. That got the attention of Paul Scarpa, the men's head tennis coach at Furman University in Greenville. He offered me the head coaching job for the women's team, and I accepted. I had been there just a year when Clemson came calling again, this time offering me the opportunity to take the reins of the women's team. Of course, I couldn't turn down my alma mater. I coached the women's team for 15 seasons, from 1983 to 1997. Fortunately, during my tenure, we had a win-loss record of 254-160 and won five straight ACC titles the first five seasons I was there. I would say my proudest moment as coach came when we won all nine flights in the 1983 ACC tournament. It has never happened before and very likely it will never happen again.

What was the secret to my coaching success? First and foremost, always to be honest with my players. In return, I ask them to play tennis with honor, integrity, and humility. I also try to instill in them that a good heart and great feet win a lot of matches. In addition, I tend to minimize the number of drills, as I feel that they produce ball strikers and not tennis players. I like good old fashioned competitive sets almost daily, since they mimic the pressure that it takes to win. Don't get me wrong, constantly drilling has its benefits. However, it's kind of akin to knowing how each chess piece moves— then not being able to play chess. More than anyone else, much of my coaching style was influenced by Chuck Kriese. But I also had my own style. I felt strongly that I needed to coach based on my own personality, even though Chuck's was foremost in my brain. To be true to myself and never fake it was my mantra. My style must have been working since eventual tour player, Gigi Fernandez, exploded onto the professional tennis scene just a year after working with me. If the reader hasn't heard of Gigi, she came from Puerto Rico, arriving at Clemson as a freshman player the same year that I took over the reins. She had a skill set and talent unlike any other player I had ever seen. She had a very functional slice backhand but wasn't satisfied with it. With my help, she soon had an excellent one-handed backhand. To make a switch at that stage of one's tennis journey was a monumental feat and her ability to do so landed her as one of our top players. Her first year, she advanced to the NCAA singles finals, by way of a play-in match in which she qualified, for a spot in the round of 64. The writing was on the wall regarding her talent, and she turned pro after that tournament. She went on to become one of the top doubles players in the world, reaching world number one in the rankings. She amassed 17 grand slam titles and two gold medals in the Olympics.

Interestingly, in 1997 I was offered another position at Clemson that would nearly double my salary and how could I say no? It was funny how it happened. I was called into the athletic director's office and thinking to myself, *am I about to be fired?* Nope, quite the opposite. He offered me the job as Director of Football Operations. I remember replying, "But sir, I've never even played football. I'm just a tennis guy." He insisted he still wanted me, telling me that I was the only person they were considering for the position. Of course, I accepted and my career as women's tennis head coach morphed into 18 years as head of football operations under three different coaches: Tommy West, Tommy Bowden and Dabo Swinney. And what a ride it was. The change was difficult at first. I worked a lot of long, hard hours. Eventually, after a couple of years, I got the program organized, allowing me to finally enjoy the excitement and thrill of running Clemson football. Fast forward to 2014. After the Tigers win over Oklahoma in the Russell Athletic Bowl, Dabo presented me with the official game ball in honor of my dedication to the program. That was pretty much my swan song, as I retired from Clemson in 2015. My time and focus turned to coaching my son, Noah … in what else? Tennis. With the help of my ex-wife, Sophie Woorons, a former Clemson player and participant in the French Open, we partnered to produce a hard-hitting left hander with modern ground strokes. On the subject of hiring an outside coach for Noah, I believe that when kids are young, the parent coaching dynamic works well. As the child matures, the parental duties of nurturing the emotional, social, and spiritual development are clearly the responsibility of the parent, while the tennis coaching often is better left to an outside coach. This will likely be the course we'll take as Noah matures, but for the time being, we'll pave the way for the next coach, whomever that might be.

Looking back at my life, I have certainly been blessed. Tennis has given me far more than I ever could have imagined. So many of my friends today are old college teammates, as well the countless players I've met throughout the years. It truly is the sport of a lifetime. I tell parents of the juniors that I coach that their child doesn't have to play pro or even college tennis, but the skills they learn on the court will serve them well into their adult years. Learning hard work, discipline, and how to handle success as well as failure, are valuable life skills. In addition, wherever their lives or jobs take them, they can join a tennis club and network with others in the community. No doubt, playing tennis gives a multitude of benefits beyond the simple joy of hitting the yellow ball. I hope your own journey will give you the same joy, friendships, and priceless memories that it did me!

WARD'S SKINNY ON ANDY

Meet my good friend of approximately 46 years now, Andy Johnston. We met playing on the Clemson University Varsity tennis team under Hall of Fame Coach, Chuck Kriese. Andy has a success story unlike the others in *Tennis Life*.

As the reader knows, Andy's journey began as a walk-on tennis player in 1975 at Clemson. I happened to be a junior at the time. Andy had no delusions of grandeur, nevertheless his immediate goal was to make the team. There was a new sheriff in town, and it was 25-year-old, Chuck Kriese. Though Chuck went on to become the greatest coach in Clemson history, the beginning was rough considering that he was new to coaching, that zero players on the roster had been recruited by him, and that he'd inherited a team with a variety of issues. Andy happened to arrive on campus just in time for Coach Kriese's unique walk-on opportunity for new blood, the event affectionately referred to by alumni as morning madness. He had no problems doing the early morning workouts with the others and embraced the challenge—most likely because his father had been a full colonel in the military and provided a family version of boot camp as his son was growing up! Needless to say, Chuck was impressed and soon after the madness ended, Andy was invited to join the team. I can tell you there was no way that I would have chosen that kind of path. The coach who had recruited me, Dr Duane Bruley, didn't have the same lofty goals that Coach Kriese had, and quite frankly, none of my fellow players at the time would have met his criteria. For my peers and I, it was problematic and what could he do? We were set in our ways and not motivated enough to work as hard as Andy. Even though he never made the top six, it should be noted that once he graduated, he came into his own and could beat most of the players on Chuck's team.

Andy's accomplishments at Clemson are legendary and to honor his journey in *Tennis Life* is special. During his first year at the helm of women's tennis, he led the Tigers to 30 wins, still a school record. He produced 51 All-ACC selections, 13 All-America honors, received four ACC Coach of the Year awards and was inducted into the Clemson Hall of Fame in 2016. Andy invested his time, heart, and soul into making his players better and that investment paid off with a multitude of ACC crowns and NCAA top finishes.

Now, he's investing that same time, heart and soul into his son, Noah. Time will only tell regarding Noah's progress but from my observations thus far watching his growth, as both a young man and tennis player, Andy and his ex-wife Sophie are doing a wonderful job. Andy is quite satisfied with coaching his son up to this point. They have instilled a profound love for the game into Noah. Add the numerous hours of hard work on the practice court, coupled with the arduous journey traveling around the country to compete in national tournaments, well that's proof that Noah cares deeply enough at this stage to take it to levels beyond the juniors.

I recently sat down to catch up with Andy and asked him his thoughts on the decline in American men's tennis. He replied, "Americans have become softer and would rather watch Tic-Tok or play video games than to train harder." He suggested other issues, specifically citing junior tennis and the rampant amount of cheating by players, as well as the lack of trained referees to police the tournaments. He went on to say, "Consequently, many juniors are turned off by this and gravitate to other sports, mostly of the team variety. Individual sports are quite taxing, and tennis is no exception. With failure comes responsibility and not every young tennis player can handle that." Andy also has disdain for the third set tiebreaker. "It doesn't always guarantee the better player will win and by doing so it takes out the critical element of physical conditioning." In a nutshell, he said that junior tennis is not developing really good players like in years past, and for this reason and probably other factors, American men are no longer among the top in the world.

I also asked him what advice he would give to aspiring juniors. He replied, "Don't chase points for the rankings. Don't pay so much attention to your UTR or others around you with that same concern. More important than ranking is to develop a complete game that will last and evolve over a lifetime. Long term is the path toward success, not short-term rankings. The bigger picture will have no age group restrictions so think big, think future and work toward playing the best players at any age, size, or venue."

Today, not only does Andy coach his son but he's a teaching pro at Spindle Tree Racquet Club near Clemson. I'm so proud of him for what he has accomplished, proud of his amazing young son and proud that he's a good friend of mine. He came from the school of hard knocks and only knows how to work hard—to include building a tennis club in Anderson, South Carolina! Andy goes at it with one hundred percent commitment whether he is teaching a club player, working with Noah, or even helping an old friend like yours truly. Andy has an intimate understanding and knowledge of tennis and when it comes to playing intelligently, he is one of the smartest players I know. Like his chess analogy, Andy puts stroke production aside in a battle and just figures out how to make the right moves to get the W. Back in the day at Clemson, when we were both on the same team, I was fortunate to be the better player. But surely it was because I began playing at a very young age and competed nationally throughout my junior years, while he didn't take up the game until the age of 15. I have no doubt in my mind that he would have been the better player had he started younger. Fast forward to today, and Andy has never given up a set to me in our many fun battles. I find it amusing that 40 years later, I can't win a set from him, yet in those days, Andy couldn't win a set from me! I guess the cream rose to the top.

There are several fine qualities to describe Andy and modesty is one of them. He doesn't care about traveling around the country to get a national ranking. He would rather compete when convenient, and then simply beat everyone on the other side of the net. A few years back, Andy entered a Men's 55 and over event in Greenville, drawing the top seed, a very good player out of Virginia. I heard from an eyewitness just how good his opponent was. However, Andy dispatched the guy 6-2, 6-2! Andy plays an old style of tennis using long, flat, and linear strokes that knife through the court with incredible velocity due to lack of spin. Add to that, the top seed was quite taken aback with Andy's attire—he certainly didn't appear to be sponsored by Adidas or Nike. My buddy likes to wear a long sleeve shirt that is more in tune with a championship surfer dude rather than a matching Adidas shirt, shorts and shoes. To top it off, Andy comes in unseeded and destroys the guy! Upon the match's conclusion, the opponent simply asked him, "Who are you?" Andy went on to win the tournament, handily disposing of every one of his opponents. Keep in mind, most of these tournament players do nothing but tour the country and compete, while my good friend just teaches every day, and when he can find the time, practices by playing fun sets with my sidekick, Brad Huff!

Andy would no doubt be among the top ranked players in the sixty and over division should he decide to play for more titles and trophies. Alas, they are not his fancy anymore. Father Time is a factor as well— that undefeated foe in every tennis player's life, as the wear and tear on Andy's knees have finally caught up with him. He recently had the necessary operation. Unfortunately, he thought he was Superman and could fast tract the recovery process by playing way too soon! Another trip to the surgeon and the MRI detected more extensive damage which would require a second operation. As much as I would like to beat Andy like I did forty plus years in the past and play him with his bad knee, I will be patient and wait for him to heal, and likely the guy will wreak havoc on me yet once again. If anyone asks Andy who wins between us or Brad or fellow pro, Mike Lissner, Andy always replies in his ever-modest way, "We are all about even." Get well soon my dear old friend, and though I promise to allow another victory for you, it will happen clearly and decisively with my only solace being your comment afterwards, "We are all about even." Funny, great guy, super father, and friend. So proud of Andy Johnston and just wishing him a full recovery so that he can once again rule the court that he plays upon. A genuine, down to earth person, I am so thankful to have rekindled my friendship with this Hall of Fame coach after all these years.

NOAH JOHNSTON

From the author: All the contributors in *Tennis Life* have either played on the tour or coached. However, it only seemed natural to follow Andy Johnston's chapter with one about his 14-year-old son, Noah. To include such a promising young phenom, one whom I've personally witnessed explode onto the junior tennis scene, seemed like a no-brainer. I thought it would be interesting for the reader to hear his perspective as a current junior, in comparison to the hindsight of the much older, veteran players represented within these pages. Please take note of this talented kid's name because when he arrives onto the pro scene, you will have heard about him here first! Since Noah is still a young teen, his chapter is based on notes I took when interviewing him. The casual Q & A was held in the family room of his Seneca, South Carolina home, his dad present to give added details should his son's youthful mind roam from the task at hand. Noah is the son of Sophie Woorons and of course, Andy. Both parents played tennis professionally, Sophie, having a tad more worldly experience to boast about since she played in the French Open. She also played on one of Andy's teams while a student at Clemson. She still competes in senior events around the world and is among the top players in her age group worldwide. As the reader knows from reading the previous chapter, Andy's tennis game flourished under Coach Chuck Kriese. He went on to win several tournaments after Clemson, competed nationally in USPTA events, and eventually coached the Clemson Women's Tennis team to 254 victories.

Noah can't clearly recall his father rolling a tennis ball to him as a two-year-old, but he's been told it happened on a regular basis. Developing his hand-eye coordination at an early age was part of his parents' strategy in preparing him for tennis. He also went on to learn other sports, such as snow skiing, soccer, and football. It wasn't long before he was skiing with skill in Chamonix, France, as a nine-year-old. Andy insists the French Olympic coach said he was the best he had ever seen at his age. Noah still loves to ski but his passion for tennis is his primary focus and appears to have his undivided attention. Over the course of the last several years, Sophie and her father, Lucien (aka Pappi and former gymnast coach for the French national team), have provided the foundation and technical aspects for Noah's game. He drills with Pappi for a couple of hours twice a week and hits with Sophie and Andy when schedules allow. I've watched Andy and Noah from the sidelines, and to observe father and son in practice, one might be convinced they're watching an aging touring pro versus a teen touring pro. Consistency and depth are common factors when they hit, and I've seen them use just one ball—quite frankly, they don't miss! In fact, Andy recalled having a 100-ball rally with his son when he was only seven. Thus, between Pappi, Sophie, and Andy, Noah receives an interesting and effective blend of family coaching that seems to be working well so far.

I asked Noah about his general practice routine and practice partners, other than with family members. He practices two hours per day, seven days a week—playing some sets, tiebreakers, and incorporating a lot of drills. When playing sets in practice, he said the focus is not on winning, but to work on consistency and good strokes. However, as a tournament approaches, he'll put more emphasis on winning. Unfortunately, he has a difficult time finding playing partners his own age, and in the small town of Seneca, finding players better than him is even more of a problem. He used to battle Andy's good friend and teaching professional, Brad Huff, on a regular basis, but it has become pretty much a one-sided affair in Noah's favor, as he continues to grow stronger and mature. He works out with two other pros now, Kim Oshiro, a former number one in Brazil at ages 12 and 14, and Sander Koning, a former number one at Clemson and former head coach for the Georgia Southern men's tennis team. Noah told me that at this juncture of his junior career, he's pretty happy with his game even when working out with these two talents, but one area that he would like to improve is the return of serve. His goal is to make it a "five out of six" by improving his placement, depth, and consistency.

When it comes to tournaments and the issue of nerves, Noah said that a couple of days before an event, he starts feeling the jitters. He tries to manage them by listening to music—interestingly, no musical group in particular. But once he steps onto the court, the nerves calm down and he's ready to play. Speaking of tournaments, he has been playing in them since the age of six. In fact, in his very first event, a 10 and Under Challenger, he won every match. The following year, he won the 10 and Under Intermediate in the Southern District Championships. His tennis prowess was certainly evident early on.

Here's the fun little Q & A session I had with Noah, his answers candid and to the point:

Q: Do you do any off-court training?

A: *I don't because I prefer to chase a tennis ball than to run circles around a track.*
Q: How do you process a loss versus a win?
A: *A loss bothers me more than getting a win.*
Q: Is temper ever an issue with you?
A: *I don't get mad too much. I have confidence in my game and feel that my technique works. Unless something like the wind, sun, or court conditions are a problem. I try to stay balanced physically and hope that will help battle the things I don't like to deal with.*
Q: How do you deal with bad calls by your opponents?
A: *I do my best to accept the bad calls because they aren't going away. It seems they are made more by players ranked between 70 and 100. The top players call the lines more honestly.*
Q: What is your biggest challenge as you continue grow?
A: *Steadiness and stamina. I pride myself on being consistent and try to minimize my unforced errors.*
Q: Do you appreciate the money spent and sacrifices made by your parents to further your tennis aspirations?
A: *I try to.*
Q: What are your goals for your tennis future?
A: *Right now, I'm just focusing on winning the U.S. Nationals.*
Q: Who are your favorite players and why?
A: *Carlos Alcaraz, Jannick Sinner, and Diego Schwartzman. Alcaraz because of his intensity, Sinner because of his backhand, and Schwartzman for his love of the game and pushing it to the edge. Maybe Stan Wawrinka for his amazing power but his flame has pretty much burned out.*
Q: If you have one bit of advice to give to other juniors, what would it be? A: *Stay calm and don't be scared to hit the ball. Because if you get scared, then you're not going to play as well as you could have.*

As one can see, Noah has put in the groundwork; the foundation laid both on and off the court. I think his future is so bright, he will always be wearing shades!

I'm a huge fan of his and can't wait to see how his game evolves with age, maturity, strength, and ability. His tennis life is certainly on track for something very special, and hopefully the reader has gotten a special glimpse and preview of this champion in the making.

WARD'S SKINNY ON NOAH

Let me just say that Noah's success is no accident, and his progress is well worth watching. When competing on the same court with him, I have witnessed firsthand what he brings to the game and it's truly off the charts. He hits with such velocity and spin, that he dominates from the baseline. I don't enjoy playing against him because quite often, I let his shoulder-high shots go by me thinking they're going to sail long, and then lo and behold, they fall inside the baseline. If you try and crowd him at the net, he simply uses a full swinging topspin lob over your head unlike anything I have ever seen. I'm truly impressed with his ability to take both success and failure in stride. As he reported, he disdains losing more that he enjoys winning. He has a very mature outlook about his tennis—it's more about proper execution and trust in his technique than being victorious. When he does get the W, he doesn't gloat, brag, or even talk about it thanks to his excellent parenting. An example of that parenting? Let me start with Andy. To listen to him speak to Noah about his ongoing tennis philosophy is interesting, fun, and kind of amazing. I like to think of it as a sort of holistic approach, since Andy preaches the simple basics to his son on a day-to-day basis. He tells him, "Just hit it deep, don't miss, don't get mad, don't gloat about your victories. Work hard and listen to your mom and grandfather. Of course, Sophie is the other huge ingredient in the mix that has helped create their son's success. She brings the critical technical elements to his game, or as Noah put it in our interview, his mom brings him the much needed speed and agility.

So, keep your eyes out for Noah Johnston and stay tuned, as I predict this young man could be a household name in the tennis world. I get the feeling if he stays grounded and committed to the principles instilled in him, he will have earned his chapter in *Tennis Life* alongside so many other talented players. My sincere thanks for your participation, Noah, and best of luck in your evolving tennis journey.

BREAKING NEWS—LAST MINUTE ADDITION! Right before *Tennis Life* went to press, Noah, seeded number nine, captured both the singles title and doubles title in the 14 and Under at the Fila Easter Bowl Championships in Indian Wells, California. Dominating one of the toughest fields in junior tennis, he won his first gold ball in both events and to top it off, he was also awarded the Sportsmanship award. When being interviewed after the singles victory, he glanced down at the trophy and said, "I've never even seen a gold ball ... it just feels so good." With mom/coach, Sophie Woorens, in attendance, and dad/coach, Andy Johnston, back home in South Carolina cheering his every shot on YouTube, Noah delivered a masterpiece, announcing his arrival to the tennis world. Likely the first of many more titles to come, a big congratulations to Noah and his team. Post Easter Bowl, Noah's USTA 14 and Under ranking climbed to #3 in the nation.

Oh, but the dream week doesn't stop there. Flying back that night to South Carolina via Miami, they missed their connecting flight to Greenville. Forced to spend the night, they realized the Miami Open was in progress, with the finals being played the next day. Who was in the finals? None other than one of his idols, Carlos Alcaraz. They bought tickets and Noah had the pleasure of watching Alcaraz win the singles title!

CHUCK KRIESE

I grew up in the old neighborhood section of Indianapolis and was introduced to tennis in a city park at age 13. I attended Cathedral High School, a parochial school where I not only played tennis but ran cross country and played basketball as well. Upon graduating, I was close to enlisting in the military. My dad being a schoolteacher with six kids, the cost of higher education was prohibitive at the time. But as luck would have it, Tennessee Tech offered me a scholarship to play and study there. That one phone call from Coach Larry Ware changed the direction of my life forever, as I might have been a gunner in Vietnam or perhaps never even making it out of combat, still a sobering thought to this day.

I graduated from Tennessee Tech in four years with an undergraduate degree to teach high school math. Then out of the blue, I get a phone call from my college coach to work for Harry

Hopman's tennis camp in Amherst, Massachusetts. I was offered $70 a week for ten-hour days. I vividly remember Mr. Hopman approaching me after a terribly long day, asking me to hit with his wife, Lucy. I couldn't turn him down. He showed up after the session, reached into his wallet, and pulled out a $20 bill to give me, but I declined. The following week, the same chain of events occurred and once again, I turned down his $20. The next week, he called me into the office, and I honestly thought I was going to be fired. Instead, he offered me a job at his academy in Port Washington, New York. It was one of the most prestigious academies in the nation. Future greats such as Vitas Gerulaitis, John McEnroe, Ricky Meyer, Peter Fleming, and Mary Carillo, could be found working on their games there. It appeared the $20 was a test, and my refusal to take it showed Mr. Hopman that I wasn't just about the money. Don't get me wrong, I was tempted to take the extra cash, but it just didn't feel right. That being said, $20 back then could have bought me 80 red solo cups of beer!

I eventually left Port Washington and went back to Cookeville, to work on my master's in Health and Physical Education, as I always wanted to be coach. I got to be an assistant coach for a year and was also an assistant track coach for one semester. Things looked up and I assumed I might get the job at my alma mater. However, to my dismay I wasn't offered the position, and grudgingly had to swallow my pride. Having a masters in Heath and Physical Education, I was fortunate enough to have highly motivated professors and mentors at TTU. I knew a lot about fitness (and was young and hungry to coach) but had very little experience. I think that's what hurt me. Before leaving campus on my last day in Cookeville, I stopped in the office of athletic director and head football coach, Don Wade. I asked him to please remember me if the job ever opened. I was unaware that he had played football for Clemson University back in the day (I didn't find out until years later), and when an opportunity opened up for the Tigers' head coaching position, he got me a job interview with athletic director, Bill McClellan. Amazingly, I got the position and there I stood at the age of 25, the new head tennis coach of a major university. It was really a holy shit moment for me, as I was pretty certain that it might not last long once they figured out that I was so green and inexperienced. I decided to work as hard as possible and to make our team the most fit in the country. I was a bit unsure of how to approach the new position and that's an understatement. I was charged with taking over a program that was in a transition of sorts with the departure of Dr. Duane Bruley, Dr. William Beckwith and his assistant coach, Dr. Joe Mullins. For me to suddenly be thrown into the fire was difficult for the existing team. My initial thought was to try to emulate the best two programs in the country, UNC and UGA, and their respective coaches, Coach Cliff Skakle and Coach Dan Magill. My problem soon became that neither one of these fine gentlemen suited my personality and style, thus I decided to make the program my own and focus on what I knew— hard work and extreme fitness.

So, I began my coaching at Clemson with the goal of having the hardest working team in the nation. Having had the short stint as assistant track coach at Tennessee Tech, as well as some tough basketball training, I knew how to get student-athletes in shape. Just as well, the Hopman teaching and coaching experience gave me much needed confidence. It was a bit of a shock for the guys I inherited since they weren't used to a regimented and rigorous daily practice. I expected some resistance but embraced the opportunity to put my signature on the program and with no hesitancy, I asserted myself on day one. I live by two adages—that hard work eliminates small thinking and also that courage never goes out of fashion. There was need for a blue-collar work ethic and white-collar expectations. My sister's husband and my best friend in life, John Comella, (who sadly died at age 35), gave me a book titled, *Winning Images.* I lived by the tenets of that book and wanted Clemson to have the image of the hardest working program in the country. I also followed the principles of another book, *They Call Me Coach,* by Coach John Wooden, and it became my coaching bible.

One moment in particular stood out my first year at Clemson. I had the team out on the track after practice, stopwatch in hand, when my team captain, Steve Vaughan, grabbed one of my players and literally shook him. He told him that he was proud of being in good shape; that running was good stuff and to just suck it up— with enthusiasm! Steve was a great leader, one who worked hard each and every day to get my messages across. The challenge to finish the daily running ritual at 100% under my watchful eye and stopwatch was a shock to most of the guys, but that moment Steve spoke up stands out as a nice turning point for me. I realized the culture was finally changing and had hope that my methods would produce positive results. Teams across the country started taking notice of our training protocol. Tennis went from a country club sport to an athletic sport, with several schools following suit. It became commonplace for players to hit the weights, the track, and adopt a more vigorous training regimen in general. To this day, I'm very proud of that.

When some new recruits arrived, they knew up front what I expected of them, which of course helped tremendously. The first players were Mike Gandolfo, Mark Buechler, Dick Milford, and David Loder. When recruiting, I looked for someone who played from the heart and had a good work ethic, the aforementioned guys fitting the bill. Through trusted friends in the tennis community, I was able to verify this essential quality for a student-athlete to join my program. If the person had a good junior ranking, all the better, but not the driving force for me. To summarize in a more entertaining way, what I was looking for first and foremost were "stallions" or talented hard workers. Second in line were the "workhorses" or hard workers with less talent. Lastly were the "show ponies", talented non-workers who I was good at recognizing and stayed away from. It was the introduction of "morning madness" where I provided an opportunity for any and all players to make the team. My teams have always had a "no-cut" but "a-very-high-bar" policy for entry. This is where the weeding out process took place (the show ponies never made it out!). Two fine gentlemen, Andy Johnston and John Anderson, made it through and achieved much in the process. Andy remains a lifelong friend to this day.

Ward asked me who I thought the most talented player had been under my tenure at Clemson. There are several that come to mind but the one that stands out the most is Richard Matuszewski. I first noticed him in an indoor tournament and though he wasn't a highly ranked junior, there was something about him that got my attention. He was smooth, with a great pair of hands and a mind for the game. The son of first-generation immigrants from Poland, Richard learned the game in his backyard from his father and came to Clemson with a partial scholarship. It seemed with every ball that Richard struck, his game would improve. He was a lowly number thirteen at the start of his freshman year. However, he made the top six by spring and won a conference title. Each year he got better, making the main draw of the U.S. Open his senior year and ultimately achieving a career high world ranking of 47.

I can't overlook other great players that come to mind: Jay Berger, Mark Dickson, Pender Murphy, Mike Gandolfo, Lawson Duncan, Kent Kinnear, Jean Desdunes, Craig Boynton, Miguel Nido, Rick Rudeen, Mitch Sprengelmeyer, Nathan Thompson, John Sullivan, Vince Van Gelderen, Brandon Walters, and so many other memorable student-athletes. In all, we had 36 players that played on the pro tour and 11 made it into the ATP top 100. In fact, I stay in touch with many of them. Let's just say my former players are trophies to me and my relationship with them grows in significance as the years go by!

Reflecting on my time at Clemson, I wish I could have a few redo's. Certainly, in a more perfect world, I would have preferred to have been an assistant tennis coach for three or four more years before taking on the head coaching job. Secondly, I never gave my guys the opportunity to enjoy their successes. In other words, I didn't allow them to "marinate the wins". I made them go right back to work and I would change that if given a second chance.

Lastly, I truly believe that during our 13 years of producing top ten teams, three of them should have been number one in the country. We should have won the national title but didn't and that's on me. I blame myself to this day for not being able to run with some of the great momentum we'd worked so hard to create.

As far as regrets, I have at least two that I often think of, the first one regarding family. I devoted my life to coaching early on, taking too much time away from my first wife and kids. My priorities were not always in order of God, family, and then job, as my father had often stated during my youth. Thankfully, I learned how to balance job and personal life as the years passed. I'm proud to say I just celebrated 23 years of marriage and have six wonderful children and four grandchildren (and counting). Another one of my regrets goes back to the 1984 NCAA Men's Singles Championships in Athens, Georgia. The significance of the occasion can't be overlooked, as it was the first time I had ever coached a player who had reached the final of this most coveted college event. Freshman Tiger, Lawson Duncan, was about to face UGA's number one player, Mikael Pernfors. He had beaten Pernfors in straight sets in a dual match about a month earlier. For all the rounds leading up to the final, Lawson used the same routine for a long warmup prior to match time. On the day of the final, for whatever reason, we were sequestered inside a small room before the match (I think it was where they strung racquets), and we didn't do the normal warmup ritual. To this day, I know that I should have been more proactive with the warm-up routines and been more active from the sideline. Lawson lost to Pernfors in straight sets. It was crushing. The no-ad scoring surely didn't help either, as Lawson never got his game into gear. I'm fully to blame. What a great champion he was. He later reached the ATP top 50 and was one of the best clay court players in the world. I look back and realize more than ever now, that a coach must be fully aware of the routines and preparations that can be controlled. Both pre-match and post-match are extremely important.

Speaking of Lawson, his 70-14 record during the 1983/1984 season may have been one of the reasons the NCAA put restrictions on practice time and number of matches. I sincerely believe that liberal coaches and administrators didn't want to have to chase our hard work. They decided that lowering the bar was an easier solution. Please bear with me while I get on my soapbox, but the restriction of work ethic is laughable. No, let me rephrase that ... it's extremely sad and very problematic in the pursuit of excellence. The abbreviated matches and bastardizations, such as stopping the matches before the end are very shortsighted. For players, the opportunities for learning and growth are being taken away. The agenda for the ITA tennis committees are greatly responsible for the dumb-downs that are being forced through. They have essentially penalized work ethic, and instilled things that are customized for talented non-workers, plain and simple. Forcing through the rule of no-ad scoring has done the greatest harm. It has now made the simplistic and primal race to four become more important than the hard to learn physical, technical, and tactical skill sets that have always taken years to develop. It has led me to wonder and suspect if the fondness of random results by ITA administrators has become a profitable endeavor for those who benefit from the marketing of our sport. Sadly, the no-ad scoring promotes more cheating than ever before in college tennis, and now in the youth ranks as well. The eight-point swings on game point are just too tempting and profitable for the pressured player not to make a bad call and take a point they didn't deserve. Good sportsmanship is also being forced to the sideline by no-ad scoring. The promotors say its real purpose is to shorten play. I believe that has always been a red herring! The real reason seems to be to help promote more random results. Thus the scoring system now holds more merit and is more important than the physical and technical sets of tennis that take years and years to learn. It's a tragedy that our tennis administrators are so shortsighted (sometimes even arrogant) in destroying some of the most precious heirlooms of the sport. It seems to be happening in other sports, as they are being compromised as well by abbreviations. Whether it's baseballs being juiced to allow more homeruns, shot clocks and three pointers for basketball, rally scoring system for volleyball, or numerous other gimmicks, it seems that whatever minimizes the depth, the history, and the artform of sports in general, is being done for marketing purposes. The marketeers will always say that it is about time. Once again, that's a ruse. As the reader can see, I don't take things like this sitting down, and will always do my best for the integrity of the game. I have a deep passion for our sport, and I truly believe that protecting the history and heritage of the sport should be a prime focus for all of us. If we allow the artistic depth of tennis to be minimized, we will lose it.

After 33 years as Clemson's head coach, I retired in 2008, and in the same year, I was appointed technical director of the Southeast Asia Tennis Federation, where I coached and trained top juniors in that part of the world for the next two years. I was able to travel in multiple parts of Asia and do coaching seminars in seven different countries in that part of the world. One of our juniors, a young lady by the name of Noppawan Lertchewakarn, won four grand slam events. She was the first Asian in history to win a grand slam! She won both Wimbledon singles and doubles in 2009 and was ranked number one in the world the same year. With those wonderful experiences and my time serving as USA Junior Davis Cup coach in the early 1980's, I was able to coach five grand slam championship performances and four other finalists in those world events. In 2013, I was named head coach for the Citadel Bulldogs in Charleston, where I continue to coach to this day. Once again, I'm working with fine young student-athletes who inspire me to get up early every morning—to pass on whatever knowledge and expertise I can, and to share my undying passion for this great sport we call tennis.

WARD'S SKINNY ON CHUCK

Penning *Tennis Life* has led to a series of so-called revelations for me. The deep seeded passion for tennis the contributors in this book continue to have at this stage of their journeys is a joy to hear. However, as it pertains to Chuck Kriese, his level of passion for the sport just might be unsurpassed compared to the others, and it was never more evident than when I sat down with him recently to catch up with him after all these years.

I spent two years playing under Chuck at Clemson and will admit right away that I was too young to understand and appreciate him when he arrived. Since I had been recruited by Dr. Duane Bruley, Chuck's unusual style of coaching made it all the more trying for me. His mantra to outwork every other team in the country meant lots of demanding work, both on and off the court. Chasing a ball for hours on the court suited me just fine but doing drills on the track was not to my liking and let us just say it was obvious in my rebellious attitude of which I displayed to Chuck on day one! I was pretty much the wiseass that I can still be to this day, and here's how it all went down. He introduced himself to the team with a one-hour oratory on his background in physical fitness and the new, innovative way of getting in shape known as interval training. He explained that it dispelled the myth of doing long distance running around a track, and instead, focused on maximum exertion in short and frequent distances with the maximum distance being a quarter mile run. At the end of the speech, he announced, "Tomorrow, you will be running six miles for time." With utter disbelief and disgust, I questioned him in front of the rest of the team as to why the six-mile run if it was no longer useful as he had reported? He looked at me in astonishment and replied, "Ward, I want to see you in my office before you leave here." I soon found myself with him behind closed doors. It was far from a pleasant experience, as I just couldn't keep my mouth shut and questioned him yet again about the validity of the run. He replied that he was doing it for our mental toughness. Well, his answer just wasn't good enough for me, and I left his office flabbergasted and pissed, knowing full well the party was over! With a chip on my shoulder, I managed to comply the next day, running the six miles as fast as I could. I never got used to Chuck's running routine but grudgingly admit that I never got tired in any match from that point on, and all credit is due to him. I now appreciate and admire him for sticking to his guns. I also applaud him for a characteristic that he embodies and cherishes more than anything—honesty. He says it like it is, with no filters for political correctness. That is just Chuck.

Our two-hour interview seemed to fly, because to hear this man reveal so much with such amazing passion was priceless. It also brought back fond memories of some of his profound maxims. They helped guide his genius and I thought I'd share a few here:

Hard work eliminates small things.

Courage never goes out of fashion.

Morning madness weeded out the show ponies.

Fatigue makes cowards of us all.

The more you sweat in peace time, the less you bleed in war time.

No one achieves any knowledge, skillset, or training until they actively seek it through hunger of an inquisitive mind.

Greatness comes when you hate or disdain losing, and love winning.

Permit your players to marinate the win.

If you're not five minutes early, you are late (which would lead to Dawn Patrol! A known military phrase, Chuck made it his own at Clemson. If you showed up one minute late for practice, then you were subject to the following: With a stopwatch in Chuck's left hand, a clipboard in his right, and a miner's light shining from his cap, you were required to do several 440's!)

Coach Kriese transformed collegiate tennis and put Clemson on the map, just like Coach Dabo Swinney did with our football program. Now down in Charleston, he endeavors each and every day to inspire, teach, coach, nurture and make each one of his Citadel players better. Chuck has never tanked a day in his life and for all of his lucky players at the Citadel, I hope they cherish the years with this man who has been National Coach of the Year four times. But that's just the tip of the iceberg. I'd like to take a moment to celebrate the sheer magnitude of his achievements, and they are as follows:

- All-Conference player at Tennessee Tech
- Winningest Coach in ACC history with 685 victories (now 750 plus and counting)
- Ten ACC team titles
- NCAA Elite 8 (seven times)
- 16 top ten finishes in the NCAA
- Produced 36 All-Americans
- Four National Senior Players of the Year
- 11 players reached the top 100 on the ATP tour
- Inducted into six Halls of Fame including the National Collegiate Tennis Hall of Fame, Clemson Athletic, South Carolina Tennis, Tennessee Tech Athletic, Tennessee Sports Hall of Fame, and Indiana High School Tennis Hall of Fame
- USA Junior Davis Cup coach and USA national coach
- Technical director and coach for the Southeast Asia Tennis Federation
- Coached the 1st Asian player in history to win a grand slam event, when Noppawan Lertcheewakarn of Thailand won the junior girls singles and doubles titles at Wimbledon in 2009
- Over 16,000 juniors have attended his tennis camps
- Guest clinician and speaker, and gave coaching seminars in 17 different countries

- Hosts American Tennis Radio Show each week
- Has authored four tennis books, including *Total Tennis Training, Winning Tennis, Youth Tennis* and *Coaching Tennis*. The first book, *Total Tennis Training,* produced an unsolicited testimonial from the world class player out of South Africa, Kevin Anderson. He came up to Chuck and said, "Thanks, Coach. My dad taught me how to play tennis in our backyard with your book." *Total Tennis Training* has become the third bestselling tennis book of all time.
- Has also co-authored three editions of *Where the Tigers Play* and *History of Clemson Athletics*

Chuck, it is my sincere hope and desire, that the reader appreciates what you stand for and all that you've achieved after reading your chapter. I know I do—the scars have healed from those miserable timed runs around the track, and only good thoughts and feelings remain. I now have a sincere appreciation for what you stand for, your amazing body of work, and the methodology behind your morning madness! Thanks so much for being part of my Clemson experience and my life today, and of course for sharing your incredible journey in *Tennis Life.*

STEVE KRULEVITZ

My tennis career began after my golf career ended at age seven. My dad, Kenneth, a physician, and former number two singles player on the University of Maryland tennis team, introduced me to the game of golf when I was just four years old, hoping that one day I would make it to the PGA tour. But as fate would have it, a rainy day forced me off the driving range and over to the tennis courts, and once I hit on the backboard, I was hooked. I was also an avid baseball player, enjoying the little league games and competition. Nevertheless, something about tennis got my attention.

When my dad saw how interested I was, he looked up former Maryland teammate-turned tennis instructor, Maury Schwartzman. Maury was extremely busy, so he recommended his assistant, Dave Applefeld. Shortly thereafter, my thirty-minute lessons began at the Druid Hill Park Courts. I made it a point to have my mom drop me off at least a half hour before my lesson so that I could hit on the backboard, and then have her pick me up a half hour after the lesson so that I could revisit the backboard. This was my weekly ritual and within a year, Maury took notice of my dedication. It was then that he felt the need to teach me personally.

My first tournament was at age nine in the 12 and Under at Congressional Country Club in Bethesda, Maryland. My opponent was Richard Healy, a pretty good tournament player. Much to my dismay, he moon-balled me to death, beating me 6-0, 6-1. This left a sour taste in my mouth and thought maybe I should devote more time to baseball. But Maury insisted that I give it one more try and so I did, entering the Baltimore Jaycees on the red clay courts at Clifton Park. It would be the first of many encounters with my good friend and fellow competitor, Harold Solomon. He was the top seed and heavy favorite. Playing in the first round, we battled into the third set with Harold eking out the third, 6-4. I remember him being extremely upset that his dad, Lenny, hadn't stayed to watch the match. So, after it was over, I tried to console him until his father returned to retrieve him. It was that day that Maury convinced me to continue playing, as I was the only kid that managed to take a set off Harold.

For some reason, Harold's dad took a liking to me. His business partner, Frank Hirsch, happened to live down the street from us. One day, Lenny knocked on our door, approaching my dad with the suggestion to take Harold and myself to events outside of the area, where we could encounter tougher competition. Dad embraced the idea and that was the beginning of a lifelong relationship with both Harold and Lenny—one that I will be forever grateful for. Harold's work ethic and Lenny's strategic advice truly inspired me to become a better player. That summer, I ended up playing Harold in the finals of seven tournaments in a row!

My rivalry and friendship with him continued as we progressed into the older age divisions. His father was a fine businessman and often referred to as "The Fox". He earned this nickname due to his prowess as a brilliant entrepreneur and savvy tennis coach. Owing to the cold weather in the northeast, Lenny moved the family to Miami Beach for the long winter. By doing so, he gave Harold the opportunity to play virtually every day of the year, something that most of us could not do unless blessed with indoor courts. I enjoyed spending time at their home in Miami, playing with my friend and soaking in wisdom from the Fox.

Fast forward to the age of fifteen when I was mired in a slump. I just couldn't get out of my own way and those were tough times for me. Wins eluded me, but nevertheless, I qualified for the national championships during my first year of the 18 and Under at Kalamazoo. The draw came out, pitting me against the number six seed from Miami, Mac Claflin. Mac was an outstanding player and on paper, he had me beat long before the match began. But when Harold's father drove up in his Cadillac, the prognosis changed. Lenny had seen Claflin dominate the junior events in South Florida and knew of his prowess between the lines. He took me aside and told me the following. He said, "I want you to juice it, that is to hit out on every ball, GO FOR IT and DON'T THINK." I followed Lenny's sage advice, upset Claflin, and made it all the way to the quarterfinals. My slump was over and getting the win gave me the boost of confidence that I so desperately needed.

I found myself ranked in the top ten in the U.S., and soon the scholarship offers came pouring in. The one that interested me the most was from Coach Dale Lewis of the University of Miami. I liked Miami for the weather and the fact that the school had a top tennis program, as well as a renowned coach in Mr. Lewis. My sights were set on attending but when all was said and done, it just didn't work out. Fortunately, I had other options to choose from, Utah and Arizona topping the list. My dad recommended that I go to Utah. So, I accepted their offer, spending my first two years of college there.

It was during my freshman year at Utah, and on our spring break road trip to California, when I was swayed to make a change. I was taken in by the incredible weather, the beautiful landscape, and the California girls. The cherry on top was the amazing campus and tennis complex at UCLA. The seed was planted, and Southern California was calling my name. Off went a letter to Coach Glenn Bassett. He answered, offering me a full scholarship with the warning that I'd have to be redshirted my junior year. In case the reader is not privy to NCAA rules, upon transferring during my era, you had to sit out for the first year. I accepted anyway and used the time to work hard on my game and studies.

Now 1973 and my senior year at UCLA, I was chomping at the bit to play. The competition on the west coast was probably the best in the nation, precisely what I longed for after sitting out for one long year. The practice I put in while sitting out paid off. I made it to the quarterfinals of the NCAA championships and proud to say, became an All-American.

In preparation for the next step of my journey to go out on the tour, Coach Basset was kind enough to arrange ways for me to earn money. I taught tennis lessons in my spare time and was able to pad my savings account enough to give me a running start. With no international ranking, I traveled to Europe where I began the laborious task of playing the qualifying tournaments to get into the main draw. I played in Spain, France, and Italy, but it was the Italian Open that turned the corner for me. I not only navigated successfully through the qualifying, but through the main draw and into the quarterfinals. In the third round, I found myself in the massive stadium, with a boisterous partisan crowd cheering on local favorite and world number 24, Antonio Zugarelli. Though it was an early round match, being the second most important clay court event in the world made it very special, and to play a local hero made me feel like a Roman Gladiator back in the day. The contest had the atmosphere of a final, the crowd cheering my opponent's every good shot. However, fortunately for me, I literally didn't miss a ball in the first set and went on to enjoy one of the most significant victories in my life. Getting to the quarters of the Italian Open, and about to face the Argentine great, Guillermo Vilas, was a defining moment in my career. Even though I lost to Vilas, the satisfaction of banking my first substantial paycheck, and the fact that I was one of the last eight players standing, pretty much validated my years of hard work. It appeared that I had made it on the tour—a dream come true, and when I arrived back in the U.S. six months later, I was ranked 84 in the world.

The most satisfying win in my career came in a Davis Cup match playing for Israel (I became a dual citizen). It was 1978 and Austria was in town. The Tel Aviv venue was a packed stadium known as the Ramat Hasharon Tennis Center, and I was facing a very tough opponent, the Austrian number one, Hans Kary. A few choice words were exchanged between us before stepping onto the court, strengthening my resolve to beat the guy. It ended up being a very tough five set win, but I was extremely proud to have won the point for Israel.

Ironically, the most memorable loss in my career came after my full-time playing days were over. It was the 35 and over event sponsored by Reebok and held at the Billie Jean King Tennis Center in New York City. To get there I had to win my sectional qualifying which was the M.A.T.A. (Middle Atlantic Tennis Association). The goal was to win the New York City segment and then go to Newport, Rhode Island for the finals. I would like to stress this was not about money since it was an amateur event, but more about the love of the game, as I longed to play on the grass at Newport, the Hall of Fame grounds made famous by Jimmy Van Allen. The guy on the other side of the net standing in my way was the tough Australian, John James. It was a massive struggle, the match going to a final set tiebreaker, and you know the outcome—a devastating loss. Ah, so close and ensuing regrets. I hate to admit it, but the pressure got to me. I knew there was no tomorrow or next week. For this special event, it ended suddenly for me and what a big disappointment since I wanted it so much. The next year, and on the exact one-year anniversary of my devastating defeat, I had the chance to play John James once again. It was the Reebok teaching professional tournament at the National Tennis Center in Flushing Meadows, New York. The second time around, I got the best of him with a score of 6-0, 6-1. Though it took me twelve months to avenge the defeat, it was satisfying, nonetheless.

MY ADVICE TO JUNIORS

I am a believer in hard work and lots of practice, but playing tournaments is the key. This is where you test yourself every time—under the pressure of real competition. It's great to be able to execute any given array of shots in practice. However, to do it under the gun in tournament events is the real challenge. When you can play well in a tournament, you confirm what you have been working on, and consequently your game and confidence will grow. You can't play enough tournaments!

To play up or not? That's a good question. Often, there is tremendous outside pressure on the player, usually coming from the parents, but also from one's peer group. Playing up an age group can alleviate some of that pressure and is a good way to work on your game. But to make it on the ultimate level, you have to learn how to handle pressure and that means competing in your own age group.

There's nothing more important than to keep it FUN. Tennis is not a life-or-death situation. Keeping things in perspective helps lower the pressure, thus allowing you to play at your best. If the experience of practicing and playing is not fun, then it won't work. Enjoy. Make it fun and you'll be moving in the right direction.

I'm a big proponent of going to college, as there is nothing more important than getting a good education. The tour life is not an easy one and thankfully, I had my kinesiology degree to fall back on if needed. I was genuinely interested in pursuing the vocation, but happy to say that my tennis career managed to pay the bills, affording me an amazing lifestyle that I will never forget.

NERVES AND PRESSURE

Every player must deal with this subject, and I believe that everyone gets nervous. I'm a big believer in reading books by sports psychologists. In fact, I remember reading the book by Dr. Jim Lehr which discussed how to win matches by keeping the nerves in check. He advocated deep breathing, arranging strings between points, and momentarily turning your back on the opponent to regain focus. If your mind stays occupied, then the nerves will be less of a factor. There are many books like Dr. Lehr's, and I strongly recommend the one that suits you the best.

I recall a match years ago during the North Conway tour stop. I was playing a tough lefty from Tennessee in the third round by the name of Terry Moore. This was a very big tournament, with top competitors from around the world using it as preparation for the U.S. Open, just around the corner. I vividly recall being ahead 6-2, 5-1 and thinking I would soon be in the quarterfinals. Next thing you know my racquet got so heavy and I couldn't swing it. Before I knew it, the set was lost. In the final set, I'm down 4-1. Suddenly, thoughts of Lenny the Fox came to mind, and his simple advice of, "Don't think." So, I didn't, and the pressure lightened. Then Terry started choking! I ended up surviving in a final set tiebreaker, getting the lucky win that should have been a foregone conclusion an hour earlier. Don't kid yourself. Everyone gets nervous, but some players handle it much better than others. It will always be a problem and yours alone to solve.

REGRETS

Possibly one. Ion Tiriac, a colorful Romanian doubles specialist, French Open doubles champion with partner, Ille Nastase, and sought-after coach, offered to take me under his wing for a fee—to train and travel with him and Nastase. If I had done so, who knows what could have been? When I played the tour, only the top few guys had the luxury of a full-time coach. A coach helps keep you focused, protects you from extracurricular activities that can sidetrack your performance, and makes certain you are ready to play. I can't change the past but feel sure a coach would have helped me tremendously.

I'm incredibly grateful for the journey I've had, and the experience of tour life. I enjoyed traveling the world, meeting new people, playing in front of enthusiastic crowds, the adrenaline rush of competing/succeeding, and the fellowship with my peers. There's much to be thankful for but I couldn't have done it alone. I am especially appreciative of the financial, emotional, and coaching support from the following people that made it all possible: Dr. Kenneth Krulevitz (Casey—my dad), Lenny "The Fox" Solomon, Harold Solomon, Maury Schwartzman, Glenn Bassett, Dennis Ralston, Lew Gerard, Eddie (Hondo) Dibbs, and my wife Ann.

I hope you enjoyed my story and gained something from my own experience in this great game we call tennis.

WARD'S SKINNY ON STEVE

It's been an eye opener to revisit Steve's impressive tennis resume, and I would like to brag about his achievements as follows:

- Top 100 in the world from 1974 to 1983
- Played in 32 major championships
- In 1977, won gold medals in singles and doubles (with partner, Larry Nagler) for the U.S. in the Maccabiah Games in Tel Aviv, Israel

- Tour wins over Raul Ramirez, Vijay Amritraj, Jose Higueras, Adriano Panatta, and many others

- Coached tour players, Gilad Bloom (Israel), Jaime Yzaga (Peru), Reed Cornish and Vince Spadea (U.S.)

- Won 2 singles titles on the tour and had numerous doubles victories

- Inducted into USTA Mid-Atlantic Tennis Hall of Fame in 1993

- Inducted into the Maryland State Athletic Hall of Fame in 2019. In impressive company with the likes of Babe Ruth, Jimmy Fox, and Johnny Unitas. One of only three tennis players inducted to date.

- Coaches at the Gilman School in Baltimore, Maryland and led the Greyhounds to 12th place finish at the high school championships in Kentucky. Also led his team to seven consecutive conference titles in the Maryland Interscholastic Athletic Association. He set the MIAA record for most consecutive titles and most championships in the history of the league.

- Author of *Lightning Strikes, The Life and Times of a Professional Tour Tennis Player,* 2017. It describes his life growing up in Baltimore, Maryland, and as a professional tennis player.

I'm proud to help Steve celebrate a wonderful career that just keeps on giving. He gives back successfully, as shown by the vast array of records his teams have earned under his watch at the Gilman School.

Steve's passion for the game is as strong as ever, spanning six decades and counting. I hadn't spoken to him for over forty years and to rekindle our relationship was special, as he is not only a great tennis player with an interesting tennis journey, but his fine achievements and passion for the sport are inspiring to all that meet him. His energy seems just as strong as the seven-year-old kid's, who once pounded balls on the backboard sixty plus years ago.

Growing up in Maryland myself and competing among the top players in my respective age groups, I fondly remember the older guys, including Steve. The State of Maryland provided the tennis community with many talented players, and I was lucky to see firsthand the growth and development of not only Steve's skill sets, but of his peers, Harold Solomon and Fred McNair. They collectively fed off one another, ultimately making it to the big stage.

If you would like to read more about Steve's journey, check out *Lightning Strikes*. I appreciate his contribution to *Tennis Life* and hope his experience will motivate aspiring juniors to take it to the next level as he did. Many thanks for your story, old friend!

BILLY MARTIN

I was born in Evanston, Illinois in 1956 on Christmas Day. When I was seven years old, my family moved just down the road to River Forest. My mother and father, both being avid recreational tennis players, immediately joined the River Forest Tennis Club. My dad also became a member of the Tennis Patrons Association, an organization that helped raise the money necessary to develop local junior players. Soon, I was learning the basics of the sport from one of the club pro's, Rudy Witsman, and later began working with the head pro, Dennis Konicki, a Big Ten champ for Northwestern University.

A few years later, I became even more enamored with tennis thanks to the U.S. Men's National Clay Court Championships, which had been taking place at the River Forest facility since 1935 (now held in Houston, Texas), and pretty much in our backyard considering we lived only three blocks from it. One of those tournaments sparked my desire to make the sport even more of a priority. It just so happened we housed a player for that year by the name of Billy Lenoir. In those days, when prize money wasn't much, it was commonplace for players to stay with members of the local tennis community. I got to know Billy during his stay with us, looking up to him as a sort of mentor. He had already logged a high school win against the future great, Arthur Ashe. I loved to watch him compete. He was unique in that he hit two handed for both his forehand and backhand. He inspired me, and as a result, my dream of being on the tour was set in motion.

By age ten, I was competing locally in junior tournaments. It wouldn't be long after, that my parents (my mother mostly), carted me around the country, where I competed on the national circuit, as well as the year-end event, the Orange Bowl. I must say my junior tennis career was quite successful, the competition and related lifestyle helping me tremendously in later years. I learned how to compete, handle my nerves, travel, socialize, and win modestly, while managing to lose very infrequently. I achieved the number one ranking in every division throughout my junior career except for the 12 and Under, where interestingly, I played the author of this book in doubles at the National Doubles Championships in Chattanooga, Tennessee (stay tuned for Ward's account of that match). My junior ranking allowed me entry into tour level matches while still in high school, and one of my most memorable wins as a 17-year-old came in the quarterfinals of the Washington D.C. Grand Prix tournament. In a tight final set tiebreaker, I beat Stan Smith, the world number seven at the time. It was a major confidence booster knowing I could play with the big dogs.

Upon graduating from high school the following year, I accepted a full scholarship to UCLA. Surprisingly, my parents made a deal with me that if I won the NCAA Singles Tournament, then I could leave college for the tour. Lo and behold, I won it my freshman year, under UCLA coach, Glenn Bassett. I felt compelled to take advantage of the amazing position I found myself in. The memorable five set win against George Hardie propelled me to number 50 in world, the ranking points allowing me to get straight into the main draws of all the tournaments, including the majors.

My first few years on the tour after leaving UCLA were an eye opener. While the money was good, my crazy success in the juniors didn't continue through to the world of professional tennis. I eventually learned that working harder than the other guys was not enough, as it had been as a junior. Now I had to study my upcoming opponents' weaknesses and work at attacking them. Once I realized that, I had some good runs in 1977, and there's one win I'll never forget. It happened at Wimbledon in the third round against the third seed, Guillermo Vilas. I knew it was going to be a challenge, since I had practiced with him and played against him before. But I thought the grass surface would suit my game more and went into the match with confidence. I was also fortunate to have had lessons with Bjorn Borg's coach, Lennart Bergelin, and practice sessions with Rod Laver prior to stepping on court. I was also careful not to play the match in my head before entering the stadium, adopting a nothing to lose mindset. My strategy worked. I beat him in three straight sets, my serve and volley game pressuring him convincingly. I was so pumped, that I showed up to the post-match press conference in a white Superman sweatshirt! I continued my run to the quarterfinals, where unfortunately I lost to Vitas Gerulaitis in four sets.

Interestingly, when it comes to my most memorable loss, Vilas gets the honor as my opponent again. It was just one year later at the French Open, and he was the defending champion. Clay being his favorite surface, and with the slow conditions, he couldn't have been more at home. It was a very long and grueling match, going five sets. I was up 4-1 in the final set, up two service breaks and an ad. I remember the shot vividly—I approached the net and had a relatively easy forehand volley. But the moment and my nerves got the best of me. I froze, losing the point, the game, and ultimately the match. If had properly navigated that one all-important shot, I feel sure I could have pulled out the win.

What about hindsight? If I could go back in time and do things differently, there's one thing that stands out more than anything else—my early exit from college. A second year at UCLA would have gone a long way in helping me mature as a player and a person. Though I had played tournaments since I was ten, I was always playing for the love of it and bragging rights. The only pressure up to that point was to collect a trophy and ranking, while all my expenses were generously being covered by my parents. By quitting college and joining the tour, suddenly tennis became my job! The duress associated with having to win to justify my existence on the court, was now a reality. Knowing I had my parents' blessing, leaving after my freshman year seemed completely logical. Looking back now in the rear-view mirror, I can see the benefits that I would have gained by staying longer. That being said, I'm okay with the decision I made back then and have no serious regrets about it.

Just like many of my peers, I have some entertaining tour stories worth repeating. After my memorable win over Stan Smith in D.C., I wanted to go out on the town. The gentleman who put me up for the week offered to let me take his nice new Porsche for a spin after my big victory. Keep in mind, I was only a teenager and just had my best day on the tour in my budding career. Crazy, right? Could it get any better than this? Well, my dream drive came to a screeching halt when blue lights flashed behind me, and I was pulled over. When asked to produce the proper insurance and registration for the vehicle, I couldn't find the documents anywhere inside. Of course, the officer was instantly suspicious. With no cell phones at the time, I couldn't contact my host. I explained the situation but to no avail. The officer put me in his squad car and drove me to what I thought was my host's house in the affluent neighborhood. He knocked on the door, and the man who opened it recognized me as the guy he watched beat Stan earlier in the day. He yelled to his guests, "Hey, this is the guy we watched beat Stan Smith this afternoon!" The officer being reassured that I was not just some young punk driving a stolen car, used the man's phone to call my host. The police officer was satisfied with the conversation, took me back to the Porsche, and let me go off into the night. You will never guess who the man was that opened the door—The White House Chief of Staff at the time, and the former Secretary of State, Donald Rumsfeld.

Another fun memory that sticks out in my mind was playing in the annual Robert F. Kennedy Pro-Celebrity Tennis Tournament. It was held in New York City, just prior to the U.S. Open. Various celebrities took part in the event, alongside top ranked players. My partner was Senator Ted Kennedy, and we made it to the finals before losing to Brian Gottfried and Bill Cosby. I had the pleasure of meeting the Kennedy family, including Arnold Schwarzenegger and his wife, Maria Shriver. Fast forward one year later. I'm at the airport in New York, gathering my luggage and heaving my tennis bag over my shoulder, when I hear a shout from an entourage of people coming toward me. The familiar voice asked, "Billy, do you need a ride?" It was Ted Kennedy. I was amazed that he recognized me, even if it had only been a year since we partnered together.

In 1982 at the age of 27, I was forced to end my playing career due to a condition called hip dysplasia that caused immense pain. Hip replacement was a possibility, but the surgery wasn't nearly as advanced then as it is today, so I chose to forego it for the time being. Enter my old UCLA coach, Glenn Bassett. He offered me a job as his assistant coach and urged me to complete my degree at the same time. School never came easy to me and the thought of studying again was a bit daunting. However, the athletic director informed me that if I aspired to be head coach in the future, I had to have a degree in hand to fulfill NCAA compliance. I'm proud to say, I took it a step further and got my MBA, via UCLA's archrival, the University of Southern California.

After several years as assistant to Coach Bassett, I took the helm in 1994 as head coach. Sixteen years of competition and 11 years assisting at UCLA, helped mold me into the successful head coach I am today. I take tremendous pride in nurturing my players, knowing their dream to play professional tennis was once mine. There are so many obstacles to face other than simply hitting balls across the net better than your opponent. I also try to help with the issues that student athletes must deal with, such as maintaining grades/eligibility, team status, dislike for classes and studying, pressure from home, and of course, the pressure to make the tour.

I'm beginning my 29th year as head coach and have loved the evolution of my tennis career more than the anyone can imagine. One could say that I'm living vicariously through my players now and enjoying every minute of it. I like to get to know each one and try to relate to their unique, individual personalities. My philosophy is never to let them think that I want it for them more than they do. I always try to empower them with self-motivation and encourage them to take the bull by the horns to call their own team meetings—without my presence. When a peer group speaks out to one another with constructive criticism, I feel that resonates more than if it was from me. I welcome all my players to step up and become a leader, and it doesn't necessarily mean they have to be the number one or two on the team. I look back fondly on two such students—MacKenzie McDonald and Marcos Giron. Both great players and leaders, they had a passion and commitment to win, which rubbed off on the team in a very positive way. Now both are competing successfully on the pro tour. I'm also proud to say my teams have earned 14 straight top NCAA finishes, with five of those finishes being in the nation's top five, as well as nine consecutive 20-plus winning seasons. Thanks to the success of my amazing players, I was named the Intercollegiate Tennis Association, Division One, National Coach of the Year and I was inducted into the ITA Hall of Fame.

Having coached for so long, I'd like to share what I believe to be good, sound advice for up-and-coming juniors. Let me start by reflecting on some of the things that I did to improve each year when I was one myself. As my competition aged and improved, it was necessary for me to keep up. And I can tell you with certainty that some of the all-time great players (several now coaches) made a big difference for me, their tutelage a huge help. I'm a proponent of developing a well-rounded game, along with adding very strong weapons to your stroke arsenal. To make it successfully on the professional circuit these days requires the possession of a very powerful ground stroke, with at least one distinctly outstanding shot that will help dictate play. I was blessed with a very solid ground game and a pretty good serve and volley, but always looking to improve. It was a meeting with former Aussie great, John Newcombe, that gave me momentum in perfecting my serve and forehand—two shots that he excelled in. He actually invited me to his tennis ranch in New Braunfels, Texas. Established in 1968, it's still going strong today. While there, I studied film of his amazing serve and forehand, and soon incorporated his technique. I liked his style, his competitiveness, his genuine love for the game, and in particular, his generosity in helping me improve. I'm forever grateful and thankful to this great champion.

It's normal to assume an aspiring tour player has the basic fundamentals. But to achieve more, a player should spend a good deal of time overcoming his or her weaknesses, while simultaneously nurturing that essential big weapon that virtually all great players possess. To that end, I feel professional instruction is preferable. When I played as a junior, nobody had a full-time coach, and the tennis academy concept was in its infancy stage. It's ultimately a personal decision as to which method to choose. I don't believe that an academy is for everyone but it's certainly a viable option. You should have a coach in some form or fashion, and preferably a former player who has both knowledge of the game and experience in competition. The person you choose should have the type of personality that can adapt to the player, because there's no one size that fits all.

My last bit of advice is to strongly consider going to college and play for two years. The education obtained, maturation, and match play experience, along with the daily practice routine, is an essential stepping stone to the tour.

Now for the subject of nerves. Virtually every player out there has to deal with the pressure and the handling of associated nerves. In the old days, the topic of mental toughness was rarely mentioned. However, an old friend of mine, Bjorn Borg, epitomized this concept. Bjorn was so calm, cool, and collected as the saying goes, and never seemed to get nervous. His expression always appeared as a blank stare. I managed nerves in my own way, and for the most part it worked, although as previously mentioned, the nerves and situation got to me playing against Vilas. I believe the tendency in a nervous situation is to rush things. I always told myself to slow it down, work/build the point, and go to a happy place in my mind.

Modern day players handle the nerves similarly. For instance, Maria Sharapova would turn her back to the court, trying to get her thoughts and nerves in check. Borg, on the other hand, kept every emotion inside while playing. After Wimbledon one year, we practiced together on his island retreat, playing nonstop tennis and Badminton. He literally broke a badminton racquet in anger! For the first time ever, I saw a bit of a temper, one that he never displayed while on court in any event I saw him play in. I can't be sure, but I think it might have been his nerves that finally contributed toward his decision to retire at such a young age. Keeping all the emotions inside is problematic but in deference to Bjorn, he had more pressure than most of the great players in his day, and possibly the nerves got to him in the end.

I think that about wraps up the tale of my obsession with tennis. For those of you who have now heard my story, or perhaps even saw me play, please know that I love this sport, and I'll be forever grateful to have lived this incredible life revolving around the fuzzy yellow ball. And if by chance your travels bring you to Los Angeles, please consider a visit to the UCLA tennis complex and take in a match or two. If I don't look anything like my player photo, it might be because it was taken about forty years ago! I can promise the reader one thing—my passion for tennis is as strong as ever, and I'm so very pleased to have had the privilege of sharing my memorable adventure with you.

WARD'S SKINNY ON BILLY

Speaking on the phone with Billy Martin, some 42 years after we faced each other in the finals of the Boys Western 14 and Under in Ohio, was incredibly special. While discussing our match, it was evident who the better player was. There are so many reasons why. However, the obvious one is the fact that he didn't remember our match, while I have replayed it many times in my head over the years, the outcome never changing. Billy was the winner by the score of 6-4,10-8. This was before tiebreakers were conceived and I'd like to think I could have won if there were breakers.

Another encounter I had with Billy came in the National 12 and Under doubles in Chattanooga, Tennessee. I teamed up with Scott Smith from Winter Park, Florida, this time with a victory, defeating Billy and his partner, Bill Tompkins, from Ft. Lauderdale, Florida. I'm enormously proud of this most inconsequential win against a guy that ended up being named the Junior Player of the Century by Inside Tennis Magazine!

Any tennis player growing up in that era knew full well that Billy was one of the finest junior players in the history of our sport. He was a relentless competitor, extremely consistent and obviously detested losing, as he never seemed to come out on the wrong side of any given contest. He captured the 1973 and 1974 junior titles at Wimbledon, U.S. Open and the Orange Bowl. He won the NCAA singles championships in 1975 over George Hardie (thanks George for sharing that memory), while leading his UCLA Bruins to the team championship that same year and winning all nineteen of his dual matches!

Ranked as high as 32 in 1975, he defeated the world number three Guillermo Vilas at Wimbledon in 1977 and enjoyed 143 other match wins during his professional career. Billy is the only person in tennis history to win the NCAA team championships as both a player and a coach, and as a result, was later inducted into the ITA Hall of Fame. He had an amazing all-around game and contemplating his comments about the need to have big weapons, I can only surmise this might have been part of the reason that he did not break into the top ten, win a major or become a household name. The respect he has earned from yours truly, and virtually every player that I have spoken with in *Tennis Life*, is off the charts. Billy is truly a legend in our sport and anyone who played this fine gentleman knew they were in for a titanic struggle. His love for the game transcended quite naturally into coaching at UCLA, enabling all his players to soak in his wisdom, knowledge, and expertise.

Such a gentleman and ever so modest, thanks so much for sharing your story, Billy. I can't wait another 42 years to see you again in person—or the reunion will end up taking place six feet under. I must get out to Los Angeles and visit with you on the sidelines soon. Go Bruins!

FERNANDO MAYNETTO

I grew up in Lima, Peru. As a child, I fondly remember accompanying my father to the Lima Lawn Tennis Club on weekends, where I would watch him play with his friends. Sadly, I lost my father to cancer soon after, when I was only nine and a half years old. To cheer me up and get me out of the house, my cousin, Alfredo Hanza, continued taking me to the red clay courts, the difference being that a racquet was now in my own hands. I quickly became hooked. Alfredo would be the catalyst in my tennis journey, as he had been ranked as high as number three in Peru. I then became close to a player by the name of Miguel Maurtua, who was two years older than me. He came from a wealthy family and helped nurture me along the way. He was like a big brother and helped me with equipment, balls, and anything else I might need to be successful in the sport. He also encouraged me to study English so that I could go to college in the States. It seemed I was a natural athlete, and it took me just three years to make the national team. I punched my ticket to Bolivia, to play in my first 14 and Under international tennis tournament. I began to represent Peru regularly, playing junior tournaments including the South American Championships, the Banana Bowl in Brazil, and the highly coveted Orange Bowl in Miami, Florida. The Orange Bowl is where I had my first good victory—by winning the doubles championship with my partner, Ricardo Ycaza. At just 15 years old, I was invited to be the reserve player for the Davis Cup team. I'm proud to say, it would be the start of an 18-year relationship with the tournament, both as a player and captain in 1987 and 1988.

During my senior year of high school, the Peruvian Tennis Federation fell on hard times and didn't have enough money to send everyone on the team to the Orange Bowl for the final tournament of the year. Thus, three of us were vying for the one open spot. My coach ultimately made the decision to hold a round robin, in which the winner would get to go. Since my family didn't have the money to send me to Miami, and because I needed to compete in the tournament to secure a tennis scholarship for college, I knew I had to win the round robin. And that's what I did. I went to the Orange Bowl and soon after, was offered college scholarships. Where did I go to college? My hometown mentor, Miguel, ended up at Penn State two years before me, and had promised me that if he could get into Penn State, he would get me a tryout for the team. Following the Orange Bowl my senior year, I found my way there and just as Miguel had promised, he got me a tryout for the team. Unfortunately, there was a slight problem—I'd never played on hard courts and that was all the Penn State tennis team had. The pace being unfamiliar to me, I couldn't beat any of the other players and as a result, no scholarship was offered. But I was given another opportunity with Wingate Junior College. It was there that I met Steve Vaughan, who was attending Wingate with a half tennis, half basketball scholarship. He took me under his wing, and I ended up traveling home with him on the weekends to

Greensboro. He even went as far as to set me up on dates, his dad spotting me $20 to make sure the girls had a good time! That year playing for Wingate, I ended the season undefeated, winning the regional tournament and then the National Junior College Singles Championship. Steve and I would travel together that summer, playing junior tournaments all over the south. During a tournament in Charlotte, we both caught the eye of Clemson's coach at the time, Dr. Bill Beckwith. He offered me a full ride scholarship and a half scholarship to Steve. I refused to take the full ride unless Steve got the same deal. Dr. Beckwith agreed that if Steve could make the team, he could have a full ride, and so he did, squeaking in at number six. I played number one all three years I was there, and Steve rose to number two for both his junior and senior year. In 1977, immediately following graduation, I went down to Florida for three months to help Harry Hopman with his tennis camp. Unfortunately, while there, my student visa expired, and I was forced to return to Peru. Once back in Lima, Miguel and I joined forces again to form our own tennis academy, working as partners for a few months. In the meantime, I applied for a visa to go back to the U.S. to start playing on the Penn Circuit. Miguel was going to join me and help fund my start. I went back first, but Miguel never followed due to family issues. That affected my funding, and I was left with little money to start the circuit—think I had like $150 in my pocket. With a little financial help here and there, I was able to get by. After completing the first round of Penn Circuit satellite tournaments, I finished tied for 15th place with two other players. Out of all the hundreds of players that competed in the satellite, only 16 got into the Masters, where ATP points were guaranteed. I was called to the tournament director's office along with the other two players. Director Brian Early, put three pieces of paper into a trophy cup. Only one piece had the number 15 written on it, meaning one of us would get in by luck of the draw and the other two would have to play a match for the 16th spot. Lo and behold, I picked the golden ticket, assuring me my first ATP point. By the end of my first year, I was ranked 155 in the world. That got me to my first Grand Prix tournament.

How would I define my time on the Grand Prix tour? Like so many others, as a journeyman. I had an average ranking of 175 for approximately three years. I hit my high ranking of 104 for a few weeks in 1981, allowing me to enter the main draw of the French Open, Wimbledon, and US Open that year. As mentioned earlier, I was also a Davis Cup player, as well as captain for Peru. I had some good wins on the tour but one of my most memorable matches was interestingly a loss. It was at the 1982 French Open against Ivan Lendl—first round on center court, a large crowd in attendance. The atmosphere on center court against one of the top five players in the world was electrifying and despite the thrashing I received, I'll never forget the feeling of stepping onto that legendary court against one of the best players in the world. My friend, Miguel, who was living in France at the time, came to watch me play. What I enjoyed most on the tour was the excitement of traveling to new cities and countries, and then meeting and forming bonds with players from the various cultures and backgrounds. It was always fun to discover new tournament venues and the local cuisines. My most memorable trip has to be the one to Africa in 1983, as I enjoyed so many out of the ordinary experiences! Players had big incentive to travel and play there. The Nigerian Tennis Association would give players a $5000 bonus on top of the prize money won in the tournament. In addition, I was entered straight into the main draw of both the Ogun and Lagos challenger tournaments. But there was one small catch. The prize and bonus money were given to the players in Nigerian currency, basically forcing us to spend it all in Nigeria. One of the players, who had played in Nigeria before, told me to go to the Pan Am ticket office and buy airline coupons with the money. Interestingly, after a few of us took his advice, the Nigerian authorities got wind of our creativity, and when the rest of the guys tried to do the same, they were turned down!

Then there were the unusual cultural eye openers. When rooming with Sashi Menon at the tournament's hotel in Ogun, he explained with a straight face that our third "roommate", a giant lizard, had purposely been placed in our room to eat the ravenous mosquitos and would not bother us when we slept. Looking back, surely he was pulling my leg since I didn't hear of anyone else having one in their room, but it makes for a good story, right? We also had no access to conventional showers. Instead, when we wanted to bathe, the staff would bring us buckets of water, one large one with murky water for the body and one small one with clear water to wash our face. Fun, fun. Driving to Lagos for the next tournament, we saw burned cars on the highway. Seemed that was just a prelude to what we would see upon arriving in Lagos—their tallest building had been vandalized and then set on fire. It was an unnerving time to be in Nigeria. Tensions between the civilian and military aspects of the government had been rising, as evidenced by the destruction we had witnessed. In fact, we stayed at the Venezuelan ambassador's residence in Lagos as a precaution. I remember the room being incredibly hot, and we had no choice but to open the windows and be eaten alive by giant mosquitos! Thank goodness one of the players I was traveling with, Carlos Di Laura, had brought along a spiral smoking mosquito repellent. But even with that, we spent all night trying to kill them. Grateful to leave Lagos after my exit from the tournament, the next stop was Tunis, Tunisia, about an 11-hour drive. What a difference a country makes. Tunisia had some of the most beautiful Mediterranean beaches and spiciest meat couscous I've ever had. I liked the couscous so much, I had my fill of it. My ass was on fire, and I had the runs for two consecutive days! Maybe too much information? Sorry, some experiences really register in one's memory bank, even sentimental memories of the bad stuff. A different type of pain in the ass? Carrying the heavy tennis laden luggage through the airports and being forced to run with it to the gates. Even worse, having to go up and down steps with it at train stations. It's amazing how much a player accumulates when being on the road for long periods of time, more so back then being prior to 9/11. And since money was an issue, it wasn't easy to go back home to Peru to dump what I acquired along the way. Ranking fluctuations between 100 and 200 in the world didn't quite cut it. But I still loved every minute of it, even the miserable ones.

When my career was winding down, I played a match in Chile, where I met the mother of my firstborn son, Nicholas. Later, during one of my frequent trips to Chile to visit Nicolas, I was introduced to my wife of 35 years, Paulina—mother of our daughters, Tania and Natalia. After Natalia was born 1993, I reached out to my old buddy, Steve Vaughan, to see if he knew of any coaching opportunities in the States that might be a good fit for me. Within weeks, he asked me to come to Naples, as he thought he had something that would be perfect. My family and I fell in love with Naples. I knew instantly it would be our new home. Hired as a tennis professional along with Steve at Grey Oaks Country Club, he and I grew the program together. Fast forward 25 years, I'm the head pro there and I still love pulling into the parking lot for work every day. In all those years, I've seen members that have come back from back injuries, knee replacement, shoulder surgery and even brain injuries. They have inspired me never to give up and to embrace this amazing life that we've all been given—to live each day with joy, enthusiasm, and compassion.

Juniors that aspire to play the tour ask me what my recipe for success is. Number one is having the love to play the game. When I was a youth, I couldn't wait to get out of school and meet my friends to hit. Also, develop good skills and technique early on. I believe as kids we learn more by watching than be being told because we can relate better to the game. Lastly, don't get hung up on being sponsored right out of the gate. I've heard juniors say, "I can't start playing in the pros if I don't have a sponsor that gives me 100,000 a year—I won't make it." Or this one, "If I don't make it in the top 200, I can't survive." As I mentioned earlier, I started with literally nothing but my passion to play opened amazing avenues for me. I may have not made the big bucks on the tour, but I got to play with the greats, travel all over the world, and learn five times more than any education ever could have given me.

In closing, I attribute much of my success in the sport to my undying passion for the game of tennis. The journey and later adventures were what propelled me to play at a high level. Being exposed to and part of a special group of athletes is what kept me improving and staying motivated. Money was always an obstacle, limiting my ability to travel better, eat well, sleep in nicer accommodations, have better equipment and pay for a better coach. But I always ask myself, if having all those things that money can buy had put more pressure on my life, then it might have limited my enjoyment of the game and the adventurous travels. The notion is like the cliché, "money doesn't always buy happiness", just expressed in my own words. One last thought. I can talk about the injuries that slowed me down, hurt my ranking, caused the inability to compete and loss of playing income. Of course, I wish I hadn't had to deal with them, but at the same time, they taught me other lessons and gave me greater rewards in my life. I believe that everyone has their destiny and that the word "if" can play a regrettable role, which personally, I don't like to associate myself with. I feel very fortunate that I played at the higher level ... period, and that I managed to enjoy every amazing experience. I owe it all to the classic, age-old sport known as tennis.

WARD'S SKINNY ON FERNANDO

It was 1975 when I first had the pleasure of meeting Fernando. It was my sophomore year, a mere 47 years ago. Fernando had just transferred to Clemson from Wingate College, along with his teammate and doubles partner, Steve Vaughan. It didn't take long for the two guys to assimilate with the rest of the Tiger tennis team. Even more impressive, Fernando was our number one singles and doubles player all three years he was at Clemson. But when you're the star of the team like that, it's only human nature for your fellow teammates to want to beat you any chance they get, and of course, I was not an exception. I managed to triumph over him and am I going to gloat about it? You bet! My victory was set in motion by our coach at the time, Dr. William Beckwith. He had the top six players on our team battle to play in the upcoming Princeton Invitational Collegiate Tournament at Princeton University in New Jersey. The annual prestigious event highlighted the top two players from 16 colleges, to play in a singles and doubles draw, consisting of 32 players in singles and 16 teams in doubles. So how did Coach Beckwith decide who would represent Clemson? There would be a series of challenge matches played amongst our entire team, with the last two players standing punching their tickets. I don't know what got into me during those challenge matches, but I came out on top, and in the process beat my good friend Fernando in straight sets. I'm proud to say it was the only loss he ever had to a fellow Clemson teammate during the three years he played there.

So being the top two players, Fernando and I headed to Princeton for the tournament. Our first doubles match was against the top seeded, All-American team from Columbia University consisting of Rick Fagel and Henry Bunis. Their reputations were frightful, since the week prior to the Princeton Invitational, they had taken part in an ATP tour event, with Fagel barely losing a three-setter to one of the world's best players at the time, Guillermo Vilas. Warming up with Fagel on the opposite side of the court, I can vividly recall the pre-match jitters, thinking we had no chance against the guys. However, Fernando became my fearless leader, his confidence rubbing off on me, and we put on a display that is the most memorable in my 50 plus years of competitive play. Under his watchful and encouraging eye, we played intelligently and patiently, as our opponents battered missile- like forehands at us. To compensate, we hovered near the net, hitting one volley after another at their feet. Of course, they picked on me being the weaker player. But I rose to the occasion. Cool-hand Fernando served out the match with precision, focus and brilliance unlike any other player I've partnered with in my entire life. I'll never forget that moment in my tennis journey even though we didn't win the tournament. I consider myself very lucky and will be forever thankful to have played a few matches with the great Fernando Maynetto. I still wonder after all these years how I was able to beat this amazing player. It had to be Fernando's higher level of play that motivated and inspired me to raise my game, stepping out of my comfort zone for that one week in my life.

Though his world ranking did not penetrate the top 100, I personally witnessed Fernando battling numerous number one players in the three years we were at Clemson together and he always competed on a high level. He could handle pace, big serve and volley games, or whatever the foe could throw at him. His reply was an amazingly solid one-handed backhand, great touch, an efficient serve and volley, great footwork, and a tennis IQ unlike anyone I have ever played with. Fernando has been teaching tennis ever since exiting the pro tour. It's safe to say that he is well liked and admired by the membership at Grey Oaks Country Club in Naples, Florida, where he's spent the last 25 years as head tennis professional. I'm so grateful that we've stayed in touch and that our friendship has not wavered after all these years. Mr. Maynetto, thank you so much for being a part of my life, sharing your amazing story with our readers, and of course, giving me my two most memorable moments on a tennis court!

RICKY MEYER

I grew up in Great Neck, New York, a region of Long Island. As a teen, I played for the Great Neck North High School tennis team all four years and I'm proud to say I had a 56-0 record in singles. That earned me a spot in the 1973 Faces in the Crowd, a monthly Sports Illustrated feature. Then I won the New York State High School Doubles Championship, twice with my brother, Bob, and once with Peter Brill. I reached the rankings of number two in the East in the 16 and Under, and number two in the 18 and Under. Thankfully, those stellar stats garnered several college scholarship offers, my choice being not too far from home—The University of Pennsylvania. I started out as the number three player my freshman year, ascending to number one during my last two years. I had the pleasure of playing alongside many fine partners, including Steve Yellin. Playing for a college team helped me to mature both mentally and physically. I didn't think about playing on the tour until my senior year. Even though it delayed my professional debut, I considered it to be the best way to develop both mind and game before facing the likes of my childhood idols on the world stage. As a result, I'm a strong proponent of going to college and have no regrets whatsoever. I always had my Wharton School of Finance degree to fall back on if I discovered the circuit wasn't for me.

Before I get to my time on the tour, I'd like to share the details of a very special match that occurred when I was a college student. It happened in the finals of the Eastern Men's Clay Court Championships, which just happened to take place in my hometown of Great Neck. I faced a 40-year-old eye surgeon, also from the state of New York. His name was Richard Raskind. We were good friends, having just played together on the U.S. Maccabiah team which had toured Israel the year before. Richard was the captain of the team and looked out for me, sort of like a big brother. After the tour, we would often meet up and practice together back home. However, this would be the only time we would ever face each other in a tournament. A very amicable match for obvious reasons, I ended up coming from behind to win it, 3-6, 8-6, 6-3. For those not in the know, this is a notable event because Dr. Richard Raskind would go on to become Renee Richards, tennis's first transgender pioneer. Amazingly, and as of this writing, she is still practicing ophthalmology at the ripe old age of 87! She became my eye doctor the year following our match and still is today.

Once on the tour, I played both singles and doubles, facing the highs and lows just like everyone else. My first big singles win came during the Sarasota tour stop in 1979 where I had to go through qualifying. I beat world number six, Bill Scanlon, in the second round of the main tournament, and then world number one, Ilie Nastase, in the semi-finals. I lost to Johan Kriek in the final but consider the event to be one of my most memorable. The following year, in 1980, I reached the televised third round of the U.S. Open by beating Trey Waltke and Chip Hooper, solid affirmation that I had finally made it on the tour. My opponent? None other than John McEnroe. I lost the first two sets. Winning the third set with two consecutive aces was a huge adrenaline boost for my confidence. Serving and volleying was my game and to do it successfully against one of the all-time best in his own backyard? It was certainly an amazing feeling. I ended up losing to him in four. However, playing on grandstand court at Flushing Meadow and giving McEnroe a scare, confirmed all my years of hard work—my dedication to the sport finally paying dividends. If the reader desires to see a glimpse of our interesting match, it can be found on You Tube with Tony Trabert commentating.

1981 was perhaps my momentous year on the tour for two reasons. By February, I'd broken into the top 100 in the world for the first time, reaching my career high ranking of 83. And in December of 1981, I hoisted the trophy for the only singles tournament I ever won on tour, a Grand Prix event in Sofia, Bulgaria. I also won two doubles tournaments—Napa with Chris Mayotte and the South African Open with Frew McMillan. Jay Lapidus and I also reached the finals of the Paris Indoors beating world number one, Ilie Nastase, and world number three, Adriano Panatta, in the semi-finals. I attribute that breakthrough year to my big serve and volley. The concept of taking time away that it provided, not only worked when hugging the baseline, but was also a factor when I moved towards the net. My forceful approach always put pressure on my opponents, as they were forced to hit outside their comfort zone. I covered the net extremely well and with good instincts. It was the style that I embraced and preferred to play, even though it didn't translate well on softer surfaces, such as clay. I also benefitted from some sage advice given to me by former top five player, Brian Gottfried. Once when we were practicing together, he couldn't reiterate enough the importance of being as fit as possible—not putting in the necessary training was totally unacceptable. He said it was not okay to lose a match because at six all in the third set you got tired; that being fit has nothing to do with talent. Embracing his advice was a critical element for my very physical style of play. Finally, I knew how to manage my nerves. I truly never feared those demons because being nervous is inevitable and part of the process—something that every player faces. I chose to manage the pressure situations by breathing deeply. It was as simple as that.

Who was the toughest opponent I ever played? John McEnroe without a doubt. I faced him a total of seven times in singles and doubles combined, losing every time, the most notable loss coming in the previously mentioned U.S. Open match. He had a pair of hands unlike anyone that I had ever played. Not only could I not predict his incoming shots, but I don't think he even knew where they were going! He was creative, innovative, and brilliant, and of course, a great competitor. I was very close to a doubles win against John and Peter Fleming in the 1982 U.S. Open. Alongside my partner, Eric Fromm, we lost a close three set match to them on the grandstand court. McEnroe would end up being one of the greatest doubles players of all time, and by no accident since he had the greatest volley of all time in my opinion.

Looking back, if I could have changed one thing about my game, it would have been to add a two-handed backhand to my repertoire. Obviously, the most common strategy when playing your opponent is to pick on the weaker side. And my one-handed backhand was weaker than my forehand. Keep in mind that most of my practice partners and peer group grew up hitting one-handed backhands, except for Gene Mayer and Michael Fishbach. One of my coaches, Warren Woodcock, had a beautiful one hander—the two hander not in his teaching vocabulary. Well, you know what they say ... better late than never. Now when playing recreationally, I put my right hand on top, meaning it's closer to the strings, rather than at the bottom near the butt of the racquet. The left hand is for the power and strength, and I find the only challenge is flipping the forehand grip so to speak. By applying this technique, I simply put my forehand grip in the middle so that I can comfortably slide my left hand below it. This may seem a bit unique and unorthodox but strangely, it works well. Certainly, the game of tennis has evolved to the point where most modern-day players are hitting the backhand with two hands, making a big difference no doubt.

Here is my advice for junior players. First and foremost, I recommend playing close to the baseline. By doing so, you take time and distance away from your opponent. You'll also develop faster hands, more efficient strokes, and make your opponent feel rushed, likely forcing him into committing more errors. Secondly, develop a big serve. My big serve was no accident. I learned to envision the serve toss like an elevator going up, the contact point with my strings as high as possible. In addition, Coach Woodcock had me jumping into my serve at age 16 to increase my serve power, and I practiced the shot more than any other. My daily practice routine included almost two hundred serves, comprised of one hundred first serves and an equal number of second serves, of course rotating between the deuce and ad court. I can't stress enough how much practicing the serve was overlooked by most players back in my day—as it is today as well. Finally, finding a great coach is critical for a junior, as proper fundamentals are most often learned through a good instructor. In my youth, I was blessed not only with Warren Woodcock, but also John Nogrady, who taught me sound mechanics early on.

The reader may find this difficult to believe, but I have no regrets looking back on my tennis journey. Being an athlete during my 20's had numerous benefits, to include lasting friendships with fellow juniors, collegiate and tour players. I thoroughly enjoyed seeing the world, meeting so many interesting people along the way, and visiting places most people would never have the opportunity to set their sights on. I found it fascinating to learn about other cultures, the plight of a few providing eye-opening experiences that I will never forget. I was fortunate enough to meet kings, queens, and presidents. Playing against so many talented players and defeating close to a dozen of them ranked in the world's top ten, in both singles and doubles, says that I played at the highest level possible. And of course, reaching the round of 16 at the Australian Open was a major accomplishment. To this day, I am extremely proud of all those wins. You can be assured, that if I had the chance to do it all again, I would.

WARD'S SKINNY ON RICKY

My path crossed Ricky's in Springfield, Ohio, at one of the nation's premiere junior tennis events, The Western. We happened to join forces at the event as doubles partners in the 16 and Under division. We played one of the best teams in the country at the time, Victor Amaya and Pat Dupree. We didn't win but it was a hard-fought contest, and we gave them one heck of a battle. I tried to hold up my end of the bargain, but Ricky was the man and because of him, we almost pulled off a major upset that day. Thus, I have some advice for all you juniors out there. It's simply to hook up with a partner like Ricky, put a saddle on him, and just ride! All kidding aside, the pleasure of meeting and playing alongside him was an experience I will never forget. And getting in touch with him for the purposes of this book after all these years—it's as if we haven't missed a beat.

To include Ricky's insight in *Tennis Life* was a no brainer due to the fact he achieved so much in his career. I personally witnessed his tennis IQ and wisdom on the court. His practice regimen was unique and effective, and any juniors aspiring to achieve what he did or beyond, I strongly urge them to reread his advice to juniors.

Being brought up in the greater New York area, Ricky feels that his talented peer group, as well as growing up playing on clay courts, indirectly forced him to develop a well-rounded arsenal of shots. His prowess certainly showed up on the tour, especially when facing the great John McEnroe at the 1980 U.S. Open. Though he didn't beat him that day, anyone watching the match would have thought he had a solid chance. However, as we all know, the top tier players have that extra tennis-specific DNA that propels them to more victories. Nonetheless, it's my opinion, subjective of course, that Ricky falls into the category of special players. I'm a firm believer that anyone who makes it onto the big stage does not necessarily have to win a grand slam or major tournament to be considered as such. And to watch the video of Ricky playing McEnroe at the Open with legendary tennis players and commentators, Tony Trabert and John Newcombe, singing the praises of his mighty serving, well—that speaks volumes.

I'm very proud of Ricky and forever grateful that he nearly carried me to an amazing junior upset back in the day. Another great player now in the books of *Tennis Life,* and a truly wonderful human being. Thanks for sharing your journey, Ricky.

EVAN PHILLIPS

I was born in Georgetown, British Guiana in 1950. Now known simply as Guyana (and spelled differently as of 1966), it borders Venezuela to the west, Brazil to the south, Suriname to the east, and the Atlantic Ocean to the north. It also has the distinction of being the only English-speaking country in South America. Growing up there in the 1950's and early to mid-1960's was a very significant period in my life. The country was engaged in a bitter struggle for independence from Britain. There were worker's strikes, riots, shootings, episodes of arson and other acts of violence around the country. I remember the strong scent of teargas as I rode my bike to school. Independence was finally achieved in 1966 bringing with it some much needed stability.

Being a British colony during my childhood, cricket was the most popular sport in Guiana. However, at the time, my father was playing grass court tennis. In fact, he was on the 1957 Guiana championship team, alongside the country's top player, Ian McDonald. They beat Jamaica in what was referred to as the

Brandon tournament back then, the premiere lawn tennis event in the Caribbean. My father being a natural coach, he taught myself, my brother, and my sister how to play. Before I knew it, I was the national junior champion at age 14 and never lost another local junior match before aging out. In 1968, I was invited to play in the junior event at Wimbledon. It was a significant tournament as it was the first year of the open era of tennis. I played one of the better kids and lost easily in the first round. However, I met and roomed with Italian, Adriano Panatta, for a couple of days, a future French Open champion and the only man who would go on to defeat Bjorn Borg at Roland Garros—twice. After Wimbledon was over, I stayed in England for five weeks, playing tournaments every week, gaining a much better understanding of competitive play, something I didn't really have access to back home. In retrospect, I wished I'd played Junior Wimbledon at the end of those five weeks rather than before. I might have had a much better outcome during the first round.

A few weeks after returning to Guyana, I was offered a tennis scholarship by Oral Roberts University in Tulsa, Oklahoma. I found myself on an extremely strong college team, very likely one that could have been considered top ten in the country, if not higher. Unfortunately, we couldn't get an official ranking, as the university was new and hadn't been accredited yet. My Hall of Fame tennis coach, Bernie Duke, developed the "picture-postcard" recruiting method. Basically, he sent a postcard to every tennis association in the world, asking if they had any tournament players who were interested in a tennis scholarship in the U.S. What was the result? Two Davis cuppers and several high-level players who would probably have played on tour if there had been any money in the game back then. Our number one player, Pekka Saila had a win over Tom Okker, who was number seven in the world at the time.

When I first practiced with my teammates, I found the pace of the ball to be a bit overwhelming. But after a few weeks, I adjusted quite comfortably. Unfortunately, a decision one afternoon in early October would change things. Starting to rain on the courts, I decided to go over to the soccer field to get a workout with the soccer team. I fell chasing the ball, the result being major knee surgery the next day. I didn't play on the team my freshman year but managed to keep my scholarship. I filled the extra time tutoring the basketball team and courting (no pun intended) fellow student, Mary Anne Parker. We were married the following year and at the time of this writing, we've been together 51 years. Along the road to knee recovery, about a year or so later, I played a couple of tournaments in Florida over winter break, one being at legendary Holiday Park in Fort Lauderdale. I had a very close loss to Brian Gottfried, a future world number three. It was great to experience the electric atmosphere at Holiday Park and I'll never forget watching Jimmy Evert give a lesson with a laundry basket!

It wasn't until my senior year that my knee was strong enough to play higher level tennis. Playing as the team's number two player, I went 23 and 1, my only loss occurring in Boulder, Colorado—my first time playing high altitude tennis. After graduating that summer with a Bachelor of Arts degree in Sociology and English Literature, I set my sights on the Tulsa City Championship. I made it all the way to the finals, defeating my good friend, Paul Lockwood, a highly ranked junior who played number one for Oklahoma and eventually coached there for 22 seasons. That fall, I entered graduate school, and a year and a half later had my Masters in Writing and Rhetoric.

What was next? Living, working, and playing in paradise. I took a job teaching English on the beautiful island of Barbados. I not only taught English but coached the tennis team and managed to find extra time to play cricket for one of the top clubs. I also played several tennis tournaments, the most significant event being the Virgin Islands Championship in St. Croix, which I won. That win would produce a job offer as the head pro at the Frenchman's Reef Hotel in St. Thomas. I accepted, and my wife and I moved there later that year, which is where, by the way, I would meet the author of this book.

Living in St. Thomas created the perfect environment—giving lessons and playing in tournaments. I really enjoyed coaching, especially teaching the local kids. The teaching and tournament playing soon turned into a somewhat elaborate, yet unassuming business enterprise, since my wife and I bought the tennis concession at Frenchman's Reef. And thanks to Mary Anne's business brilliance, we were able to turn our tennis shop into a beach boutique, tripling the gross. We later opened similar businesses at two other resorts, as well as a wholesale business. It was quite a busy little operation, and I was grateful that I could continue to coach and play tournaments through it all. I was the leading player in the Virgin Islands for about fourteen years, winning over a hundred tournaments in singles and doubles, while giving over 20,000 hours of lessons. Most of the tournaments were played in the Caribbean, many of them USTA opens in the Virgin Islands and Puerto Rico.

In 1976, I had a successful year competing. I played for Guyana in the Commonwealth Caribbean Team Championships, just as my father had in 1957. The prestigious Brandon Trophy at stake, my country was victorious. The event is like a Caribbean Davis Cup, and in the exciting finals, we defeated Jamaica. In five sets, my brother, Cecil, won the last reverse singles match. Unbeaten in the tournament, I was voted most valuable player. We also won the women's event, claiming the Phillips Trophy, with my sister, Debbie playing number one on the team. To say the least, my father, who donated the Phillips Trophy for the women, and who taught us all to play, was a happy camper.

After returning to St. Thomas, I traded in my racquet for the new Prince oversized racquet, winning five strong tournaments in a row. I truly thought it was some kind of magic wand and later that year, as if to confirm my fanciful thinking, I was selected to play on the Caribbean Davis Cup team against Canada. Unfortunately, when I was in Ottawa practicing for the tie, I turned my knee and injured it once more. I had surgery in Toronto the following winter. I wasn't sure I'd ever play at a high level again but managed to play and win tournaments in the Caribbean and U.S. over the next several years. In between events, I worked with several local kids on a pro bono basis to improve their game, enjoying the challenge of coaching and watching my students' progress. Even though groups of students were more financially rewarding, I concentrated on private lessons, simply because I didn't believe I could coach them as well in a group setting, especially in their earlier days of development. I used my own style as a coaching model, attaining good results. I focused on basic flat ground strokes, like those of Chris Evert and Jimmy Connors, as well as under spin backhands. I also believed in full-service motions and volleying prowess, giving the kids solid all-around games. I'm proud to say that several of my students were ranked in the top five in USTA Puerto Rico and probably would have been even better if the cost of traveling to the U.S. for tournaments and more exposure, hadn't been so cost prohibitive. Nevertheless, I helped several of them obtain tennis scholarships on the mainland. The coaching part of my tennis life was, and always will be, very important to me.

In September 1989, category five Hurricane Hugo, hit the Virgin Islands, leaving extensive damage. Most hotels were closed for several months, and the economy of the islands practically came to a screeching halt. Our shop at Frenchman's Reef was severely damaged. Unable to come to an agreement with the general manager on how to reopen, we decided to close it after 14 years. A couple of months later, while on vacation in Virginia Beach with a good friend, I was introduced to golf. Immediately intrigued by the game, I spent the next 18 years playing, coaching, and even administering the game, as president of the St. Thomas/St. John Golf Association. Even though I could get by with a compromised left knee on my golf swing, it became more and more difficult for me to move quickly and change directions on the tennis court. I managed to win a couple of tournaments over the next few years, but by my 40th birthday in 1991, I knew the only competition going forward would be on the golf course. I spent most of my time working in our businesses and golfing whenever I could. I caught on to the game rapidly and within two years was playing to a nine handicap. I became one of the better golfers on the island, playing on the St. Thomas team in the annual Eastern Caribbean Championships for four years.

During the years of tennis and golf in St. Thomas, Mary Anne and I, with the support of our employees, held a number of charity events with some of the tournaments we ran. We raised approximately two hundred thousand dollars for very worthy causes in the Virgin Islands. I am forever grateful to my wife for making all our endeavors work so well. I truly believe that the combination of our retail business, as well as my coaching and playing tournaments, provided the means for an incredible life—one that allowed me to continually pursue my passion for all things tennis. Even though I didn't make the kind of money from playing that tour players make today, the notoriety I gained from playing and coaching opened many doors for us in the business world and society where we lived.

In 1995, unfortunately there was another direct hit from a major hurricane. After twenty years in St. Thomas, we decided it was time to leave the island. It was not a decision taken lightly, as we both truly loved it there. However, recovering from a major storm on a small, isolated island is extremely taxing. Medical care became more difficult to come by for certain ailments. Thus, we moved to Tucson in 1996, settling into a retirement way of life. I worked hard on my golf game, got down to a 4.7 handicap, and did quite well in local tournaments. But soon I was bored and realized that I missed teaching. I passed a certification course from the U.S. Golf Teacher's Federation and in 1999, started coaching on the range at the La Mariposa Sports and Fitness Club. I also secured a substitute teaching position and two years later, I was an adjunct professor in the writing department at Pima Community College. Teaching both writing and golf was a great combination for me. Then in 2004, the owners of La Mariposa, having learned of my tennis background, entreated me to coach their three sons. I decided to take the plunge on the courts again and in doing so, had to let my classroom position go. Well, the tennis began to flourish and eventually, I had to stop coaching golf as well. In the beginning, I only wanted to teach four to six kids on a part-time basis but found that I couldn't say no, and the program just kept growing. My goal was to teach them to play tennis at a high level, but still allow them to have a normal life. This included going to high school, being interested in and fully aware of the importance of academics, and then going to college, hopefully on a tennis scholarship. I was able to achieve these goals with several students. When it comes to tennis academies, I've never been a fan of them. I don't believe kids should leave their homes and go to a place where they spend most days hitting tennis balls for hours at a time. While tennis is a wonderful game, too many hours spent on it can interfere with important things in life. Kids need a healthy balance between family, academics, sports, and social interaction.

I'm proud to say that I've developed a very good coaching system and have posted approximately 50 videos on You Tube, featuring methods from the system I used in St. Thomas, to include hitting the ball off the front foot as much as possible and using topspin on the forehand within the weight transfer foundation. From 2004 to 2019, my instruction efforts moved along very well, growing to about 40 kids and two assistants. In 2020, Covid hit, forcing me to take a year off, and at the time of this writing, I've returned to coaching but on a smaller scale.

So how do I feel about the state of American men's tennis today? Basically, I think that with the money spent on junior players, there should be more promising talent. An American male player hasn't won a major tournament since Andy Roddick did so in 2003. So why isn't American tennis better? I believe the problem is embedded in our general coaching system and that some of it needs to be changed. Tennis is a great sport, but it is one of the most difficult to learn, when it comes to playing at a high level. Even with all the videos and other resources available, it is practically impossible for any young player to be ranked in the top 20 in their section without a lot of lessons. The fundamentals, including swing patterns and footwork take a lot of time to master. Because of this, it's extremely difficult, if not impossible, to develop good basics in the early stages of development if the instructor is spending time with more than two kids. In a group, especially a large one, there is simply not enough time for each player to execute correct swings an adequate number of times while hitting the ball. What's my assessment of a typical junior group lesson? Students are first asked to jog around the court and then stretch. They then form two lines, hit two balls, then move to the back of the line. The instructor can't stop for very long, if at all, to correct a swing. The kids are hitting balls individually for ten minutes each and waiting on their turn for 50. Even if this type of group meets three times a week, there's very little fundamental tennis being taught. Most kids in these types of clinics develop such poor stroke and positional habits in their first year of tennis, that they can never overcome them. It's therefore unlikely they'll ever play at a high level and then ask themselves, what when wrong. This cycle is repeated over and over and over, ad infinitum. Therefore, most kids who start group tennis instruction are lost to the possibility of playing championship tennis. In many instances, parents do recognize the importance and necessity of private lessons but they simple can't afford them. Decent instructions can easily cost $10,000 a year. And then when a kid starts to play tournaments and one includes the cost of travel, food, accommodation and entry fees, the total can really add up. The result? Only kids from wealthier families can afford to play and the others get left behind even though they may have more talent. Adding insult to injury, the USTA junior development program doesn't invite the top juniors to their camps until they're about 11 or 12, and after they've been working with private coaches for five to seven years. By the time kids who started clinics at age six get to age 11, thousands of them have left the game, primarily because they've only received instruction in clinics, and are still basically beginners who can't compete at a decent level. What's my remedy for this situation? We would have more talented juniors if the USTA had a strong grass roots program, whereby they have a good system with effective coaches who are trained to teach beginning kids. A method to choose the kids for this program should be devised, and the USTA should cover all the costs, so that the kids don't have to pay for it. Our tennis organization has a lot of monetary resources at its disposal. It makes approximately a quarter of a billion dollars annually off the U.S. Open. Much of this money is wasted by the Sections, by financing perfunctory or artificial junior development programs that have absolutely no chance of developing good players. There are simply too many of these meaningless programs. They should be a lot better.

I have one other thought regarding the state of American men's tennis. Tournaments like the Tulsa City championships I took part in were very common back in the day. In my USTA section, the Missouri Valley, there was a high-level tournament practically every week in the summer months, and several others throughout the rest of the year. This was also the norm in most, if not all the other sections. There were adult and senior rankings, besides just the junior rankings, and these were important to the players. Many college players competed in those tournaments, along with the top juniors and seniors. It gave former college players, who didn't think they could play pro tennis, a reason to keep playing, and many of them did for a long time. Suddenly, around the mid-eighties, there were less tournaments and those that were held, had less people playing in them. I believe this is when the NTRP rating system started to get more popular. Unfortunately, the NTRP tournaments appealed more to recreational players, and the hole this put in the regular tournament schedule caused many former college players to stop competing seriously. As a result, top juniors could no longer compete against them, and the situation led to the demise of U.S. tennis on a world class level. However, I'm hopeful that the ITA tournaments today are helping to rebuild the old competitive system.

Now 70, I'm proud to say that I'm still coaching juniors. To this day, I can clearly remember the first junior tennis tournament I played in Georgetown, British Guiana in 1963, and the first lesson I gave in Tulsa, Oklahoma in 1970. I believe my accident on the soccer field as a college freshman, and the knee surgeries that followed, helped to clarify my approach to the game. I enjoyed competing but wasn't going to be able to do it as a tour player. Therefore, I was very happy to play as a big fish in a small pond and as a result, win a lot of tournaments. I loved coaching, which I was able to do extensively, and with enthusiasm and success. I must say it's been a great ride and I look forward to continuing my tennis life in one form or another.

WARD'S SKINNY ON EVAN

In 1977, fresh out of college, I ended up in beautiful St. Thomas after working as a mate on a charter boat delivery out of Ft. Lauderdale. I got caught up in the fun island life and bummed around paradise for a few months. Looking for a court to practice my game, I was referred to the Frenchman's Reef Hotel and long story short, that's how I met Evan. He was the head tennis professional there and his office and teaching court was just fifty yards from the azure blue waters of the Atlantic Ocean. We became practice partners and good friends.

It hurts my ego to say this—Evan was always the winner when we practiced. But then again, he was the best player on the Caribbean circuit and to practice with him was something special. He used the old green Prince racquets, hitting very flat and linear strokes with depth and precision better than most. He had all the shots and if only his knees had been healthier, as those crucial body parts were compromised by injury and wear and tear. A bonus for me, he had me take over his position as head professional when he wanted to travel, and goodness knows, that extra cash came in handy since downtown Charlotte Amalie was a happening place in those days.

I was thrilled when Evan and I had a chance to play doubles together in a professional tournament in San Juan, Puerto Rico. Players from all around the Caribbean competed as prize money was the attractive "chum". I won a few rounds in the singles but fell short of the real money. Evan, however, was a different story. He competed quite well and advanced to the singles finals where he was slated to play world ranked player, Terry Ryan of South Africa. As far as the doubles, Evan and I played very well together. Our games complimented each other. My aggressive style coupled with his steady stewardship proved effective and we soon found ourselves in that final as well. The schedule called for the singles final to begin the next morning at 11:00 am, with the doubles final to immediately follow. The next day arrives, and the singles final gets played. The match lasted almost three hours, the hot tropical sun combined with the hard courts, as tough a foe as his opponent on the other side of the net. Terry won a nail biter via tiebreaker in the third set. The match ended at 2:00 pm and my dear partner, Evan, was lying in the locker room fighting off cramps, totally exhausted. The tournament director summoned me to the front desk and alerted me to the fact that hundreds of spectators had stayed for the doubles final and that we needed to start asap. One small detail I haven't divulged yet is that we were to play the tournament director's son! Of course, there was no way he was going to back down since his son was in the finals. I pleaded our case but to no avail. Quite literally, I almost had to pick Evan off the locker room floor to go with me onto the court. The tournament director's son and his partner were good, and not to say we could have beaten them under different circumstances, but I think if we were fresh, the outcome might have gone one hundred eighty degrees in our favor. I desperately tried to take most of the shots, but the guys were just too good and though we never gave up, the extenuating circumstances didn't seem fair in the end. I don't recall how much we won but the winner's check was certainly more appealing than our check. Oh, and FYI, Evan did avenge the singles loss to Terry Ryan two years later, when he defeated him in the finals of a tournament in St. Thomas, in straight sets.

That was the only tournament we played in since the circuit ended soon thereafter but suffice to say, playing with Evan was a privilege. Injuries and opportunity aren't always distributed equally in life and that fact certainly inhibited his ability to play on the bigger stage. Nevertheless, on the smaller stage of St. Thomas and surrounding islands, he was the dominant force, respected by anyone who knew him.

If by chance you happen to be in the Tucson, Arizona area, you might catch Evan out in the dry desert air, working with a potential junior upstart in tennis or golf. Though he is in the twilight of his career now, I have no doubt he will prolong his tennis life as long as physically possible. After all these decades, I can now properly thank this warrior player for giving me the chance to make a few bucks while unemployed and granting me the opportunity to compete professionally with him in San Juan. But mostly, I am so happy to have stayed in touch with this fine man after all these years and I'm very proud to call him a dear friend.

KEITH RICHARDSON

I was just five years old when I started hitting on the red clay courts of Confederate Park in Rock Hill, South Carolina. The tennis courts were practically in my front yard, as well as a concrete hitting wall that I utilized almost every day before school began. My brother and I didn't have the luxury of a private coach or state of the art equipment. But we did have a sort of mentor in local businessman and player extraordinaire, Joe Roddey. He provided us with racquets and limited instruction, setting in motion my passion for the sport. For obvious reasons, the red clay surface would be the preferred one for me, but interestingly, my best tour wins would come on the hard courts. I started out as a baseliner, and the only time I would venture to the net was to retrieve an opponent's drop shot or to hit a short ball. However, being forced to transition to mostly hard courts during my four years at Appalachian State University, I soon learned the art of serve and volley, embracing and becoming adept in the style.

Going to ASU was an easy decision for me, one of the best moves that I made for several reasons. My older brother David was already enrolled there and playing on the team. Even though I received other scholarship offers, including one from Clemson University, I knew that I would probably play in the middle of the lineup rather than at number one where I played all four years in high school. I also knew the Southern Conference would be competitive. In addition to playing in the conference, my coach, Jim Jones, scheduled matches against many very tough ACC schools. Lastly, I loved the location of Boone and the scenic mountains surrounding the beautiful campus. I'm proud to say my college career stats were comprised of 109 wins and 11 losses, with four of those losses coming in the NCAA tournaments.

My thoughts on skipping college and making a beeline to play on the tour? I'm an old school kind of guy and recommend going to college for more reasons than the goal of obtaining a degree. For myself, I wasn't good enough to skip school and go straight to the tour, and most of my peers were in the same category. Quite frankly, most aspiring tennis players could use at least a year or two in college—unless they are superstars destined for immediate success and greatness on the tour. I can't stress enough the importance of having a fallback, and for me, earning a degree in Business Administration was just that. I had four great years to hone my tennis skills, develop a more well-rounded game, and stuff a degree in my back pocket in case I couldn't support myself on the tour.

Shortly after graduating from ASU in 1975, I joined the W.A.T.CH circuit with hopes of accumulating the critical ATP points that would buy me entry into bigger tournaments. It was a grind for sure, but I gradually won matches and points, enabling me to move up and play at a higher level. My goal of making it was finally realized in 1977, when I broke into the top 100 in the world. That magic number was the threshold whereby I was able to get into tour events, including the majors. Luckily, I had the perfect travel partner in my wife, Marilyn. She was a huge boost for me since tour life can be very lonely and frustrating. She kept me focused and at the same time, helped take the edge off the tour grind. She was also the perfect antidote for a loss, as we could enjoy taking in the sights of the various countries that I was competing in.

Looking back, I'd say that my most memorable win came in the Stockholm Open tournament, at a very cool old venue called the Kungliga Tennishallen. Built in 1943, the rustic setting and old wooden seats placed between the courts were special, the setting one that I will always cherish. The draw was unkind to me—I drew the number six in the world, Eddie Dibbs for the first round. Thankfully, the tournament was indoors, and the unique tile surface was faster than greased lightning. That didn't necessarily favor my style of play but perhaps it took away from Eddie's ability to control the battle from the baseline. As a result, it made him approach the net more often than he preferred. Thus, I ended up with the highest ranked win in my nascent career. Unfortunately, the high from my win would be short lived, as I lost a three-setter in the next round to very tough American, George Hardie. But the bonus of earning extra ATP points from defeating a top ten player was significant. I went from being ranked 92 at the beginning of the event to 63 at the end. Needless to say, I was pumped, and keen to continue working my coveted "job", as earning a living on the tour was pretty much my goal.

In this highly competitive sport, and as the reader knows, there is but only one survivor at the end of any tournament. That's the daunting reality for a tour player and something you have to deal with the minute you lose a match. However, I chose to embrace my losses as so-called benchmarks, and in effect, used them as positive teaching moments to grow my game, rather than as negative events. I had many of those teaching moments along the way, but a few stand out more than the others, particularly at the 1977 Wendy's Tennis Classic in Dublin, Ohio, just outside of

Columbus. This was a special event since it benefitted the Buckeye Boy's Ranch, a local orphanage. Even more special, the orphans participated as the ball boys. I had to face the world number one, Guillermo Villas, who was in the midst of a winning streak that would ultimately tally 46 wins in a row. Our match was on a Tuesday evening. He had just played the night before, winning the South Orange, New Jersey tournament, so I was hoping he might be a bit worn out. I concocted a game plan—my intention not to be victory number 23 for him. Though I had never played him, fortunately I had watched him on television that summer, as it seemed he was the featured player almost every week. Thus, I knew trying to beat him from the baseline would be a losing strategy. My plan? To get him out of his comfort zone as soon as possible, by bringing him into the net with a constant barrage of drop shots. Growing up on clay, I had developed a very good dropper and to successfully get him to the net was my goal.

I walked onto the court that evening prepared and ready to play the best player on the planet—in a packed stadium and on his best surface. The match began with my nerves in check and my focus on the previously mentioned strategy. Lo and behold, I jumped out to a 5-2 lead in the opening set. I had a set point and decided to throw him a curve ball. I rushed to the net on my serve, giving him a big delivery to his stellar backhand. In retrospect, maybe I should have gone to his forehand, but I didn't, thinking I could surprise him since I hadn't ventured to the net the entire set. Villas hit a blistering reply at my feet, got the error, broke my serve, and went on to beat me by the score of 7-6, 7-5. This was a pivotal moment in my career considering that I came close to taking a set off the world number one, giving me much needed validation that I could hang with the great ones.

There is one other loss that gets honorable mention. The year was 1978 and the venue was the Mutual Benefit Life Open in South Orange, New Jersey. The tournament director was the highly regarded and esteemed, Gene Scott. This was a very important event, as it was the last tune up for the U.S. Open. I defeated talented Eliot Teltscher in the first round. Several elite players having entered event, the next guy I would face was none other than John McEnroe. John was the second seed and Guillermo Villas the top seed. It should be noted that the courts were very soft since heavy summer rains drenched the court 24 hours prior to match time. I thought the slow conditions might play into my hand, as I intended to do the same thing against McEnroe that I did to Villas—drop shot him to death. The difference was that John excelled at the net and bringing him into the net was risky. But I knew playing my ordinary game would not be enough, so why not try something different? That's precisely what I did but with very little success—the guy was just too good. Fast forward to the second set. It was a one-sided match up to that point, with John up a set and a comfortable 4-1 lead in the second. He hit an overhead that landed a couple of inches inside the baseline and the line judge called it out. John went nuts and rightly so! I walked over to the older gentleman sitting in his chair and urged him to take another look at the mark. He declined to check it, maintaining the ball was out, while McEnroe went ballistic on the other side as he had famously done on other occasions. He argued vehemently with the chair umpire but to no avail. I calmly waited for the resumption of play and once it did, fortune changed in my favor. McEnroe made errors out of understandable frustration, while I hunkered down, capitalizing on the sweet turn of events. The boisterous summer crowd quickly got on my side, chanting my name, and throwing beer cans onto the court, protesting the way McEnroe so notoriously acted. Certainly, a combination of the alcohol, his temper tantrum, and their desire to see another set, the crowd continued to chant my name repeatedly. The electric atmosphere spurred me on as I reeled off five straight games and won the set—I was pumped! But not for long. He calmed down and handily beat me in the third set. I must confess that McEnroe is a very nice guy off the court but once he walks on, it's game on. In my opinion, and after witnessing his implosion firsthand, it was evident the guy was a perfectionist and could not handle a bad call, regardless of the fact he was in absolute command of the match and the score at that time. Despite the loss, I was pleased to add another benchmark to my resume, as continued validation that I could hang with the best.

My ability to stay on the tour was helped by two important factors, the first being the availability of some cash in my bank account as the costs were prohibitive. Thankfully, that problem was solved while working my first job as an assistant tennis professional at the WCT Peachtree World of Tennis in Atlanta, Georgia. While there, I was able to practice as well as play in local tournaments, including the prestigious Georgia State Open, which I won. In the process, some members recognized my talent and decided to put up ten thousand dollars to sponsor me. Their intentions were to supply the necessary expense money for a year on the tour, which at that time would cost, what else? Approximately ten thousand. Their return on investment would be two thirds of my winnings. This took a huge burden off not only winning every week but losing and thus watching a dwindling back account balance.

The second part of the equation was my best friend/wife and traveling companion, Marilyn, being by my side every step of the way. My investors understood the importance of providing the funding necessary to have her travel with me. As I discussed earlier, tour life can be very lonely and having her presence was critical for my success. As a matter of fact, here's a little side note regarding her unwavering support and passion for the sport. When we got married in 1975, she agreed to spend our honeymoon in Corpus Christi, Texas ... so that I could compete in the NCAA Tennis Tournament!

I would say the players I admired the most were Borg and Vilas. I loved Borg's game, his mental toughness, his extreme fitness, his quiet demeanor, and all-around nice guy persona. We came together at an ATP event in Cologne, Germany, where I had an afternoon match scheduled against the tough Hungarian, Balazs Taroczy. Up walks Borg's coach, Lennart Bergelin, and asks me if

I would like to warm up with Bjorn. Of course, my response was an emphatic yes, and for the next ninety minutes we batted balls across the net. I would normally hit much less on a day when I had a match scheduled but hitting with the great Borg was an opportunity of a lifetime, and I was content to hit until he had enough, regardless of my afternoon contest. It was an unforgettable moment in my career, one that I will never forget.

I admired Guillermo Vilas because he was the toughest opponent I ever faced in competition. I mentioned my early lead over him in the Buckeye Classic, only to let it slip away. The guy had ice water in his veins, playing with precise ground strokes and amazing confidence. He showed me how mentally tough he was, and though I was statistic number 23 in his 46-match winning streak that summer of 1977, it was a pleasure to compete against this all-time great.

Upon reflection and of course hindsight being 20/20, I would definitely have done a few things differently in my tennis journey, the most significant change being to my serve. There was a great coach and friend by the name of J.W. Isenhour, a former North Carolina State coach. He worked his magic on one of his players, John Sadri, in the early 1970's, as well as others throughout his coaching years. If only I had engaged his help. The thought of getting a freebie occasionally was something my game lacked. But I was reluctant to make a change and stuck with my adequate delivery. In hindsight, improving my serve might have dramatically changed the direction of my career.

The other regret has nothing to do with my physical game but more about my decision to skip most every player's dream, Wimbledon. I qualified to play two of the four years that I played on the tour but chose to stay at home for a variety of reasons. The grass court venue didn't suit my game, and in those days, it was pretty much exclusively serve and volley tennis. To play proficiently on grass, it would have required practicing and playing the tune up events, costing an exorbitant amount of money. I certainly wish I could go back in time and reverse my decision. If I could, at least I would have in my possession the genuine Wimbledon towel!

To the subject of nerves, amazingly it was never a problem for me when I played. I knew I always had the next tournament to look forward to, and sooner or later, I'd get a lucky draw and a win. That said, if I wasn't nervous, I had a right to be—does that make any sense? Being nervous meant the match meant a good deal. However, once the contest began, my nerves were never an issue and I just simply competed. Of course, I felt pressure to win, since not only did I put this burden on myself but felt the push from my sponsors as well. It was certainly foremost on my mind but somehow it made me work harder, thus performing without the nerves that can often get in the way with most players.

If you are a junior player reading this, my advice for your success is quite simple—develop a complete game. Play tournaments with emphasis on winning matches and register them in your mind to help your confidence. Compete locally, regionally, and of course nationally, since playing the most talented competition out there is the best way to improve. Plan on going to college and pick a school and coach that will help to nurture your still-developing game. There are exceptions to every rule but accepting a college scholarship and playing at least one year, if not four, makes good sense. Keep in mind that back in the day, tennis careers were pretty much finished by age twenty-eight, thus the pressure of giving up four years for college was considerable. So many of my peers would forego this valuable chance to mature both physically and emotionally, while simultaneously developing and improving their respective games. Success on the tour is limited to the special few and having a degree to fall back on takes the pressure off in so many ways (though the prize money is more fairly distributed these days). Once your prime playing days are over, there's a very strong possibility you'll have to enter the work force.

Though my life on the tour was short lived, I had some unforgettable matches with legendary players. Altogether, it was a wonderful experience, and to realize my dream and have a job as a touring tennis professional still seems surreal to this day. Thanks to *Tennis Life,* I was able to share my humble journey and hope the reader gets something positive out of it.

WARD'S SKINNY ON KEITH

It was in May of 2021 at the Atlanta Senior Invitational Tennis tournament, that I had the pleasure of meeting Keith for the first time. Of course, I had to look him up on internet when the draw came out, discovering that his tennis pedigree was much higher than my pay grade.

Before our first-round match, I asked him to be a contributor to *Tennis Life,* in an attempt to distract him from the task at hand and hope he'd throw the match to be a nice guy—just kidding, Keith! We started the warmup, and it was an eye opener. He was clearly the better player, the thought that I might lose love and love entering my mind. After all, I was not tournament tough. Much of my on-court time now consists of teaching 3.0 to 4.0 club level players, occasionally supplementing that with ball machine work and hitting sessions with other local pros. So why did I enter the tournament? To see if my game was ready for prime time. Or should I say, to see how far off it was from being ready for prime time. I wanted to see where I stood amongst such tough competition, and to draw Keith Richardson was a daunting task for me. However, having defeated some very good players in between my many losses, the challenge was once again exciting, and anything was possible. I would compete the best I could regardless of who was on the other side of the net—I was going to play to win. The match was probably more competitive than Keith envisioned, but the better player came out on top. Proud to say I gave him a run for his money though, the score being 6-4, 7-5. I actually led 5-3 in the second set, only to lose the last four games. But employing Keith's wise philosophy of using his losses as benchmarks, I'll categorize the match as a very good learning experience and the belief that I could compete with the top senior guys in the United States. Learning from one's loss is the best way I know how to turn a negative into a positive. So, I've since improved my second serve and rekindled the old serve and volley technique I employed throughout my collegiate career at Clemson.

Getting to know Keith has been a blessing, even though it took a thrashing in Atlanta to begin and ignite a new friendship. I truly admire his tennis journey. To go from an assistant tennis professional in Atlanta, to the W.A.T.CH satellite circuit so that he could eventually compete on the tour, was an onerous process. Kudos to him for making it happen. Keith Richardson, another fine addition to *Tennis Life* and I'm so very honored to share his story. Thanks for the kind butt kicking in Atlanta, buddy!

LAURIE FLEMING ROWLEY

Let's just say that when I was growing up, my family ate, slept, and breathed tennis. Thus, playing competitively was inevitable. My father picked up his first racquet attending the California University of Pennsylvania—in what else, the town of California, Pennsylvania. As captain of both the football and baseball team, his friends teased him the moment they got wind he'd started playing the sissy sport known as tennis. Thankfully, he ignored them. He was very athletic, passing his genes on to me, my younger sister, Carrie and my brother, Scott. Even my mother played regularly in a doubles league before raising a family took precedence.

In 1963, when I was eight years old, my father decided he wanted to move the family far away from the cold Pennsylvania winters. He took a job as guidance counselor in Broward County, Florida. We bought a house in Fort Lauderdale, about a mile away from public tennis courts known as Holiday Park—a very special place back in those days. The fun we Flemings had. We played tennis day in and day out. When waiting for a court to open, we'd pass the time by playing cards and Simon Says. My how times have changed! Now while waiting for a court to open, kid's eyes are glued to their cell phones. And Holiday Park was where the Fleming kids and Evert kids friended each other—the old-fashioned way. We all became close very quickly. I have fond memories of my sister Carrie and I walking with Chris, and her younger sister, Jeanne, heading to their house only blocks away from the courts for lunch and ping pong. It was about this same time in the mid 1960's, that Jimmy Evert, Chris's dad, would put Holiday Park on the map as a breeding ground for a who's who of exceptional players, many of them coached by him.

Chris and I became inseparable friends off the court and fierce rivals on the court. In the early years off the court, we'd laugh, sometimes even start dancing at the drop of a hat. We were so close that we occasionally wore matching tennis dresses. At one point, we were known as the Lauderdale Lovelies and people thought we looked so much alike, that a local bank considered using our so-called resemblance in a television commercial. Hmm, but wait, did I say inseparable off the court? Not all the time. Not when Chris relished being the victor no matter the situation. I'll never forget the one day we were playing a tournament in North Miami Beach, across the woods from a monastery. She dared me to run onto the property and ring the bell five times. I replied, "You go first." She complied and then retreated to parts unbeknownst to me. The monks none too happy, scoured the woods, finding me instead. They threatened me with jail but acknowledging it was just a youthful prank, let me go. I returned to the tournament to find Chris sitting in the stands with a deadpan expression on her face, seemingly unconcerned as to the dicey result of her scheme. And then there was the boyfriend issue when we were both 16. We met a very special guy at a regional tournament by the name of Stephen "Pike" Rowley. Chris went out on a couple of dates with him, then decided she was more interested in somebody else. So, Pike and I started dating, nearly causing the end of my friendship with her. From that point on, we made an agreement not to go out with each other's ex—which was never again an issue for me as I married special Pike, a few years later!

Our rivalry on the court is well documented. Chris wanted to be beat me and I wanted to beat her. Equally talented in most respects, we played a similar game. But we handled our determination and desire quite differently. My former junior coach, Fred Weinman, probably said it best about me: "Laurie does not possess Chrissie's killer instinct on the court." With Chris, it was a no holds barred, take no prisoners attitude when trying to win. With me, I lowered my expectations, so as not to be disappointed with the outcome of a match. That differing mindset is reflected in our head-to-head stats. In all the years competing against her, I managed to beat Chris in practice and a high school doubles match, but never in an official match. She was downright invincible on the court. However, taking her out of my tennis career equation, I have much to be proud about. I was ranked among the top players in the nation throughout my junior career. I won the Orange Bowl in the girls 14 and Under and 16 and Under divisions and was also the national champion for 1969 and 1971. I won two national singles titles and one doubles title. Post high school, I toured professionally from 1973 to 1975 and then played World Team tennis for the Florida Flamingos for a year.

My time on the tour was an eye opener, shedding light on my priorities in life. Upon graduating from high school in 1973, I made my pro debut in the inaugural Family Circle Cup in Hilton Head, South Carolina. I downed the world top five player, Julie Heldman, in the first round, one of the original nine women on the Virginia Slims Circuit. I'll never forget—she yelled and complained the entire match, saying things like, "I can't believe I'm losing to this kid!" She really didn't behave well that day but then again, she was known for such outbursts. I considered the win to be a validation that I could play with the big girls. And thus, I began the whirlwind tour, playing at Wimbledon, the U.S. Open, French Open, and Italian Open, just to name a few. But being so young and having been sheltered most of my life, the tour was a lonely place for me. I expected the older players to befriend me but that was not the case. I got homesick, sometimes crying during my phone calls home. Thank goodness I liked to draw, and I always had my sketchbook along to keep me occupied in between matches. The next year, Pike and I got married and I stayed closer to home for the most part, traveling back and forth between tournaments and Clemson University, where he played for the tennis team. I unexpectedly became pregnant, and my tennis career was put on hold. I think in some ways, I felt relief, since I was tired of the traveling. I've always been a nesting person—I like to have my own place with my own things on the walls. And my most important priority had been realized … I was about to start a family. A bit premature, but nonetheless I was thrilled. Four years later, at the age of 23, I wanted to make a comeback but only if Pike and our son, Brett, could come with me. My husband quit his winter job as a teaching pro, and we traveled the winter circuit together. But keeping a child quiet in the stands was a challenge, especially an energetic four-year-old little boy. One time, Pike was cheering for me so enthusiastically, that he didn't notice Brett slip away. Humorously (not back then of course), he ended up in the linesman's chair! As one might expect, I was a tiny bit distracted with what happened and lost the match, my comeback pretty much ending that day.

Looking back at my tennis life, I've asked myself on occasion what I would do differently. Certainly, nothing to do with the coaching aspect. My father coached me, and I credit him with my tennis skills and success as a junior. In fact, he was so enthusiastic about teaching my brother, sister, and I, that he asked Jimmy Evert for advice about discipline and attitude when drilling us. Eventually, he got so good at giving lessons, he started his own clinics and private lessons elsewhere once we'd flown the coop. Another subject—did I regret not going to college right after high school? No, not really. In fact, from 1982 until 2005, in between carpooling my kids here, there, and everywhere, I took one class a semester at Florida Atlantic University and completed my art history degree, something I'm very proud of. As far as the tour being a lonely place for me, I think if I could have traveled with someone, maybe even Pike early on, perhaps my performance would have been much better. In a strange way, losing matches rewarded me, sending me back to my comfort zone, while conversely, winning kept me away from it. A conundrum for sure. Years later, I would ask myself, should I have pushed the nesting desire aside a bit longer—until I was a little older? Mind you those were only fleeting thoughts and I have absolutely no regrets. I wouldn't trade Pike, my son, Brett, and daughter, Carrie for anything in the world. They are no doubt the biggest win of my life!

A final thought and some simple advice for the aspiring junior: Make certain tennis is YOUR dream and not somebody else's. If it is your dream, work hard. Be prepared for setbacks and losses without losing your vision—just believe!

WARD'S SKINNY ON LAURIE

I had the pleasure of practicing with Laurie on numerous occasions, either after school or on weekends at Holiday Park. I practiced with Chrissie as well and to be honest, there wasn't much difference in their games whatsoever. Each had very flat two-handed backhands, as well as similar linear forehands. Neither player came to the net unless forced, relying mostly on maneuvering, and outplaying their opponents.

We all know how famous Chrissie became and kudos to all her achievements. As for Laurie, I can't help but reflect on something she said about giving up the tour to make a life with Pike. I am quite certain, that had Laurie and Pike traveled together, and Laurie had remained on the tour longer than her brief two-year stint, she would have become a household name just like Chrissie. But that was not her chosen path and much respect to her for her life choices and conviction.

I can't help but reminisce about a match that happened 49 years ago in the finals of the Broward County, Florida District Championships. It was Laurie Fleming from Cardinal Gibbons High versus Chrissie Evert from St. Thomas Aquinas High. It would be a preview of so many more court confrontations to come between these two friendly rivals. Laurie battled her in three close sets, coming up just short against arguably one of the greatest women players of all time. That match will forever be stamped in my mind, as the quality of the tennis was spectacular, and Laurie showed she had the game to go to the next level and beyond.

Just like so many of the other greats in *Tennis Life*, Laurie is unique in that she gave up her tennis journey so soon. Family was the most important path for her. However, anyone who ever had the pleasure of watching her grace the tennis courts couldn't help but be in awe of her natural talent and skillset. Laurie Fleming: a truly great tennis player, person, and dear friend to this day. Thanks for sharing your story!

BUNNER SMITH

Had it not been for my father, Bunner Smith, Sr., a tennis professional at the Oratani Field Club in Hackensack, New Jersey, and a winter resident of Sarasota since the late 1940's, I most likely would have been a baseball player. He put a racquet in my hand at the age of five. I would spend most of my youth playing on six red clay courts right on Sarasota Bay. There over the next ten years or so, I hit on the wall, played with old men, and started to become a pretty good player.

It was the introduction of Ken Wagstaff and a new club known as the Bath and Racquet Club, which helped to really propel my game. I was introduced to top local talents in Buster Brown, Chris Baxter, and Susan Vinton. Ken offered me a free membership in exchange for maintaining the courts and the opportunity to play with better players in a private setting. Soon, the sport took time away from baseball, the game I thought would be my primary focus. I was lucky to have a practice partner in Susan Vinton. She was one of the best players in the state, ranked number three behind Chris Evert and Laurie Fleming. She was in the same situation as I was, with no real local competition in the area. Her steadiness in the backcourt helped me learn to play using an aggressive serve and volley style, resulting in some very good wins along the way. I vividly recall Susan's admission that she disliked my chip and charge tactics, since most of her peers didn't utilize a slice one-handed backhand, and none of them came to the net ... unless it was to shake hands. She was cute, and I had a crush on her, so I stayed back a lot until the score got close. Once it did, then I would serve and volley to beat her—she hated to lose. Playing with her a few times a week improved my backcourt game but playing against her ultimately exposed that my groundstrokes were not good enough. She finally left to become pro and join the Virginia Slims tour in 1972.

My first state tournament occurred in the mid 1960's where I came up against the number one player in Florida and the country, Brian Gottfried. Up to that point, I had won every local 12 and Under and never played such a talented kid my age. To this day, I remember the match vividly. Brian didn't miss anything, and even though I didn't win a game, the fact that he was two years older took a bit of the sting off the loss. It was at that moment I embraced tennis, splitting my time between baseball and tennis. Some in my peer group included Sam Vuille (number one in Florida every year that he played) Mike Green, Jim Oescher, and the Reilly brothers. My parents would drive me across the Sunshine Skyway bridge at least once a month to practice with them. However, it was an event in St. Petersburg that really inspired me, where the Australian legend, Harry Hopman, hosted a tournament there known as the Masters. The entire Davis Cup team would spend the week prior to the event practicing at the Sarasota Bath and Racquet Club. To watch these greats practice every day left an indelible memory and planted a seed that one day I could play on the tour like them.

The Florida junior tour was among the toughest in the nation, and it seemed whenever I played well, I would make it to the semifinals only to lose to Sam Vuille or Mike Borling. It was a bit disconcerting but expected, as these guys were the best in the state and few of my peers had the goods to defeat them, including myself. In 1972, I became number ten in the state after losing a tight three set match to Mark Joffey, another top player in Florida. College offers started rolling in. The University of South Florida was the first to recruit me. But the coach and I didn't get along, probably because of my long hair and rebellious attitude. I also had an offer to play at the Naval Academy and visited the campus, totally awestruck. However, I knew that if I was subjected to the hazing and discipline I was in for, I wouldn't last two weeks before being kicked out. In the end, it was between Florida State and a small school in Statesboro, Georgia, called Georgia Southern, I ended up taking the full scholarship at Georgia Southern.

That same summer, I got into a big station wagon to play in the national junior tour with fellow players, Grey King (semifinalist in Kalamazoo), Sam Vuille, Vance Dickinson, and Mike Green. I got to meet the enigmatic Vitas Gerulaitis, Brian Teacher, and several other amazing junior players from Southern California. Unfortunately, I was more interested in having a good time than winning. My good friend, Ken Friedman, had a 1963 Corvette, and together we tore up the road, from the Westerns in Springfield to the Nationals in Kalamazoo, while hitting every city in between. Probably not the best training for Nationals!

The summer after my freshman year in college, the birthday rule changed, and I was eligible to play junior tournaments another year. I stayed in Savannah (just 49 miles east of Georgia Southern) simultaneously playing Georgia junior events and working as an assistant pro at the Chatham Tennis Club. I won every tournament I played, including the state 18 and Under championships in Atlanta. That got me the number one ranking in Georgia but with an asterisk, as I really wasn't a Georgia resident. Even though I was playing well, I decided not to pursue the summer national tour, as my assistant pro job was great, the head pro, Jim Nerrin, a former player who worked for Nick Bollettieri in Puerto Rico.

After the summer of 1973, I realized I could make a good living as a teaching pro. Any illusion I had of making it on the pro tour was toast. I enjoyed the rest of my time as a college player, having reasonable success. During our spring trip to Florida in 1976 of my senior year, a pro who had seen me play in Atlanta, asked if I was interested in going to St. Louis to work with Butch Buccholz. They flew me to St. Louis, and my playing audition went so well, that I was offered a job for Sports Illustrated Tennis at Dorado Beach, Puerto Rico with Nick Bollettieri—a dream job at age 21. So, in May of 1976, I found myself there. Sports Illustrated Tennis was a new concept using the Bollettieri system of corporate clinics, involving the likes of IBM and other companies. The clinics were run at major hotels in the Caribbean, Vermont, Idaho, and Hawaii. Unfortunately, Nick left for the Colony Resort in Longboat Key, Sarasota the week after I arrived. The Colony would soon become home to the legendary Bollettieri Tennis Academy.

I spent the next eight months teaching and playing around Puerto Rico, the British Virgin Islands, and the U.S., in what had to be the best time of my life. Then I received a call from Mike DePalmer, co-owner of the newly opened DePalmer-Bollettieri Tennis Club in Bradenton, asking me to come home and work for both he and Nick. So, I went back home to work ten-hour days in both Bradenton and at the Colony with Nick. The work was tiring but rewarding and hanging out with Nick into many late evenings was a blast since he loved to dance and was a big hit with the ladies. Nick drew some of the top juniors in the country, including Jimmy Arias, Paul Annacone, Anne White, Eric Korita, and countless others. In hitting with the future stars, my game got pretty good. Soon, I won the Florida 25 and Over Clay Court championships in singles and in the same year, won the 30 and Over Championships in doubles.

As a single tennis professional with no kids, it was easy to jump on the various opportunities that presented themselves. The year was 1981 and one such gig came at the urging of Mike DePalmer. So off to Las Vegas and the Cambridge Racquet Club I went, where I began working with club members and training a 19-year-old girl who was the best I had ever seen. Her name was Rita Agassi (yes, Andre's sister) and I practiced with her nearly every day. Rita had trained with an impressive name before me—former pro player, Pancho Gonzalez. He would show up occasionally to watch our sessions to make sure I wasn't doing anything with her that he didn't like. I was in awe of his presence for sure. He ultimately married her despite their 20 plus years age difference. Andre, was only nine years old at the time, and I watched him hit a few times with his other sibling, Phil. I could tell he had incredible talent. The Agassi's knew about my Bollettieri connection and it's possible my time working with Rita led to their decision to send young Andre to Florida to train with Nick, but I'll never know for sure. Las Vegas was also the place where I won my only pro title and it happened at the Las Vegas Pro Indoors. Seventeen-year-old, Mike DePalmer, Jr., and I beat Phil Agassi and Greg Menster in the final. Mike would go on to have a great career, reaching the top five 18 and Under in the U.S., world's top 35 in singles and world's top 20 in doubles. Mike had trained with me back in Bradenton, and I'd like to think I helped him with his volleys and doubles success.

After the six months in Vegas, Nick called me up and asked me to start up an academy in Baltimore, Maryland. Which of course, I did. Being director of the Nick Bollettieri Mid Atlantic Tennis Academy was the dream. They furnished me with a car, apartment and a year-round program based on the system Nick had devised, whereby I would be training six or more players at a time, using drills and live ball play. As a result, the summer of 1981 saw the first Nick Bollettieri spin off camp and year-round program. It was highly successful and captured the best players around the region. I consider that stint among my best accomplishments as a tennis professional. But Nick being the mover and shaker that he is, decided to move the program north to the Boston area. I had close to 100 kids at the time. Because they knew me and didn't really know Nick, I felt that I should stay in Baltimore. Thus, I went out on my own and called it the Mid-Atlantic Tennis Academy. Between 1982 and 1988, we had the most successful program in the region. Almost all age groups attended the camp. Every talented player I had, I sent down to train with Nick in Bradenton.

In 1988, my father was diagnosed with cancer, and I returned to the Sarasota to help him out. I began coaching several juniors, going to tournaments, and working with Nick on projects. A bit burned out, I took a break from tennis and got a "real job" in 1999 as sales manager for the Jeep dealership in Bradenton. It would be the best thing I ever did for my future, as it gave me benefits including Social Security. My passion for tennis never waned despite my 10-year hiatus. After leaving the sales manager position, I started a non-profit tennis program for the Boys and Girls Club in 2014. During these later years, I had maintained my close relationship with Nick, and in 2019, my program merged with his and I became head pro with the Nick Bollettieri Tennis and Learning Foundation. Working with less privileged kids, helping them with school and showing them that their future could be bright was our mission. I'm proud to say, we graduated our first two students in 2021 and they both got academic scholarships to the University of South Florida through our foundation. In 2021, Nick retired from coaching at the age of 90. He is letting myself and the staff run the program as he would want to see it done, and it's now called Team Success Charter School Tennis and Training.

Looking back on my life, I was blessed to have had a father who put that wooden racquet in my hand for the first time. I've made so many special friends along the way. Especially during those early years of my junior career in Florida, including Pike Rowley, Rick Fagel, Chris Sylvan, Ward Snyder, Alan and Don Petrine, Paul Curtin, Ford Robinette, just to name a few. To this day, we can pick up the phone or communicate via social media, barely missing a beat even though several decades have passed since last seeing one another. This wonderful sport created lifelong memories and friendships that I cherish to this very day. Though I didn't compete on the tour, missing it was a blessing in disguise for me. I've had so many amazing experiences, and to have spent so much time with the greatest coach ever, Nick Bollettieri, is beyond what I ever could have hoped for. My sincere thanks to him for believing in me and being a lifelong friend. Yep, it's been some tennis life.

WARD'S SKINNY ON BUNNER

Bunner Smith is one of several very good players I have personally known in my junior and collegiate tennis journey. He, like most of my contemporaries, strived for a career on the big stage, but ultimately accepted the cold hard reality that his game just wasn't good enough. Yet he has the same emotion that is embodied in every player and coach in *Tennis Life*—a deep passion for the game. An interesting character to this day, Bunner and I go back a long way, our memorable first encounter in the Ft. Lauderdale Championships held at Holiday Park. It was in the doubles 18 and Under division when I first came face to face against his doubles prowess. He was playing alongside my future doubles partner and good friend, Pike Rowley. My partner was another good friend, Rick Quinby. It was like David versus Goliath in this match up on the first court. Pike and Bunner were among the top seeds, and certainly the odds-on favorites, while Rick and I were really in it to have fun, feeling like we had nothing to lose. The bleachers were full of Pike's fans. His girlfriend and future bride, Laurie Fleming, sat with her friends and family to witness what most thought to be a routine drubbing of yours truly and partner. The match came down to a third set, six games all tiebreaker to decide the winner. In those days, it was known as a nine-point breaker, meaning the first team to win five points would win. With the pressure mounting after each point, soon the score was four points all.

Suddenly, it was match point for each team. Pike was the server, and Rick and I had the choice as to which person Pike would serve to. Though I was the better player, I liked Rick in the deuce court because he had such a good forehand. The tension mounted as Pike hit his daunting big serve into the forehand corner. Rick smashed a down the line missile past the outstretched arms of Bunner as he tried to poach. Game, set and match to Ward and Rick! Fast forward to Columbia, South Carolina, in a collegiate event featuring several university teams vying for the trophy. This match pitted Clemson versus Georgia Southern, specifically myself and Pike as partners now, against Bunner and his partner (sorry but no memory of his name). Lo and behold, another close contest and another nine-point breaker in the third set and guess what—down to match point once again for both teams. Pike and I won it! So only two times that I ever played against Bunner and both times nail biters ending up with the W on my side of the court. Bunner took it in stride as he always does, and love that I can share such memories in *Tennis Life*.

Bunner and I have much in common. We both played our juniors mostly in Florida, endeavored to play on the big stage but didn't have the goods, worked in the U.S. Virgin Islands, and competed there, played reasonable collegiate tennis on full scholarships, and lastly pursued careers in teaching tennis (though I became a teaching pro just five years ago). I'm so pleased to share his story. His passion for tennis is over the top, and to culminate his journey with such a wonderful philanthropic endeavor as the Boys and Girls Club program is to be admired and applauded. Thanks for being a part of *Tennis Life,* Bunner!

HAROLD SOLOMON

I have been playing tennis since I was five years old. During one of our winter trips to Florida in 1959, my father introduced me to the sport, and I never looked back. Starting at the age of 11, I traveled the country, playing sectional and national tournaments. When I was 13, I captured my first big title, winning the 18 and Under at the Maryland State Tennis Championship. By this time, my family was spending entire winters in the Sunshine State, necessitating my high school years be divided between my home state of Maryland and Florida—and my junior career took off. I give credit not only to my father, who by the way made me hit what seemed like 1000 balls in a row one day, but a handful of coaches that worked with me as a junior as well: Dr. Mel Richter, Maury Schwartzman, Clark Taylor, Pauline Betz Addie, and Bob Ryland.

In 1969, I won my first Orange Bowl title. Interestingly, it was at the Orange Bowl that my father insisted I change from a one-handed backhand to two. He had seen the Canadian great, Mike Belkin, brandish a very effective two-handed backhand on a nearby practice court at the event facility. Therefore, I give my father the ultimate credit for what I consider to be the most profound and important change to my game. Then in 1970, I not only won the Orange Bowl again, but managed to take home trophies for the USTA National Clay Courts Boys' 18 and Under Singles Championship and the National Interscholastic Championship. Upon graduating from Springbrook High School in Silver Spring, Maryland, my intent was to go to Stanford since my good friend, Sandy Mayer, was going there. But just about every night, it seemed the Rice University coach, Sammy Giammalva, would call me, luring me in with the fact that he already had two excellent players in Zan Guerry and Mike Estep. I was offered a full tennis scholarship and the choice became Rice. I earned All-American status there and even at my diminutive height of 5'6", it felt like the tour was beckoning me, the thought of it just too enticing. However, the real impetus to jump ship came at the River Oaks International Tennis Tournament in Houston, Texas. I played Australian lefty, Ray Ruffles in the first round. I recall that he was very upset because I was wearing black sweatpants for the entire match. He even complained to the referee about it. Though the temperature didn't merit that I wear sweatpants, I did so to show Ruffles how tough I was. My strategy worked. I proceeded to upset him, making it through to the quarterfinals where I faced top American, Cliff Richey. I lost a close hard-fought match to Richey. I knew that I should have won it, and it was at that moment I was confident I could compete on the big stage. So, in 1972, at the end of my sophomore year, I turned pro. Later, Coach Giammalva confessed to me that he thought I would have been a good number five or six player on the team but had no clue I'd be so good.

I made the main draw for my first French Open right after leaving Rice. Breezing into the fourth round, I found myself facing my Davis Cup teammate, Jimmy Connors. One problem? I was rooming with Jimmy and the night before our match when it was time to go to bed, he wouldn't turn off the lights or the tv. I insisted he do so, but he would not oblige. It just so happened that Davis Cup captain, Dennis Ralston, and Stan Smith were staying in the room above us. I called Dennis requesting a bed swap which ended up being with Stan. The next day, I beat Jimmy in three straight sets. Ultimately, I lost to Manuel Orantes of Spain in the quarterfinals, but nevertheless, very happy with the results of my first grand slam. Two years into the tour, I played my first match against Bjorn Borg. The tournament was in Tokyo, and it stands out to me for a couple of reasons. The surface was Uni-turf, a synthetic hard court and the ball bounced very high as I recall. I won the first set 6-0, but lurking around our court was Ian Tiriac, a former Romanian Davis Cupper who played with Ilie Nastase. Word was he was trolling for a coaching stint with Borg. I could have sworn that Tiriac was coaching from the sidelines and influencing Borg's play, as the Swede's strategy changed dramatically after the first set. I lost the second set 6-0 and the third set 6-1. That would be the beginning of many of my losses to Borg.

Three years into the tour, I found myself ranked in the world's top twenty. Five years into the tour, I'd made it into the world's top ten, with my highest singles ranking coming in at number five in 1980. I'm proud to say I won 22 ATP titles, reached the finals of the 1976 French Open and had wins over virtually all the top players of my era except for one—my nemesis, Borg. Ah, Borg. His dominance over me is subject matter that I might as well get over with. Sad to say my record against him was 0-15. The matchup with him was problematic, as he was taller, stronger, fitter, and produced heavy topspin ground strokes that bounced high and out of my comfort zone, always tiring my shoulders. He had little weakness at the baseline, had an effective serve, a solid volley, and owned one of the best returns of serve of the game. And it doesn't stop there. He ran like a gazelle, had the heart rate of an Olympic runner, and last but not least, was as cool as a cucumber to no end—possibly the latter attribute irritating me most of all.

Reflecting on the tour, there so many memorable matches and moments. But a few will always be foremost in my mind. I'll start with my first tournament win over Guillermo Vilas in Washington D.C. He was ranked in the world's top five. To pull the upset near my hometown, with my family and friends at courtside is an unforgettable memory that I cherish to this day. My record against him during the tour was 4-4, which was quite the achievement really, my game matching up well versus the strong left-handed foe from Buenos Aires.

Another memorable match was over world number four, Raul Ramirez, in the semifinal of the 1976 French Open. A win would place me in my first grand slam final. Ramirez was the number one player from Mexico at the time and playing on the red clay in Mexico, he possessed the same clay court skills as myself, which meant it would be a very long contest. I remember the day being hot and humid. The on-court temperature was 115 for three straight days. And I'll never forget the exact number of large Perrier bottles I consumed against him, 23 in total. Remember, this was before Gatorade was invented. As had been predicted by the analysts, we went to a fifth set, both of us worn out. I vividly recall the moment when I was down 0-30 and 1-3. We had a long rally from side to side, possibly 20 shots, and I pulled out the critical point. I glanced over at Ramirez, saw the look on his face and knew I had him! I went ahead to win the next five games. The match lasted four and a half hours with an improbable victory. I was in the final and would be facing the great Italian, Adriano Panatta. Ironically, Panatta had done me a huge favor by defeating my archrival, Borg, in the quarterfinals and then taking out my friend and doubles partner, Eddie Dibbs, in the semifinal. On to the final, and of course, it would be memorable. I was quite sore and stiff from my long battle from Ramirez, while Panatta was relatively fresh from his easier semifinal win. After three sets, I found myself down two sets to one. But it was near the end of the fourth set that I'll never forget. I was up 6-5, 30-15, when I hit a ball deep into the ad corner and followed it into the net. Panatta hit his backhand cross court and I decided to change it up. Rather than hit my volley back into the ad corner—a shot I'd rehearsed in practice and was using during the match—I decided to go the other way, hitting it down the line instead. Panatta faked liked he was staying there expecting the volley to his backhand. However, he promptly sprinted to my volley and nailed a forehand winner past me at the net. As exhausted as I knew he was, it gave him the impetus to hang in there and propel him into the tiebreaker which unfortunately, he won. After the match, Panatta told me that if he had not won the fourth set, that the match would have been mine as he was gassed at that juncture. That was the match that got away, as a win would have enabled my eventual induction into the International Tennis Hall of Fame in Rhode Island.

Also etched in my mind? Playing Juan Gisbert in the semifinals of the 1972 Davis Cup versus Spain. I developed severe cramps in the third set. Fortunately for me, the match was suspended for darkness until the next day. That evening, while eating dinner at a restaurant, my hamstring cramped so badly that I inadvertently knocked the table over! Happy to say though that, all was well the next day, and I took the match in five sets—winning one of the most crucial U.S. Davis points in years. Following the win, I was the subject of a Sports Illustrated article written by Curry Kirkpatrick, the title including "Oles for Moon Balls". I would bet this is where my famous moonball moniker was born.

Kirkpatrick wrote, *"Solomon's arsenal consists of biding time, hitting everything back, then launching his key weapon, the "moon ball." Receiving a shot on his double-fisted backhand, he aims for the clouds, connects with plenty of topspin and puffs it up there. And puffs it and puffs it. One journalist has called Solomon's game, "A threat to low-flying birds," but in the second singles match last week Solomon was the one flying. Against Gisbert, and all those olés that always accompany the handsome Spaniard in*

Barcelona, the young American dashed around, changed pace, moon-balled it all over the place and simply administered punishment by way of patience. He beat the Spaniard in five sets and won the most crucial U.S. Davis Cup point in several years. Suspended by darkness, played over two days, and possessed of enough passion and nerve to last a lifetime, Solomon's accomplishment merely evened the matches on the scoreboards. But, following in the wake of Smith's sluggish defeat, it also aroused the entire U.S. contingent and inspired the eventual 3-2 victory."

How about some of my most memorable Borg stories? In 1980, after I won the Hamburg ATP event (the tune up event to the French Open), Borg asked me if I wanted to go to Paris early and be his practice partner for the week—specifically play the best of a five-set match for the entire week. I welcomed the challenge to practice against my toughest and greatest foe. Each day, we played the three out of five sets. The results were always the same ... three sets to Borg and zero to me. After dinner together at the end of the week, Borg calmly looked at me and asked, "So are you ready to play tomorrow?" I politely replied, "F-you, Bjorn, I've had enough!" So fast forward to the following week and the commencement of the French Open. Both Borg and I made it past the quarterfinals and damn if I didn't have to play him in the semifinals. The outcome? You guessed it. It was just like another practice match, Borg beating me once again in straight sets. Then there was the time I played him in 1976 at the U.S. Pro Championships in Brookline, Massachusetts. Even though a cold front had come through a couple of days before, I knew I was going to be sweating profusely. I was also concerned about cramping, as I had battled the issue throughout my career. The match begins and I'm playing very well, beating Borg with a one set lead and up 4-1 in the second. By this time, I've changed my soggy shoes and shirt five times. I look across the net in between games and see Bjorn calmly sitting there with barely a drop of sweat on his brow! Trying not to let that bother me, I told myself—I'm finally going to beat him. I attacked Bjorn's serve, thinking the strategy would be the difference in the match. But as in other matches, Bjorn would manage to come from behind and pull out the win, triumphing by the score of 6-7, 6-4, 6-1,6-2. I had a bag full of wet shirts ready for the laundry while he never once changed his shirt.

I do have one post tour memorable moment that I'll never forget and would like to share. It has to do with the great Roger Federer. I'd met Roger a few years back when I was on the Board of Directors for the ATP Tour. A couple of years later, my wife, Jan, and I were at a party at Mary Jo Fernandez's house during the Miami Open. Like so many of my peers, I was in awe of him. Mary Jo's husband, Tony Godsick, had recently become Roger's agent (and still is as of this writing). When I spoke with him at the party, he politely said, "I enjoyed watching you play tennis on tv when I was a junior." We exchanged mutual respect and pleasantries. Sometime later that evening, I couldn't find Jan, as she was mingling with the crowd. I finally caught a glimpse of her in the corner of the room and guess who was engaged in conversation with her? Roger, of course. She later told me that they had conversed for about 30 minutes, that he we so genuine, that he asked about the Solomon family and was truly one of the nicest people she had ever met.

If given a redo in my career, would I do anything differently? I preferred the two-handed backhand even though the stroke wasn't nearly as popular during my time. However, I'll admit to having had the wrong grip. Hard to believe but I played my entire career with my forehand grip on the backhand side! Thankfully, that little oddity didn't seem to have any long-term nightmarish effects. I also wish I'd put in more gym time, but that option was not readily available, nor an accepted training protocol in those days. And then there's the question of tennis academies. Would I have gone to one if they'd been available during my youth? Who knows? The only personal coaches back then seemed to be parents. Jimmy

Connors was never seen without his mother, Gloria near courtside. My father, Leonard, was a large influence in building my character on the court as mentioned earlier and certainly a good strategist.

Changing the topic, I have some thoughts on the state of American tennis today and I'll start with the men. Unfortunately, we haven't been on the forefront of the sport since Andre Agassi, Pete Sampras, Jim Courier, Michael Change and Andy Roddick. I feel that players from other countries generally work much harder than the American men. Personally, I've always believed in working hard. So much so, that if I heard one of my rivals was running two miles a day, then I'd run three. If they practiced for two hours a day, I'd practice more. Another issue? Missing a repertoire of big shots. The last great American player with such a repertoire was Andy Roddick, who had a monster serve and huge forehand. As far as American women, many were inspired by the Williams sisters when they were coming up. These talented siblings dominated the world stage for most of their professional career. They are finally losing out to the common foe that all players ultimately succumb to—aging bodies. Early on, they trained hard under their father, Richard, who then set them up with the best coaches. Will there ever be any American women as successful as the sisters? Were Venus and Serena just hungrier and more driven? Perhaps, since they came from Compton, California, and tennis appeared as an exciting pathway to greener pastures. Their achievements are amazing, legendary and something tennis players worldwide should celebrate.

In 1986, I retired from the tour at the grand old age of 33. Soon after, I was running the Human Resources department for my father's Budget Rental Car operations, the largest franchisee in the system at the time. In 1989, I received a call from former player and coach, Tim Gullickson, asking me to hit with his friend and tour player, Mary Jo Fernandez. Though I wasn't playing much anymore, I still remembered how to wield a racquet and stepped onto the court with her. I was encouraged that I was able to defeat her even though I wasn't competing anymore. Around the same time, I had been practicing with Jay Berger, had gotten in great shape, and felt at the ripe old age of 38, I might be able to resurrect my professional career before Father Time had the last word. In 1991, I entered the qualifying for the French Open and lost. The comeback very short lived, it was that following November that Mary Jo asked me to come on board as her coach, the partnership lasting about five years. While coaching her, she reached the finals of the Australian and French Open, as well as the semifinals of the U.S. Open. After Mary Jo, I took on Jennifer Capriati, whose ranking had plummeted to 154 due to personal issues. Within 12 months, Jennifer made it into the world top ten and reached the finals of the Australian Open. Soon after though, we went our separate ways. I would go on to coach and travel with Monica Seles, Elena Dementieva, Ana Kournikova, Jim Courier, and Justin Gimelstob, before staying home in my own backyard of Ft. Lauderdale where in 2006, I opened the Harold Solomon Tennis Institute at the Fort Lauderdale Tennis Club. As of this writing, I continue to train up-and-coming juniors at my academy, doing my best to instill the work ethic and passion I have for this sport and always will as long as I am able. It's certainly my intent to enjoy this wonderful ride for years to come.

WARD'S SKINNY ON HAROLD

Let me start out by saying that I'm going to give Harold considerably more coverage in my skinny. We've been lifelong friends, and I personally witnessed his meteoric rise to a world top five beginning way back when, from the 14 and Under National championships, to a court-side seat at his first tournament win over Guillermo Vilas. I'd also like to call him the "top seeded" player in *Tennis Life*—for a myriad of reasons. As he said earlier, he won 22 ATP Tour titles, reached the finals of the 1976 French Open and had wins over most of the top players except for Borg. He ranked among the world's top ten in four out of five consecutive years: 1976, 1978, 1979 and 1980. He ranked among the world's top twenty for seven consecutive years, from 1974 to 1980. He also reached a number four ranking in doubles playing with Eddie Dibbs in 1976. He served as president of the ATP Tour from 1980 to 1983 and later, was on its Board of Directors.

So where do I begin regarding Harold? When we were childhood friends of course (our fathers were big buds too). I've known him since we were in the 12 and Under division. We would often practice together at Indian Spring Country Club in our hometown of Silver Spring. I was lucky to share the court with such a fine player. He was always ranked among the top five in the country in every age division along the way. As his ranking escalated, mine managed to slip each year— not a good omen for me. Nevertheless, I was happy for my friend and as I followed his journey, I tried to attend his matches in person whenever I could.

I have an interesting story about Harold and me as kids. The year was 1966 and the event was the Mid Atlantic Tennis Championships at Hermitage Country Club in Richmond, Virginia. A large contingent of players from the Greater Washington Tennis Association drove the two hours south to compete. There was a competitor from D.C., an African American acquaintance and rival of mine named Weldon Rogers. He'd driven down with his father, Reverend Jefferson P. Rogers, a distinguished civil rights leader. Weldon was a leftie, an excellent competitor, and a good guy. Soon after registration, we found out that Weldon wouldn't be allowed to play in the event. Why? Because of the country club's policy which stated that colored folks were forbidden. My father, Leonard, and Harold's father, Lenny, couldn't stand for such an act of prejudice and voiced their displeasure to us, letting us know in no uncertain terms how they felt about it. Harold's father said something to the effect of, "You boys should make the decision on whether or not to play on your own. But we feel strongly, that by playing, we as your parents would be condoning the policy and be complicit in this horrible situation." The tournament director responded to the outcry by saying Weldon could play ... but only at the nearby public courts! Our parents found that completely unacceptable and orchestrated a walk out led by Harold, me, and 11 others. We simply defaulted and drove home. It should be noted that the Middle Atlantic Championships were a vital stepping stone toward qualifying for the Nationals and Harold had more to lose than anyone. Fortunately, due to his high ranking, he qualified for Nationals later that summer, only to lose in the finals to Randal Thomas. We were very young and naïve at that age, truly not grasping the seriousness of racism back then, but proud that our fathers did.

Fast forward to 1977. I was in the stands at the Washington Star International Tournament in D.C. for Harold to face Australian, Phil Dent, in the quarterfinals. Dent a formidable opponent, was ranked in the top ten at the time, and had an all-around good game with no clear weaknesses. The match lasted almost three hours, each rally taking forever, pretty much typical when Harold played on clay. The end of the third set was near and a tiebreaker was to decide the epic battle. However, there was a problem. Harold began cramping. He could barely walk, and it appeared the match might end abruptly. What happened next is one of the reasons I have the utmost respect for my friend. He walked awkwardly to the baseline to serve, everyone in the house feeling his pain as it was truly tough to watch. Dent seemed fresh on the other side and probably figured the match would be his. But out of nowhere, Harold began rushing the net! Harold to the net was a rare sight indeed but he knew that sustained rallies with cramps were impossible. So, for the next several points, he took the ball early, pummeling it down the lines and then charging the net. Phil was not only shocked to see his opponent weather the cramps but that he was moving to the net. He was so taken aback, that he missed passing shots, one right after the other, and suddenly it was match point for Harold. He got very aggressive one more time, producing a huge winner to seal the deal. The two warriors slowly walked toward the net to shake hands. However, not only were Harold's legs cramping but his hand as well. When he went to shake Phil's hand, he couldn't let go of it and almost pulled Phil over the net with him as he collapsed to the ground! The paramedics rushed onto the court and carried him out on a stretcher. I can't remember a more courageous and dramatic ending to a match in all my years of spectating. Harold's inner strength and mental toughness earned him the victory, but once the mission was carried out, his body finally had its way.

As the reader already knows, Borg was Harold's nemesis. But there were a few other foes of his that are worth mentioning, Lendl being one of them. He possessed a similar game and style as Harold, including the mental toughness, but Lendl's height advantage gave him other options. He hit his ground strokes with less spin than Borg's, so the bounce through the court was much lower and harder. He had the ability to take out his opponents through his incredible pace off both wings. Harold's record against Lendl? 1-6. As a matter of fact, one of those losses occurred in the 1980 U.S. Open, the shocking score 6-1, 6-0, 6-0. I was astounded to hear the result since the guy was not Borg and thought Harold had a chance. But to be beaten so soundly? I happened to see Harold that Christmas break and asked him about the match, figuring he must have been physically compromised, sick or something similar. He replied that the rallies were long, and Lendl just happen to win the majority of them; that in fact, he never had one break point in the match. I was still surprised as I have personally witnessed him compete against the likes of Connors, Ashe, McEnroe, Tanner, Gottfried and Ramirez and others, and no one every trounced him like Lendl did. It's testimony to how great a champion Lendl was.

The other legend that caused some issues for Harold? The great Arthur Ashe. One of their matches was played in Harold's backyard so to speak, at the 16th and Kennedy Complex in D.C., with a boisterous home crowd cheering his every point. Though the clay courts were not Arthur's favorite surface, his game translated effectively anywhere, and on that night, it appeared his devastating backhand would prove too much for Harold. Arthur reached match point and served for the match. But my fearless friend ran around his backhand and nailed a forehand return of serve for a winner. It was a momentum changer and Harold ended up with the win. Arthur's one-handed backhand was truly one of the best of all time. Any tennis historian remembers the wonderful Wimbledon final in which he played the world number one at the time, Jimmy Connors. Arthur pitched a masterpiece that day with a straight set victory over Jimmy. Yet on a balmy summer's eve in Washington D.C., Harold secured the victory, overcoming the legend and his match point. His head-to-head record against Arthur was 4-6, the losses generally coming on hard courts. Harold told me that when he played him indoors, winning was out of the question, due to the indoor playing conditions adding to the speed of the ball. Harold recalled being obsessed with the clock—as his goal was to keep Arthur on the court for at least an hour!

Lastly, the player that really bothered Harold the most was not a player at all! It was the venue we all know as Wimbledon. The All-England Club's grass courts did not suit Harold's game one iota. What made Wimbledon so frustrating for him was that it was impossible to stay back, a style that brought him 22 ATP tour titles and wins over the greats of his time (except for Borg of course). The surface in those days was not nearly as well-groomed as today and played much faster. Harold's western forehand grip made it problematic to counter the low skidding balls. A continental grip could have handled it much better, but it was just not in his repertoire. As a result, he never won a match at Wimbledon. He played there a grand total of four times, his last appearance in 1986 pitting him against a relatively unknown player, Jonathan Canter. Harold would lose to him in straight sets, and he vowed never to return to the sacred ground. The only grass Harold would ever consider playing on after Wimbledon was that found on the golf links.

I asked Harold once how he managed pressure and nerves. Right off the bat, he said "Everyone gets nervous." He went on to say that a few physiological things happen when one's nerves get in the way—the feet stop moving, the grip pressure intensifies, and the mind freezes up. Somehow, he had learned how to combat those ill effects. He battled back by fighting for every point, keeping his feet active and forcing himself to hit harder when tight. His goal was always to figure how to win and not to lose, positive thoughts always his mantra. Hmm, wait a minute, maybe not always as an exception to Harold's steadfast mantra just coming to mind. It was the time I coached Harold when he was playing Borg at the 1978 U.S. Open—yes, you read that right! I remember sitting with him before he headed to the stadium court and talking about the upcoming encounter with his nemesis. He exclaimed to me, "I have no chance!" The words shocked me coming out of a player with such a steel trap mind on the court. But then again, he was playing the one man who had his number. I suggested, "Why not try something different? Like attack his serve in the first game and come to the net?" Harold reluctantly agreed, and soon thereafter in a packed house at Flushing Meadow, he would do just that in the first game with Borg serving. Well, there went my fleeting coaching career on the big stage, as Harold nailed the return of serve down the line, followed it to the net, and then watched as a precise passing shot whistled right past him. He looked up at me in the stands in a fit of despair and shrugged his shoulders. The writing was already on the wall and soon, it was another lopsided win for Borg by the score of 6-2, 6-0, 6-2. Of course, Harold promptly fired me and would never take my advice again! Which also brings back the memory of the time I restrung his racquet for a tour event. It was in D.C., enroute to his first ATP victory. He needed his strings replaced and I volunteered for the job. I took his Garcia home with me, along with some high-end VS Gut string. I promptly delivered it back to him as he prepared for his match against Billy Martin. He pinged the racquet string to detect the tension and I'll never forget the look of disdain that spread across his face. Without hesitation and to my chagrin, he grabbed a knife and cut it out! After my initial sense of failure, of course I understood that the racquet tension had to be exact, and thus my stringing career with him also came to an abrupt halt.

Now it's 2021 and a pair of aging, lifelong tennis-addicted friends have managed to catch up in person. I made a trip to Ft. Lauderdale, to sit down with Harold at his tennis academy and ask him to contribute to *Tennis Life*. What an impressive and professional operation! Unlike other academies, his ratio of students is two to one, giving personal and quality attention to each player. He works alongside his assistant coaches daily, his hands-on approach making his academy one of the best in the world. And his philosophy is quite simple: to work harder and smarter than anyone else. He knows what it takes to make it on the big stage and can tell unequivocally after hitting a few balls and interviewing a prospect, if they are a candidate for future stardom on the tour. He's been particularly successful with female players but why? Surely, it's not because Solly, as he was referred to, was voted one of Playgirl's top ten sexiest men in 1980 and deemed "adorable" by the publication! One never knows for sure but it's more likely it all began thanks to his partnership with Mary Jo Fernandez. It's literally been a who's who of ladies that followed in her footsteps: Monica Seles, Jennifer Capriati, Ana Kournikova, Shahar Peer, Elena Dementieva, Allie Klick, Eugenie Bouchard, and even a recent, however brief stint with Naomi Osaka. The day I sat down with him, he had just finished a coaching session with two very talented juniors. His success in making his players better is more than a subjective opinion. With 100% conviction, I know he will steer his prospects to greatness as best he possibly can. Signing on with him would be a great move for any tour player, as he puts his heart and soul into coaching—just as he put his heart and soul into just about every match he ever played.

Speaking of Harold's heart and soul, this is something he won't bring up on his own but that's one of the purposes of Ward's Skinny—I will. Around 1978, in the prime of his tennis career, he became very active in the Hunger Project, a worldwide crusade to eradicate hunger by the year 2000. His father, Lenny, was already passionate about the issue. Harold used his tennis celebrity to further the project by starting the Hunger Project Tennis Festival, which was held, all but the first year, at the Woodmont Racquet and Swim Club in Tamarac, Florida. The first festival highlighted a mini tournament featuring himself, Arthur Ashe, Eddie Dibbs, and Brian Gottfried. The second festival in 1980 was even bigger and better, featuring John McEnroe, Jimmy Connors, and Vitas Gerulaitis, once again playing exhibition tennis. It raised $30,000 for the charity. The third festival the following year raised nearly $40,000, featuring several of the same players. I found an article about the event from the 1982 South Sun Florida newspaper in which Harold told the reporter, "Life is so fulfilling now. This gives me purpose, an opportunity to use my tennis, a chance to put something back in. I used to be the opposite. I was somewhat self-centered until I was about 25 or 26. This way you know you're making a difference. You have to start taking a shift—it's not okay that two million are going to die in Africa." Over the years, those festivals eventually raised approximately $500,000. By 1990, Ivan Lendl, Pete Sampras, Andre Agassi, Mary Jo Fernandez, and Pam Shriver were also involved, participating in exhibitions in Washington D.C. and thus raising more money and awareness. In fact, at the 1990 celebrity exhibition in D.C., President George H.W. Bush hosted a White House reception the following day in which Harold and his father attended. As of today, Project Hunger is still active, and we have Harold and his dad to thank for their tireless efforts in bringing to life such a worthy cause.

I think I'll end the skinny on my lifelong friend with a non-tennis story. How about a golf match in Tennessee in the year 2000? It was a very competitive match with Jack Cohen, a childhood friend, and yours truly, versus the Solomon brothers, Harold, and Mark.

There was always some money at stake, enough to make it interesting but not too much to fret over. However, the bragging rights seemed to be worth more than anything when competing with the brothers. It came down to the 18th hole, with everything riding on the par five and the pressure thick. What happened next is beyond belief. We all hit our drives in play and the second shot would be a layup, with Harold using his trusty seven iron. He could hit his irons much farther than most since he had very strong wrists and swung very hard. His next shot would curve perilously left of his intended target, a snap hook so to speak. Immediately, he heaved his iron toward a large tree in front of us. The club vanished inside the gnarly branches and never came down. I tried to climb up the tree as I hated to see Harold lose his club, and quite frankly at this point, knowing full well that Jack and I would win the epic match as a result. After ten futile minutes, the club could not be retrieved, so on to the next shots—the all-important third shot approach to the very difficult par. One would think Harold would be beside himself after putting his layup shot into the thick rough and then losing his club in a tree. Surely, it would sidetrack him from the next shot at hand. However, if you ever knew Harold or his dad, there was no quit in the name, Solomon. But on that day and at that juncture, on the last hole and most important moment in the four-hour struggle—with his beloved seven iron nestled somewhere in the tree, I just knew he had to be done. His wayward shot lay in thick Bermuda rough with the ball barely visible and the likelihood of proper extraction very slim. Nonetheless, as so many stories go with Harold and out of nowhere, he swings as hard as he can, lofts the ball up in the air and onto the treacherous green some 150 yards away making the putt! Damn if he didn't tie us—he parred the hole. Only Harold could lose his club in a tree and get his act together to hit a wonderful shot out of the blue. The guy never ceases to amaze me, and to compete with him is as much fun as one can have in life. I have so much respect for him, that it often hurts my chances to beat him but make no excuses about it. I too enjoy competing and relish the next time we play. If he throws his club in the tree once again, I'll still climb up to retrieve it if these old bones will allow. But always expect the unexpected from this little giant of a man. Just as he did so many times in his career on the ATP tour and as I said earlier, Harold Solomon gets the top seed honor in *Tennis Life*. Thanks so much for sharing part of your journey with us, my friend.

MIKE SPRENGELMEYER

It has always been my belief that for the most part, tennis is a family sport handed down by parents that played or by actively playing siblings. For my twin brother and I, it was our actively playing siblings that piqued our tennis interest. We hit our first balls at the age of seven in our hometown of Dubuque, Iowa—not exactly a hotbed of the tennis world. We lived in the middle of historic Eagle Point Park, a 164-acre park opened in 1909, the bulk of it situated on a bluff overlooking the Mississippi River. My two older sisters and two older brothers originally got hooked on tennis thanks to six concrete tennis courts conveniently located just a half block from our house. Before they knew it, they all found themselves playing junior tournaments around the state, my two brothers good enough to receive full tennis scholarships to the University of Southern Illinois. They also played the adult tennis circuit around the country during and after college.

Soon my twin and I found ourselves following in their footsteps. Growing up I knew I wanted to make it playing professional tennis. Even now, I tell my tennis students that there are three requirements one has to meet in order to have any chance of making it on the pro tour: The God given talent for the game; opportunity— meaning the player's parents need to recognize your talent, get you the equipment you need, schedule lessons from a qualified pro, and arrange transportation to junior tournaments; and lastly, the desire and dedication to reach your goals. Fortunately, I had the God given talent and my parents were all in with their support. Next, I set my goals. I wanted to be number one in the state of Iowa, earn a full tennis scholarship at the University of Southern Illinois, and to play on the men's pro tour. I'm proud to say I accomplished all three.

After graduating from college, I set my sights on playing in the tour. That summer, I entered the Iowa Open in Cedar Rapids. I drove my brother's motorcycle 180 miles to compete in the tournament. Continuing the non-conventional theme on the courts, I wore a long-sleeved football jersey and orange bandana for every match, possibly throwing off my opponents just a bit. Winning the first four rounds, I faced the number one seed in the semifinals. Fighting off leg cramps in the third set, I pulled out the win and a post-match interview courtesy of the upset. I was asked about my attire. I explained, "The long sleeve jersey gives added protection to my elbows since I've broken both in the past. As far as my orange bandana, most other players wear white ones. I'm probably the only player that consistently wears a colored one." That afternoon, I went on to beat the second seed in the final. At the same tournament, I stumbled upon an added bonus. I was fortunate enough to be introduced to Robert Lange, a businessman from Dubuque. He owned the Lange Ski Boot Company. I told him of my desire to play on the tour and he informed me that his company was building a new factory in Colorado, his intention being to expand his company into tennis. He said that if I would move to Colorado and use Boulder as my base, then his company would sponsor me on the tour and pick up all my expenses—in fact, pay me a salary. I jumped at the chance and headed to the mountain state where the Lange Company sponsored me on the tour for two years. Looking back, I must admit my main regret from those years is that I didn't approach this fantastic opportunity in the same way that I approached my junior playing years, in which I set specific goals and did the hard work to reach the goals. Once I was on the tour, I neglected to set further goals and, therefore, didn't really think or plan on what it was going to take to reach those goals. In other words, I didn't shoot higher. It was almost like I was satisfied with just accomplishing the goals I had set when I was a junior player. After all, I was a kid from Iowa and back then, all the top American players were coming out of California and Florida. As a result of my lack of planning, I played only eight matches on the tour. The bulk of them happened at the U.S. Open on four separate occasions when they were grass courts, which I loved playing on.

Ironically, my most memorable match did not happen while I was on tour. Instead, it was at a USLTA (precursor to USTA) satellite tournament in August of 1967, at the South Hampton Racquet Club, where Dick Knight and I battled on the grass courts for over five hours to log in the longest two out of three sets match, a record still standing in men's pro tennis history—at least in theory, since tennis stats weren't recorded until the open era in 1968. The score was 32-30, 3-6, 19-17, Dick unfortunately walking away with the victory. Our long play as well as a few other matches at that same venue, caught the attention of famed journalist, George Plimpton. A frequent contributor to Sports Illustrated, he wrote about our contest in the September issue. It's such an entertaining article, I feel compelled to share the portion that relates to my match:

Oddly, one of the most popular sports—tennis—does not have a record book, a lack that was particularly felt this past August when a series of marathon matches were played at Southampton and

Newport and no one could find out if, indeed, a record had been set. Length, whether of time or distance, provides a most durable and interesting part of any record book (the longest baseball game—26 innings, the longest punt—94 yards), and the comparatively few spectators who saw those amazing matches felt a mild sense of loss that what they had watched would not be permanently marked in tennis history.

Two of the three marathon matches were played at Southampton, a tournament that used to be one of the most important on the summer tour but whose luster has faded somewhat in recent years. Those who do come, look forward more to the pleasant ministrations of the community, particularly an annual party at which the tennis players are provided with a great lobster dinner, a rock 'n' roll band under a marquee and pretty girls by the score who pick that night to move to the dance rages in the wildest outfits they've got. Also in Southampton, the community takes in most of the players as house guests and entertains them, which is a hospitable and welcome arrangement quite unlike Newport's, the next stop on the tour, where most of the players are assigned to low-slung cots in a barn like hall in the upper reaches of the Newport Casino. But as for the tennis at Southampton, that is another matter. "It all depends on the court you're assigned," one of the players said. "A good court and it's tennis. But if you get assigned to 'The Pasture'—well, you can hear the players on their way to those courts mooing and bleating, because what's played down there is a game unto itself."

The first of the marathon matches took place in the preliminary round of the singles tournament. The two participants were Dick Knight and Mike Sprengelmeyer, two top-notch college players, who were in fact delighted with their court assignment—court six, set immediately behind the temporary bleachers facing the center court and in relatively good shape. It was possible to sit on the top *rows of the bleachers and look back down over the railing at their match. Despite the extraordinary length of the match, not many did. As Knight himself said, "It was not exactly the prestige match of the tournament." Both players at this stage in their careers represent the equivalent of golfing's "rabbits"—that is to say, players who must scurry from one tournament to the next to compete among themselves in preliminary rounds for the open positions in the first round of the tournament draw. Such players must get to their work early, and the Knight-Sprengelmeyer match was scheduled for 10 o'clock.*

Perhaps the most faithful spectator was Dick Knight's girlfriend, Karen Williams, who had started out from Scarsdale, N.Y. at 6:30 that morning to be on hand. She arrived half an hour or so after the match had started. Knight could look up and see her looking down at him from the top of the bleachers. Occasionally, as the match wore on, she called down to him, "Do something!" Her schedule was tight (she had a rendezvous with her parents at Jones Beach that afternoon), and as noontime came and went and the match moved on into the afternoon, she wondered if she would be able to have a word with him at all. It took three hours to play the first set of the match. Knight finally won it 32-30, breaking Sprengelmeyer's serve on the 61st game and holding his own. In the next set Knight began to have the odd sensation that he was "floating" above the court, as he put it. The night before he had driven up from Sea-bright, and the tournament there, in weekend traffic, and he'd had only four hours' sleep. He lost the set 3-6. But in the third set he got his second wind, and Sprengelmeyer, on his part, began to get cramps. At one point, at about the 20th game of the set, his arm muscle bulged out alarmingly, and he felt such pain that he wondered if he hadn't somehow broken his arm. But he persevered, the pain lessened, and he was able to struggle on at even terms, winning his serve as easily as Knight was winning his.

After the fifth hour of steady play, the quality of which was surprisingly good according to witnesses, the match took on a surreal quality: ball kids came and went (home for lunch and then returning); one of them was a nervous small girl in a white tennis dress who had difficulty bouncing the ball properly to the player, and she would run six or seven steps like an English bowler and with a small squeak of effort, bounce the ball off at erratic angles. She would run to retrieve it, return directly to the player, and place the ball on the lip of his racket with a murmur of apology. Knight remembers the enormous pile of debris by the net post—Coca-Cola cans, orange peels, towels, empty pitchers (the players consumed two full pitchers of water and two of Coca-Cola), paper cups; he also retains the odd memory of an elderly man's face peering at the match through a hole in the green canvas backstop, an intermittent witness who would disappear for long stretches. Then, with a start, Knight would notice the face back in the hole, as surprisingly disembodied as the head of a jack-in-the-box. Finally, in the 107th game of the match, Knight found himself with triple match points, love-40 on Sprengelmeyer's serve. He lost the next two points, and then Sprengelmeyer, rushing to net behind his serve, hit a good stiff volley that would have brought the score to deuce had not the shot gone beyond the baseline, not by much, just an inch, and the match was over 32-30, 3-6, 19-17. Knight threw his racket in the air. He said it didn't go up very far, "perhaps six or seven feet," and he walked to the net to shake hands with Sprengelmeyer, who was waiting, looking at him dully. Knight didn't know what to say. He said, "Mike, honest, I just don't know what to say." Sprengelmeyer couldn't find anything to say, either; he massaged the bulge on his arm, and he said, "Yes"—something as noncommittal—and the two left the court to report the scores to the tournament director. It was 3:30. They had been playing for five and a half hours.

Plimpton, G. (1967, September 18) What the Deuce is Going On? *Sports Illustrated*

Our match, along with the other two, convinced the powers that be in the tennis world, the time was right to make a change to the scoring system – thus came about the V.A.S.S.S. system (Van Allen Simplified Scoring System). In other words, tie breakers would be played at six all in the set, the die cast for scoring in the modern tennis era.

My post tour years, my life continued to include the sport. I was the Director of Tennis at the Rolling Hills Country Club in Golden, Colorado for four years, while at the same time starting Rocky Mountain Sports, a tennis equipment manufacturer and wholesaler. Simultaneously, I was also the assistant coach for the University of Colorado men's tennis team. In 1978, I moved my family of four (wife, Pat, daughter, Hilary, and son, Mitch) to Florence, South Carolina where I was the Director of Tennis for the Florence Country Club for 20 years. We then moved to Clemson at which time I was recruited by my former business partner at Rocky Mountain Sports to take on the task of sales rep and heading up the junior player and college package program for Babolat in the Carolinas. In addition, and for a limited time, I was Assistant Men's Tennis Coach under Chuck Kriese, followed by another short stint as Assistant Woman's Coach under Nancy Harris.

While in Colorado, my son Mitch was born, and at the age of two, I introduced him to tennis, using unorthodox props—a sawed off wooden racquet, a nerf ball, some large pillows, and our family room couch! I had him stand sideways at the couch with the racquet resting against it. I would throw the nerf ball to his forehand side. He'd hit it sending the ball across the room where good old dad would dive for it into the pillows on the floor. Great fun for a two-year-old kid and at the same time, teaching him the concept of where the contact point had to be. Next came a hitting wall of sorts and when he turned three, I set up a rebound net in the basement to mimic the drill. At the age of four, I had him on a regular tennis court with regular balls, and at the age of five, I entered him in his first 10 and Under tournament. At six years old, he and I played our first father/son tournament together, giving us a wonderful chance to bond and at seven, he won his first singles tournament. Fast forward to the 18 and Under, where he achieved number one status in the state of South Carolina. That lead Clemson's Coach Chuck Kriese to recruit him. I felt that Mitch had all the technical skills required to play well when he arrived at Clemson. However, it was under Coach Kriese that he became a student of the game, enabling him to become an All-American in both singles and doubles—and eventually winning the National Senior Player of the Year award, considered the tennis equivalent to the Heisman Trophy for football. He also won the Von Nostrand Memorial Award, given to the player showing the most promise as a professional. As Chuck likes to remind me, Mitch was the first college tennis player in history to win two awards his senior year. From college, he went on to play pro tennis for four years, traveling the world and playing the Australian, French, Wimbledon and U.S. Open. I am and always will be the proud parent/coach!

Having just discussed the experience of training my own son, I have some food for thought for up-and-coming juniors. Tennis is a fantastic sport, quite possibly the toughest one out there, because you must mesh and mold the physical, the mental, and the emotional aspects of the game during a match—at the same time your opponent is trying to knock you off the court. Thus, do your best to develop a strategy to work on all three aspects at the earliest age possible. I like to explain tennis to my students as a physical form of the game of chess. It involves two players starting out with the same pieces. On the chess board, you have pawns, knights, rooks, bishops, the queen, and the king. The function of each piece is analogous to a particular shot or type of play in tennis: the pawn represents just rallying back and forth; the knight represents a drop shot/lob combination; the rook, because it can only move straight, represents down the line shots; the bishop, because it only moves diagonally, represents crosscourt shots; the queen, because it can move in any direction, represents your greatest weapon, could be your serve; the king represents none other than winning the match. So, with the same pieces, what differentiates the players? What is playing out in their minds. In other words, selection and strategy. It's the same for tennis. One other thought. When the chess players sit down to play, they are completely focused on the board in front of them—they're not looking around the room. They tune everything out around them except for that all important chess set. It should be the same thing when on the tennis court. I have a great example of not adhering to this very critical practice. Very early on, at the age of 12, I witnessed Mitch's head spin on the court like Linda Blair's in the Exorcist! He was playing a tournament in Florida, and I was in the stands watching and taking notes. He would look over at me after nearly every point. Not only that, but he would also watch players on the court next to him and people coming in and out of the stands—his head turning in every direction. After the match, I told him, "Son, your energy is all over the place, everywhere but your own court." The next day, I bought him a magnifying glass and asked him, "Mitch, what do you do with a magnifying glass in the sun?" His answer, "Burn things, Dad." I said, "That's right, son. If you don't look around and just stay focused within the confines of your own court—concentrating on noting your opponent's strengths and weaknesses and what's working for you, then you'll burn your opponents!" Mitch took that to heart, carrying the magnifying glass in his tennis bag for the rest of his junior career.

In closing, let me just say it's been a fun and fulfilling ride. I've had the privilege of playing tennis my whole life and I guess it's just in my family's blood—kind of like being a circus performer maybe! I've been so fortunate that my tennis journey has provided the means for my family, a roof over our heads and even a red clay tennis court in my backyard. God has been good to us, and I feel incredibly blessed.

WARD'S SKINNY ON MIKE

I crossed paths with Mike about six years ago and personally witnessed his skills as a player, tennis coach—and a darn good racquet stringer! I call him the Guru because he understands all facets of the game and possesses knowledge about the sport unlike anyone I've seen. In my tennis journey, I've had some amazing tutelage from the likes of Nick Bollettieri, Warren Woodcock and Jimmy Evert. But that was then, and this is now. When I have an issue with myself on a specific stroke, Mike usually has the solution. A good example of this? Recently, I played in a senior tournament in Atlanta. In my first match, I was soundly defeated. I drove straight to Guru Mike's house for advice. On my forehand shadow swing, he quickly noticed that my wrist was not properly laid back. That simple shadow swing executed in his presence produced the solution and correction, enabling me to win my match the next day. In fact, I often show him videos of some of my students from Keowee Key when I can't find a solution for their problem shots—like going to another doctor for a second opinion. I'm fine admitting that sometimes the cure to an ailing stroke is beyond my pedigree. Just a 30-minute drive down the road and he will find the answer in a few short minutes!

The modern game changed so much around Mike, but he continued to learn, evolve and adapt. The high-quality strings, more powerful racquets, and video analysis at-your-fingertips training all presented new challenges to him, yet this old school player embraced it all. He can still find the answers no matter the level of the player. That's why his son, Mitch, was so lucky to have him as his coach. From the age of two to an adult playing on the tour, Mitch had his father's shrewd expertise along the way. He really worked with him on doubles play throughout the years since the doubles point requires more finesse, shot types, poaching, faking, and formations. As a result, Mitch had a commendable doubles record on the ATP tour, one that includes a 3-2 winning record over the Bryan Brothers.

Mike is a generous soul and one that enjoys sharing his wealth of knowledge to any player desirous of improving. When an assistant coach at Clemson under Chuck Kriese, he diligently charted matches knowing that the statistics were important when it came to improving play—all of this on his own dime and for the love of tennis. He is truly a student of the game and an A student at that. Mike, never stop learning and growing as a player, my friend. Together, we'll continue to share stories and work on our games to compete in national senior tournaments, despite Father Time having his way with our bodies. Thanks for being part of *Tennis Life*, Mike. It's been a pleasure to share your story with the extended tennis community.

CHRIS SYLVAN

I grew up in Fort Lauderdale and at the age of ten, started playing tennis on the public courts at Holiday Park, the old stomping grounds of multiple grand slam winner, Chris Evert. Chrissie and I played together for several years since we were basically the same age. In fact, my first instructor was her father, Jimmy Evert. When she became the nation's number one ranked player in the Girls 14 and Under division in 1969, numerous fans packed the stands just to watch her play, day in and day out. When I was a senior in high school, Chrissie invited a surprise guest to join us on our practice court. It was none other than her new boyfriend, Jimmy Connors. He had already become a household tennis name in his own right, having just turned pro and proud winner of the NCAA singles title his freshman year at UCLA. It must have been a real treat for the northern clime snowbirds hitting on the adjacent courts when they realized who had just arrived.

Holiday Park, was an incredibly special place to take up tennis in the late 1960's. And not just because of the family with the last name Evert. Some very talented juniors were trained and nurtured there, certainly giving the tennis hotbeds of California a run for their money. Motivated by my first-rate peers, I quickly developed into a decent player, reaching number four in the country as a 14-year-old. One of my most memorable tournaments after obtaining said status happened at the Eastern Junior Championships in Forest Hills, New York. I was up against a Godly like kid and future world number four, Gene Mayer, in the semifinals. Gene was the national boys 12 and Under champion the previous two years. I was quite certain that I'd get killed and just hoped to make a good showing. I won the first set, joking inwardly with myself that it was very nice of Gene to give me a set, the good showing in the bag. Amazingly, it didn't end there. I took the lead 3-0 in the second set, and being the nice guy that I am, was literally worried for Gene—that he might actually lose! Thank goodness my ridiculously compassionate thought was only fleeting, and my competitive juices won out, as I bageled him the second set. I had beaten the God of the 14 and Under! I followed up the upset with a win in the finals over Peter Fleming, future multiple Grand Slams doubles champion and John McEnroe's partner. I attribute my success in that tournament to practicing with an obscure young teenager who was a year older. The guy played fantastic tennis but had no ranking at the time and didn't play in the tournament. He just practiced at the facility under the tutelage of pro, Warren Woodcock. I remember saying to him, "You have to play in these tournaments, you're way too good not to." He didn't seem interested—at all. Well, about a year later, he was ranked nationally in the junior tennis top five. His name? Vitas Gerulaitis.

At the age of 17, I was recruited by Cal Berkeley, moved to California, and played college tennis for two years. Peter Pearson, one of the most talented players in the region, became a very good friend and fantastic doubles partner. However, I would soon find out that Peter had a very bad habit. The discovery came when we were in the doubles semifinal of the prestigious San Jose tournament. Taking an afternoon detour to do some shopping at the local Macy's, I found that Peter preferred not paying for his purchases. He had stored several must-haves under his jacket. He came up to me and said, "Let's get the hell out of here," only to be stopped red handed by store security. By association, I was forced to join my doubles partner during the interrogation. I was finally let go and Peter was taken to juvenile detention. Unable to get him released in time for the semifinal match, we were forced to default. The next week Peter was sprung, and as if nothing had happened, we played the Burlingame National Championship, winning it along with a gold tennis ball, the symbol of excellence in junior tennis. As a side note, unfortunately shoplifting was only the tip of the iceberg for what would occur later in Peter's life. After a shoulder injury in 1982 ended his playing career, he tried teaching tennis until the early 1990's. Sadly, due to chronic cocaine use, he resorted to successfully robbing banks to fund the drug habit and hotel bills. Eventually he got caught and served time. A very sad ending for such a gifted player.

During my sophomore year, my mounting wins justified being named the team's number one player. I was thrilled but as they say, be careful what you wish for! The Stanford team, under the instruction of Coach Dick Gould, decided to bring college tennis into the major spotlight. Coach Gould arranged to have night matches played in the Maples Pavilion basketball arena, in front of paying crowds. I was incredibly nervous about the prospect of performing with thousands of spectators in the house, but it was exceptional opportunity for a college player. I was scheduled to play in one of the feature matches because my opponent was the famous newcomer and sure-to-be-star, UCLA's Billy Martin. A friend of mine, he had won every junior national championship, from 12 and Under to 18 and Under, his first and second year— an amazing feat. I thought I had a chance against him since the surface was fast, and that would favor me with my big serve. The first game was a small nightmare, as I was tight as a drum and called for a foot fault on my second point, my first foot fault call ever in my young tennis career. Then came a double fault. Embarrassment joined what I like to refer to as my "demons" and I felt like running for the hills outside the venue. Lo and behold, the nerves calmed and the amazing score of 6-1, 6-1 was the result of being given the right to play number one for Cal. Ironically, several years later I married Billy's first wife, Lotta Ral, a beautiful Swedish woman and the mother of my two fantastic children.

Going forward, I was able to secure wins over very good players during my college years and thought I might have a chance on the tour. Taking the leap, I found it was a difficult place to play. It became clear that at a height of 6'5", speed was very important at the tour level. I worked hard at getting faster but had my limits. The other challenge before me was confidence. Playing on the tour was a whole different animal when it comes to this much needed attribute. It becomes mentally tougher to gain it and then actually maintain it. Here's good example of what an important role it plays. I was in Lyon, France playing a qualifying event for the Paris Indoors. I'd won my first match and was in a dog fight in the second round with a young player that I'd never heard of. I wasn't even sure of his name. I had no intention of losing to him at any cost and didn't, winning in three sets. After the match, a fellow player congratulated me on a very good win, and I gave him a quick "F ... you." I thought the guy was giving me a dig for barely winning in three sets. He looked at me and said, "Did you know he's the number one junior in the world and ranked in the top ten in France?" Who was he? Yanik Noah, the future number four in the world and only French man to win the French Open in 75 years. So, you see, that's what my determination and confidence did for me. If I'd known Yanik's impressive credentials before the match, I might have been much tighter and not performed nearly as well.

Eventually, I reached a singles career high ranking of 200 in the world and became a member of the ATP. Around the same time, I reached my career high ranking, I qualified for the main draw of the 1977 Australian Open, unfortunately going out to Australian, Geoff Masters, in the first round. I was also ranked in the top 80 doubles players in the world. This was a great achievement for a player of my status. My only real weapon, my serve, is what got me there. Speaking of which, in 1976, I had a chance to take part in a fast serve contest at the Pacific Southwest Open in Los Angeles. The first-place prize money was $5000, second place $2500 and third place $1200. $5000 was a lot of money back then. Anyone interested in competing had to qualify first. The speed was calculated using a police radar gun via a tall ladder. I was second in the qualifying round, my serve speed measuring at 129 mph. The main competition, best of six serves, was held that evening before the opening match featuring none other than Jimmy Connors. I was to compete against 15 entrants, and two players would become my closest competition—Australian, Colin Dibley and American, Scott Carnahan. I used Scott's Yonex gold steel racquet to serve, taking first place at 129 mph. Colin then fired a 129 and tied me. Scott was the last to serve. His first four were below 129, leaving only two more tries. I knew Colin was thinking what I was thinking—what if he misses with the last two? They would both serve for the $5000 prize. Well as bad fortune would have it, Scott hit it in at 130 and claimed top prize. Colin and I had to break the tie to settle who would take second and third place. We made a quick pact to split the remaining prize money down the middle, taking all pressure off to place. We both got three serves and after missing my first one, I knew I had to just get one in. I massaged a 117 spinner. Colin missed them all, and as of that event, I was the second fastest server in the world with a cool $1850 more in my pocket.

Giving advice to today's starry-eyed junior is a tough task, simply because the game has changed so much since I was coming up. For one thing, there are no wood or steel racquets anymore. As a result, the types of strokes and speeds at which kids hit have changed—the strings and racquet weight making a big difference with regards to the style used. A two-handed backhand seems to occur at almost a nine to one ratio, and it might be the single greatest difference in the men's game. The beautiful if not vulnerable one-handed backhand allowed the server to approach the net, a lost art these days. Defending with a slice is also fast disappearing, as well as approach shots and attacking the net. Instead, baseline rallies predominate. Physical conditioning and training also become a must, whereas it wasn't in the 1960s and 1970s. Also develop mental toughness early on. My number one problem during the junior years in Florida was the concept of choking (I refer to it as the "demon" as previously mentioned) or getting tight when playing against friends. I knew that if I could play freely, I could beat them handily. But it just wasn't that simple. A great example of this was playing my dear friend and frequent doubles partner, Mark Joffey. He beat me 17 straight times. Why? Because we were buddies and I feel like I was always wound up tighter than a coil spring when facing him. Apparently, Mark handled the best buds' factor much better. Well, the 18th match arrives. I'm down 1-5 in the third set. Before I knew it, I was winning point after point. It seemed Mark had gotten complacent with the lead. I managed to put blinders on as to who was across the court, coming all the way back to win the set 8-6. Had I unconsciously channeled Vitas Gerulaitis's future quote? The one he so famously spoke when finally beating Bjorn Borg? It was simply, "No one beats me 17 times in a row." Okay, so I was one match over Vitas's 17, but that's inconsequential in the scheme of things. I remember consoling Mark that evening at his house. Let's face it, when you've had 17 consecutive wins over one player and you finally lose, it's like an unexpected death in your life.

Choking also regularly occurred when playing another friend, Bill Tompkins. I had the lead in about 60% of the matches, but Bill would come away the winner. I felt hands were always around my throat, the demon always laughing on my shoulder. Something happened during the string of matches that made matters even worse. During one of the losses, I was forced to borrow one of Bill's father's racquets, as I had broken all of mine during the match. When I gave the racquet back, his father accused me of damaging his. This created bad blood between our two families. Not a good situation since we practiced at the same courts. To placate Bill's father, my dad bought him a new racquet but regrettably due to the ongoing tension, our two families never socialized together again.

Throughout juniors, I got better, and my family eventually moved from Florida to Fresno, California. The move, due to my father's career, indirectly helped me, as the faster hard courts in California forced me to change my game. The slice backhand that we were all used to hitting was being picked on by the strong California players, and the only way I could compete was to add a topspin backhand to my repertoire. Thus, I learned it. Soon the go-to shot off my opponent's racquet would only strengthen my retooled one hander and what was once a weakness had become an asset. I would carry this new tool onto the pro tour. However, my body didn't cooperate. Every time I'd gain momentum, it would stall out with a nagging injury. This would continue until I ultimately had to throw in the towel. My finances and physical health could not sustain my dream of greatness on the professional circuit.

WARD'S SKINNY ON CHRIS

Chris and I go back so far, that I can still remember swimming in his parents' pool at the age of 12—in water hotter than a drawn bath! Ironically, this leisure activity happened just prior to our parents driving us across the width of Florida to the Bath and Racquet Club, home of the Sarasota Junior tennis tournament. Yes, this was back in the heyday of American junior tennis, circa 1967. He and I were sometimes-doubles partners and friendly singles rivals, until he slid past me with an amazing result at the 14 and Under nationals in Chattanooga. Add his win in the Easter Bowl over legend, Gene Mayer, and he jumped past me by leaps and bounds. However, Chris admits that during his upset win over Gene, he had those nagging demon thoughts that should have cost him the win. But somehow, he got out of his own way, letting his talent shine through to finish line. This was an incredible victory for Chris, as I know firsthand how great a junior Gene was. We spent a few weekends practicing together, one at my home in Silver Spring, Maryland, and the other on a weekend visit to his home in Woodmere, New York. Harold Solomon and I took a bus to the Mayer's home and spent the weekend working out with Gene and his older brother, Sandy, while their father watched our every move on the court. If osmosis had been in action that day, I might have been a more successful player since I certainly had the opportunity to play with great competitors that weekend.

When it comes to Chris, I must bring up his selective memory and the entertaining subject of—racquet tossing. Let me give you the back story. It was the first year of the 16 and Under championships at David Park in Hollywood, Florida. My opponent in the quarterfinals was a kid by the name of Alan Petrine. Alan had a banner year in the last year of the 14 and Under, reaching the quarterfinals of nationals by way of an upset. The win would give him his career high ranking of seven in the U.S. He was a fierce competitor with a Popeye-like forearm and quick feet unlike anyone on the junior scene. He loved to attack the net and due to his quickness, he was a very tough out. But the day of the quarterfinal, I put on a masterpiece performance against him and got the upset. As soon as we shook hands at the net, he heaved his Wilson Jack Kramer racquet over the fence and into the adjacent lake! I did my best to stifle a smile as I watched the racquet's trajectory into the water. Who had been scouting on the sidelines and saw the toss? My buddy Chris. The next day, it was Chris and I duking it out for a spot in the finals against the top seed and Chris's good buddy, Mark Joffey. My Hollywood magic came through one more time, as I beat Chris in three sets. When the match was over, we shook hands and without any hesitation, he stood back, raised his racquet high over his head, and tossed it into the lake! To witness both rivals' racquets go into the lake back-to-back like that, well that's a memory that I'll never forget. He denies he tossed it to this day. However, Chris had a known habit of tossing racquets as a junior, further backing up my claim. How am I able speak to this? Due to a highly entertaining Miami Herald newspaper article from July 30, 1965, about a ten-year-old Chris. I would be remiss if I didn't quote the entire article as it's priceless (sorry Chris)!

By Andy McGill of our Broward Bureau

HOLLYWOOD—Chris Sylvan became a man Thursday. It took him almost two hours, losing his temper, an injured leg, and a loss in the first tennis tournament of his career. But blue-eyed Chris, the cutest 60 pounds of tennis player to bounce onto the courts in a long time, took it all like a man. And as his match ended, the little ten-year-old paced from the courts like a bold lad—his head held high and a look of anger in his eyes—along with a few tears that we won't talk about.

"I'm mad at myself for not doing better," he said. "I'm sorry for throwing my racquet all of the time and pouting 'cause I lost. Really I am. I should'a beat him. Or at least come closer than I did. That's why I'm mad ... I gave the match away."

"Him" is top seeded Mark Joffey who won his first-round match from Chris 6-1, 6-1.

Next to the article were photos of Chris in action, the captions also entertaining. One caption read: *Australian Crawl? Nope, temper*, with a photo of Chris bowled over into a contorted fit! The other caption read: *Chris lets his racquet know how he feels about it all*, and a photo of ... you got it—Chris throwing his racquet. Seems I've got some cred my friend, case closed!

Part of my reason for writing *Tennis Life* is to shine a light on players that I have known in my life who were ever so close to greatness. Unfortunately, due to the nature of this tough individual sport, they never became household names. Chris reached the final stages of qualifying in the U.S. Open on four different occasions but just couldn't get across the finish line. The players he defeated along the way were all very good. However, Chris did make it into the 1977 Australian Open at Kooyong Park (grass courts), losing a tough three setter to Geoff Masters in the first round. In doubles, he made it into the second round. With a little better luck and perhaps a mental coach for his demons, the tennis world might have known a little more about Chris Sylvan. Now that I've set the record straight regarding the infamous racquet toss in Hollywood, I have to say kudos to him, a great player in his own right and still a dear friend after five decades. I am thrilled to have been part of his tennis journey.

TREY WALTKE

Born in St. Louis, Missouri in 1955, my father had me swinging a racquet by age six and playing competitively by age ten. Three years older than me, Jimmy Connors also grew up playing tennis in St. Louis, and I would frequently find myself watching him play on the court next to me. I never got to play him but ironically, when I was ten and Jimmy was thirteen, I played his mother and coach, Gloria, at the Triple A Club while my father played Jimmy.

Between the age of 12 and 18, I traveled all over the U.S. to play in tournaments. I'm proud to say I held a national ranking of at least six or better in every year except for the 14 and Under division. I was ranked number one in the U.S. in doubles in the 16 and 18 and Under, alongside one of the most heralded juniors ever to play tennis, Billy Martin.

Just like many of my peers, the goal of competing on the pro tour was always foremost on my mind. Up until the age of 17, I had the opportunity to practice against several talented names from St. Louis. Having no indoor courts back then to escape the cold Missouri winters, we would all practice inside the National Guard Armory—five courts set up, side by side on the wood floors. Those were fond memories for me. But because my hometown peers were older, I watched as one by one, they moved out to the warmer climes of Los Angeles to play on the tour and practice outdoors year-round. Realizing my stellar practice competition was gone, my father suggested I move to Los Angeles for my last year of high school, the idea being to seek out better competition in preparation for my last year in the juniors. I lived by myself in a studio apartment in Westwood, a neighborhood that encompasses the sprawling campus of UCLA. My last class ending every day around noon, I'd frequently head on over to the nearby UCLA courts to practice with the team, thus giving me invaluable experience hitting with the college guys. After high school, I ended up at Cal Berkeley on a tennis scholarship. Becoming an All-American after just one year, I chose to leave college for the tour. I ended up playing nine years on the professional circuit, amassing victories along the way over several legends of the sport. My most notable wins include beating my hometown hero, Jimmy Connors, as well as John McEnroe (twice), Stan Smith, Harold Solomon, and Ilie Nastase. I never won an ATP event but did reach the finals in two singles and doubles tournaments and attained a career high ranking of 41 in the world in 1981. I also won team tennis mixed doubles championships with none other than Billie Jean King.

I truly enjoyed my first six years on the tour. I relished traveling to new cities and countries and playing in legendary stadiums around the world. Facing the many different talents and personalities, I feel that I became a smarter, more mature tennis player. I liked to study the players I would face, noting their tendencies and weaknesses, many times giving me just the arsenal needed to beat them. There were a couple of wins in which the circumstances were a bit unorthodox, and I would be remiss in not relaying these stories.

The first match occurred in Montreal at the 1981 Canadian Open. I was scheduled to play Jimmy in an early evening first round match. Being the third seed, Jimmy was the heavy favorite. Nevertheless, I was rather relaxed about the moment at hand. Hanging out at the hotel, I hear my name called out over the intercom, requesting that I come to the front desk for a phone call. It was the tournament director telling me I needed to get to the stadium asap, as the match in front of us was ending much sooner than expected. I immediately hired a taxi and urged the driver to high tail it since all that was at stake was a center court appointment with one of the world's best tennis players! My nerves never had a chance to materialize because all I could think about on the way over was being defaulted for a late arrival. Traffic was heavy but after finally navigating through the maze of cars, the driver dropped me off at the rear of the stadium. I literally scaled the fence with my racquets slung over my shoulders and promptly ran onto the center court, as Jimmy and the packed house of fans cheered my dramatic last-minute entrance. Still no time for jitters, I ended up beating him 6-3, 6-4. Somehow, I'd managed to play out of my mind. Interestingly, Jimmy didn't even bother to attend the post-match news conference.

The second story took place at Wimbledon in 1983 and revolves around my choice of attire. In my first-round match against Stan Smith, I delighted the old timers in the stands by showing up in long white flannel pants with cuffs and a long-sleeved white shirt accessorized with a V-neck sweater. The outfit was identical to those worn on court up until the 1930's. Several days prior to the match, the Wimbledon powers that be got word about my upcoming fashion statement, precipitating the need for extensive discussion. Having found no rules against the vintage uniform, I was allowed to proceed. Humorously, Stan Smith greeted me on the outside court by saying "Let's get this publicity stunt over with." Well, poor Stan had to look at my stunt outfit for five long sets and adding insult to injury, I got the W. The next day, I faced Ivan Lendl on center court. I came out wearing the same outfit—could my game and uniform work their magic on world number three Lendl too? Unfortunately not, as I lost to him in three sets. Interviewed by a reporter after the match, I was asked about the driving force behind my outfit. I told him that I got the idea from old photos in World Tennis Magazine and that I tried to find the pants in the U.S. before I left but couldn't. So, when I got to England, I found this little cricket shop in Piccadilly. They had exactly what I wanted. Then I added the shirt and a V-neck sweater like Bill Tilden used to wear, as well as a tie. The tie was an ATP tie, and I tied it around my waist instead of my neck. I went on to tell him that it wasn't my intention to continue wearing long pants in my matches, it was just something I'd always wanted to do.

My last three years on tour were another story. Though I still found the lifestyle exciting and fun, the wear and tear on my body begin to manifest itself, especially in my knees. Being only 5'8", I couldn't get nearly as many free points on my serve as the taller guys could and thus, had to work that much harder for every point. The long difficult battles with the likes of Becker, Lendl, Ashe and others, had taken their toll. I could also feel the financial pinch and it was more than evident at this point in my career that I was not going to make the top ten. Without that higher ranking, the expenses of travel, training, and room and board, added additional pressure. My playing days coming to an end, it was time to cut the tennis umbilical and pursue a solid income stream. As luck would have it, I stumbled upon an opportunity with Reebok in 1984, becoming promotions manager for their newly started tennis division. I was also in charge of determining which players would be best for signing when it came to representing the company. My biggest coup was Michael Chang, who went on to win the French Open in 1989 wearing his Reeboks, and to this date, the youngest male ever to win a grand slam. When Reebok closed their Los Angeles office, I left the company and founded a ten-store java chain called Arrosto Coffee Company. But by the year 2000, I was ready for a change and was offered a chance to have a tennis career again, this time as general manager of the exclusive Los Angeles Tennis Club. That valuable experience led me to being hired in 2008 by friend and CEO of Oracle, Larry Ellison. Larry wanted me to reinvigorate and run his newest acquisition, the 34-year-old Malibu Racquet Club. To this day, I continue to work diligently at making the MRC one of the nation's top tennis destinations.

To what do I attribute my success during juniors and the first several years on the tour? Well, a few things. Back in St. Louis as a kid, I was forced to play on different surfaces due to the dramatic weather changes—the indoor wood surfaces during the winter, followed by clay and hard courts when the weather warmed up. The two extremes helped me adapt to various conditions, honing the skills necessary to compete on contrasting surfaces. Another factor? I was blessed with good foot speed and quick hands. And thankfully, I had the uncanny ability to get hot. But I couldn't crack the world's top twenty or better. Why? Once again, a few deciding factors, the first being my inability to string together enough solid matches in a row. I was artistic and creative on the court, but too streaky and prone to making too many errors. I was hopeful I could achieve a higher ranking since I'd had several wins over top ten foes, but to break into the elite group, I had to produce more consistent results. Then there was another issue, the inherited one—the uncontrollable factor of my DNA giving me my short stature. There were a few players during my time, namely Harold Solomon, Eddie Dibbs and Ken Rosewall, that were actually shorter than me. Yet they achieved more. I attribute their additional successes to having a mindset like a steel trap, enough of one to overcome their physical disadvantage.

The author asked me about my most memorable wins and losses during my tennis journey. The reader would think that beating Johnny Mac and Jimmy would be the obvious ones. However, believe it or not, it was one of the matches that happened much earlier. It occurred when I was 13, just after I had watched the U.S. Open final between Arthur Ashe and Tom Okker. I had to play in a tournament that afternoon against an opponent that usually beat me like a drum. But having been captivated by the final I'd just witnessed and my fascination with the way Okker had played, I decided to emulate his play in the upcoming match. And that's what I did. I won handily, producing a score I'll never forget of 6-4, 6-2. I had played better than ever before, the improbable win pretty much taking me by surprise. I attributed the performance solely on watching Okker, and the strength and belief I got from copying this former tennis great.

Another memorable win came in the U.S. Open versus my former junior rival and doubles partner, Billy Martin. Billy had just beaten Harold Solomon in a first round upset and according to the New York Times, I was supposed to be a mere formality for Billy in the next round. Of course, I was irked to no end reading that prediction and went on to use my pride to channel a masterpiece against Billy. Certainly, there were better wins in my career but the sense of euphoria I experienced in overcoming my fears and then exceeding expectations—that was the ultimate satisfaction for me.

I do have some regrets. My goals to make the quarterfinals of a major and reach the top ten were not realized. I could say, *oh, if only I had a better serve"*, but at the same time, I'm realistic enough to know there were limitations on my serve due to lack of height. Nevertheless, I'm proud that I was always a work in progress—that I was never satisfied with the status quo and was always looking for ways to improve no matter how small the detail.

My advice to juniors? First and foremost, STOP THE SENSELESS DRILLING AND STOP DUCKING PRESSURE! I feel very strongly about that as you can see. Then how should a player spend the week training? I ascribe to the philosophy of playing sets of tennis five days a week against a variety of opponents. Then with the two days left, drill one day and take the other day to learn a different sport so that you can freshen the athletic synapses in your brain. Also, watch the great players and their shot selection, where and when they hit their shots, and not just how they do it. Last, but not least, don't give up on your dreams. Sometimes it just takes longer to kick in, so be patient and keep trying!

WARD'S SKINNY ON TREY

The great Arthur Ashe once said, that in the early 1960's, St. Louis, Missouri had more quality players than any other American city outside of greater Los Angeles—Jimmy Connors, Butch Buchholz, Jimmy Parker, and Mary Ann Eisel just to name a few. Hailing from St. Louis as well, Trey certainly belonged among those greats. During the junior years, for him to be selected as doubles partner for the great legend, Billy Martin, attests to the fact that he himself belonged in the top echelon of junior tennis. Then when he defeated the likes of Jimmy Connors, John McEnroe, Harold Solomon, Ilie Nastase, and Stan Smith on tour, that cemented his success.

Getting to know Trey once again after fifty plus years away from one another has been fun. I lost touch with him after the juniors. His star power shot meteorically up while mine ended up at Clemson University and nowhere beyond. But I'm proud to say I was fortunate enough to beat this special player in the 1969, 14 and Under Shamrock Invitational tournament at David Park in Hollywood, Florida. Humorously, in one of our recent conversations, Trey couldn't recall the match as vividly as I could—probably because it was a much better win for me than a loss for him. Our mutual friend and rival, Chris Sylvan (also a contributor to this book), mentioned my victory to Trey and he still denied losing to me even though I insisted to him it was one of my best wins. Thank goodness for archived newspapers. Trey looked it up and there was the loss in the sports section of the Miami Herald: *Trey Walker (yes, they misspelled his last name), top seeder, was defeated in the boys 14 and Under semi-finals by Warde Snyder (my first name also misspelled!), 6-2, 6-4.* Of course, then he had to remind me of his win over me in the Ten and Under in the Orange Bowl—which I conveniently forgot! Not surprising. One thing very common to all the great people contributing to this book, they are amazing competitors who hate to lose and simultaneously love to win. Trey was as competitive as anyone and I would make the following bet—if he had been blessed with a few more inches, his dreams of attaining the top ten and getting to grand slam quarterfinals would have been realized.

Trey is the ultimate gentleman and I'm proud that my tennis journey intersected with his. To defeat Jimmy Connors and John McEnroe twice is remarkable. He's proud but doesn't gloat over said achievements, as I did over my victory in Hollywood as a 14-year-old, but now that it's public knowledge and memorialized forever in *Tennis Life*, please join me in celebrating this former great.

ROBBIE WEISS

Sibling rivalry is what motivated me to pick up my first racquet. One Chicago afternoon, my father brought myself and my ten-year-old brother, Danny, to the local country club for some recreational activity. While there, my father borrowed a couple of tennis racquets and stepped onto the court with Danny to hit some balls. Being younger and just six, I could only watch from the sidelines. Admittedly jealous of my older brother, it was then and there that I knew I wanted to take up tennis. And that's what I did. Not wasting any time, I played my first tournament at age seven, my first national tournament at age eight, and at the age of nine, I was the number one ranked 12 and Under player in the country. From there, I went on to win 13 national tournaments. My next stop—college. I looked at Clemson, UCLA and Pepperdine, eventually landing at Pepperdine as a freshman in 1984. The university had a talented tennis team, making the finals of the NCAA Team Championship my sophomore year. In my senior year, I went on to become the number one college player in the country, thankfully backing up my ranking by winning the NCAA Singles Championship. Post college, I played on the ATP Tour for the next eight years, ranking as high as #85 in the world. I'm proud to say I had wins over four former world number one ranked players, defeating Boris Becker, Ivan Lendl, Stefan Edberg and Patrick Rafter. I also won an ATP Tour 250 Tour singles event in São Paulo, Brazil, as well as three challengers in singles.

My most memorable match on tour was in 1992, when I beat world number two, Stefan Edberg, in the third round of the Masters 1000 in Miami. It was an amazing win for a few reasons, but mostly because I'd had shoulder surgery the prior year. I wasn't sure if I would ever be the same, especially to play at a high level like a Masters 1000. Nevertheless, I qualified for the Miami main draw and got through the first two rounds. Walking on to the court to face the world's number two in the third round, all I could think about was not embarrassing myself. I found that I could compete with Edberg early in the match, eventually winning it in three sets. The next year, I beat Ivan Lendl in the second round at a Masters 500 tour event in Washington D.C. and then followed that up with a win over Boris Becker in the first round of a Masters 500 event in Osaka, Japan. Those memories will be forever etched in my mind as my greatest moments. To be able to walk on the courts against some of the best players of all time and then walk off the court the winner, that was truly something special.

Do I have an interesting tour story? Of course, what ATP player doesn't? Thankfully, this one is repeatable for *Tennis Life* and let's just say because of it, I will always appreciate the English language and the good ole U.S. of A. The tale takes place after a tournament in São Paulo, Brazil, ironically the site of my ATP Tour 250 win, but not the same event. I was at the airport waiting for a flight to Buenos Aires for the next gig. I decided to get some breakfast and walked into the airport's McDonalds. Sitting at a table minding my own business, I heard some yelling and loud footsteps and before I knew it, four Brazilian policemen were towering over me, screaming at me in Portuguese. My heart racing, I reached down to get my passport to show them I was an American and didn't speak any Portuguese. As I did so, I heard the cocking of guns. Looking up, I was staring down the barrels of four rifles literally pointed at my head. As luck would have it, a player I knew from Uruguay walked into the restaurant at that very moment, witnessing what was going on. He dashed over, yelling at the policemen in Portuguese. They lowered their rifles, turned around and ran out. The player explained to me that there had been a robbery inside the airport, and they were looking for someone that resembled me. I was shaken up for hours and remember landing at Buenos Aires airport still trembling. For all I know, I could have ended up in a Brazilian prison that day and will be forever grateful to the player that saved me from that nightmare.

I consider my career on the ATP Tour successful for the most part and I attribute much of that success to being tough. I didn't give away free points, making my opponents work. I understood my strengths and weaknesses and used my strengths well, my forehand being one of them. I was tough mentally when I was locked-in and was good at putting players away when I was ahead. I played good defense, always making my opponents play one extra ball. However, maintaining that toughness and locked-in mode consistently was another matter. I think if I'd been able to maintain those attributes on the desired basis, I could have reached the top 50. The top 20 though? Probably not. I don't believe I had the game, talent, or tools to be a top 20 player—the word "tools" equating to the state and health of my body. In the eight years I was on the tour, I was off two of those years nursing an injury or recovering from surgery. Having played a ton as a junior, I feel that I stressed my body too much before it was fully developed. Back in the late 1970s and early 1980s, fitness was never a part of training. I wish there had been more guidance on injury prevention then. When at Pepperdine, I don't recall lifting a single weight. We did very little group fitness as a team. Our fitness was acquired by spending countless hours on court pounding our bodies into the ground. It was just a matter of time before my body broke down. Over the course of my pro career, I had shoulder surgery, two knee surgeries, a herniated disk in my back, four sprained ankles—just to name a few woes. After my career ended, I had three ankle surgeries and a second shoulder surgery.

Looking back, I had a lot of incredible moments on the tour—along with some very tough weeks and months, where it was a real struggle on and off the court. Unless you're at the top, professional tennis players tend to lose every single week except for the lucky few. It's tough to lose on the tour that much. The challenge is to stay positive and focused on your goals, while simultaneously pushing for excellence each day. Oh, but the thrill of winning matches! Nothing can compare to playing in front of a big crowd, pushing yourself to the limits and coming out on top. Honestly, that thrill is tough to replicate once one's tour career has ended.

In 1997, my racquet was forced to gather some dust. I went back to Pepperdine for unfinished business—taking a year to complete my degree in English. However, I missed tennis and opportunity knocked. I became the Assistant Men's Tennis Coach at my alma mater for a short period of time. Then in 1999, I moved east to become the Assistant Men's Coach at Georgia Tech. Stepping away from coaching in 2002, I changed course, and became Director of Tennis at Olde Towne Athletic Club in Marietta, Georgia. From 2004 to 2006, I became Director of Tennis at Laurel Springs Tennis Club in Suwannee, Georgia. Not surprisingly, the coaching bug came back to bite me, and in 2007, I was named head coach of the women's tennis team at Cornell University. While there, I recruited the first five-star player in Cornell women's tennis history and the team registered its highest national ranking in the university's history during my tenure as head coach. Several years later, those milestones would lead to an offer as assistant coach at the University of Alabama and in 2018, I helped the Crimson Tide team reach the round of 16 at the NCAA tournament. As a result, I was named Southern Region Assistant

Coach of the Year. Clemson University took notice and hired me as their men's head tennis coach in 2019. Speaking of my latest gig as head coach at Clemson, there's an interesting little backstory for the reader. What I didn't discuss earlier, was that I was heavily recruited by Clemson, as well as Pepperdine. I'd finally made my decision to go to Clemson and intended to call the head coach the next morning to accept his offer—the coach at the time being none other than Chuck Kriese. But Coach Kriese beat me to the punch, calling me that night to tell me I'd waited too long to accept his offer, and that he'd given the scholarship away to Jay Berger. Certainly not a shabby move on his part since Jay became an All-American for the university in 1985 and 1986. But now, after all these years, I'm happy to say I'm finally a Tiger!

Do I have career regrets? Of course. If I could do it all over again today, I would switch to a one-handed backhand, and I would train much more off the court as I previously discussed. I would also be much kinder to myself. I'd take more time to enjoy the different cities I traveled, take in their respective cultures. I feel that I put too much pressure on myself and was too laser-focused on tennis to enjoy all the amazing things going on around me. What would I tell up and coming juniors? To pursue a great coach that truly knows what they're doing. Each day, month and year are too critical to be wasting time if you're not training correctly. Be sure to start training off the court once your body develops and spend as much time off court as you do on it. Get strong and be on an injury prevention regimen from the get-go. Make sure that your strokes are technically sound and if not, get them corrected at the earliest possible age. That's critical. Then compete as much as possible—to learn how to win, how to deal with adversity, and how to overcome losing which will always be part of playing. Have balance in your life and take part in outside hobbies to clear your mind of tennis. Burnout is a real problem for juniors. You don't want your fire to get snuffed out! You must enjoy the process and have a real passion for the game. Be realistic about your chances of making it on the tour and don't put all your eggs in one basket unless you are a phenom. During the academic year, take your studies seriously to get a good education. Have an outside coach train you and let your parents be there to support you just as parents. It's much healthier to separate the two if possible. And one last bit of advice—believe in yourself.

WARD'S SKINNY ON ROBBIE

As a former Clemson Tiger, it's an honor to have gotten to know the tennis team's new head coach, Robbie Weiss. Watching his impressive interaction with the team in matches, as well as practice sessions, I've witnessed his experience and professional expertise begin to transform his fine players. The team has tremendous energy and purpose. However, a little luck could go a long way in validating what he's already accomplished. Unfortunately, injuries have been a problem from the beginning, like those that plagued him in his career on the ATP tour. In addition, several of his star players were sidelined for a variety of reasons—one due to a moped accident, another from severe food poisoning, and a few others from Covid.

The jury is still out on what Robbie's legacy will be for Clemson tennis, but if I had to bet, his fine qualities as a former tour player, his years coaching other collegiate programs, and his recruiting expertise will propel the Tigers to the top of the NCAA tennis rankings. Conversing with him and hearing him reflect on his feats during the tour, what struck me most was how modest and down to earth the guy is. He calmly revisits a victory over Ivan Lendl like it was a routine day-in-the-park tennis match. However, a win over this titan in our sport is huge. I could sense a bit of regret from Robbie as he reflected on his tennis journey— why he wasn't able to attain a higher ranking after beating some of the best in the sport. As he discussed earlier, much of his difficulty in maintaining the top level of play necessary to win tournaments stemmed from being so injury prone and thus, his words of wisdom to aspiring tour players are well worth remembering. He mentioned the importance of off court conditioning, to include weight work, which was non-existent in his day. In addition, the players at the top had a physical advantage over him, as he measured in at just six feet, his weight around 165 pounds. Guys like Edberg, Becker, Lendl, and Rafter, all of whom he defeated once, were taller and heavier. Being taller and heavier normally translates into less effort needed to hit a heavy ball, giving a player more options strategically, like having a bigger serve, the opportunity to approach the net more often, or banging ground strokes from the baseline. Robbie was limited to one game plan due to his slightly smaller stature but when he was on, the best had to beware!

I've known Robbie for only a few years but like his peers who have contributed to this book, he has such a giving and kind way about him. Winning the NCAA Singles Tournament, an ATP event along the way, and reaching a career high of 85 in the world is amazing, and like so many others that I've known through my tennis journey, he never received the accolades such a great player deserves. In our individual sport where only the top guys get the bulk of the recognition, it is time to enjoy his story and incredible accomplishments. *Tennis Life* is proud to recognize this enthusiastic tennis player and dedicated head coach of the Clemson Tigers.

There you have it. Mr. Robbie Weiss: a number one junior, a number one college player, a top 100 tour player who beat four former world number one's along the way, three-time assistant men's tennis coach, head women's tennis coach, and now a head men's tennis coach. Now that's what I call a full-blown tennis life.

SOPHIE WOORONS, Ph.D.

I was born in Lille, France in 1973. My parents, Therese and Lucien, were both gymnastics coaches. They figured I would follow in their acrobatic footsteps, but my ability in that sport can be summed up in one succinct word. Inadequate. It was my introduction to tennis at age eight that showed where my true talent and ability lay. I quickly developed the passion and desire to compete in the sport.

At age 14 and as one of the top juniors in France, I was invited to train at I.N.S.E.P. (The National Institute of Sport, Expertise, and Performance). Athletes of every Olympic sport gather and train there, using the best research, the best coaches, and the best facilities in the country. The tennis program is run by the French Tennis Federation. The venue is the who's who of tennis, attracting the likes of Guy Forget, Fabrice Santoro, Amelie Mauresmo, and Henri Leconte. Only the best in France are invited to attend and fortunately for me, I made that vaunted list. The facility is a year-round training center, providing a structured regimen for education and development of advanced tennis skills. I spent the next two years there. I was able to travel and compete around France, and even went to America for the Orange Bowl. Two of my classmates, Fabrice Santoro and Sylvie Sabas, won the 16 and Under titles at the World Championships held in Miami. Another classmate, Noelle van Lottum, played the main draw of the French Open at the age of 15. Thus, practicing alongside such talented peers benefitted me tremendously.

At the age of 17, I began my career as a professional, entering $10K and $25K WTA satellite tournaments. Playing in them helped to defray my expenses and earn points for entry into the larger tournaments. At age 18, I attained a world ranking of 429. Soon after, I decided to enter the French University in Valenciennes and just one month in, I received an offer from Clemson to come play for them. Having been away from home for four years, I declined the offer. However, after graduating from Valenciennes with a B.A. in English, I reached out to the Clemson coaches, and they renewed their offer. I received a full scholarship for my last year of eligibility. Thus, in 1996, I became a Clemson Tiger, playing at the number one position on the team while studying for another B.A. and simultaneously working on my master's thesis for the French University. Interestingly, the research for my thesis was on a comparison between the French and American system of higher education, specifically with regards to athletics.

I had the best experience while at Clemson because I was back to being a student-athlete. You see, even though I had thoroughly enjoyed being on the pro circuit, the academic part of me was missing. And while attending French University was a blast, the athlete part of me felt left out. Thus, finally, I had the best balance between my two passions, tennis and school. Classes, study hall, tournaments, practices, fitness training and weightlifting—I loved it all. I felt great balance and structure in my life and as a result, I excelled. I also had two terrific coaches in Andy Johnston and Jeff Kutac, as well as ten incredible teammates—Americans and internationals who shared the same passion as I did. I had a great season beating, the number one from Duke university, number one from Stanford, number one from Tennessee, and number one for Florida, Jill Craybas, who also just happened to be number one in the country.

In the NCAA team National Championships, we advanced to the Sweet 16 in Tallahassee, Florida, after beating the University of South Carolina and then the University of Georgia. It was May and I remember the temperature being over 100 degrees, and even hotter on the hard courts. It was the survival of the fittest, and I battled and survived, going through a brand new pair of tennis shoes in nine days. My doubles partner, Jan Barrett, and I, also made the quarterfinals in doubles, earning All-American honors in the process. Our coaches, Jeff and Andy, were there every step of the way to carry us through our victories. In singles, I had an incredible run, and made it all the way to the semifinals. At the time, the champion of the NCAA earned a Wild Card for the U.S. Open. I was extremely proud of making it to the final four, defeating extraordinary players along the way, and battling with every inch of my strength and endurance. The semifinal defeat still hurts to this day. I lost my focus at 5-4 in the second, only to lose the set 7-5. I happened to glance at the other semifinal, where the two women playing, number one for Stanford (Blesinski) and number one for Florida (Craybas), were ladies I had defeated the week before, and two months prior, respectively. I knew the title was within my grasp and sadly, that's where I lost focus. Interestingly, after the match concluded, the officials pulled me aside for a random drug test because I guess I must have impressed somebody with either endurance or speed. I didn't mind except for the fact that I was completely dehydrated. It took me an hour and a half to accomplish the task, as it was rather difficult and awkward sitting on the throne while someone watched you perform. Ultimately all was well, and as expected, I was cleared. I had never taken a drug test in my life before and truly supported the need to have them.

I graduated from Clemson and started playing Pro Team Tennis. My first memorable win came in 1998 when I defeated world #89, Karine Quentrec. I played very well that day, and somehow, I was able to achieve an incredibly intense focus. Each shot placement had a purpose and I made Karine play as bad as she could possibly play. It wasn't her fault, it was my doing! And I was enormously proud.

Another great win came against world #115, Iwona Kuczyńska, Martina Navratilova's doubles partner. I simply had an incredible day. She had a big serve and incredible volleys, coming into the net many times. But my passing shots and running speed were on fire, and I just painted the corners. I beat her in three sets, turned around and won the finals in the event in straight sets.

Probably the most unusual win came during a match versus the country of Hungary, when my captain asked me to stall the match! I was up 5-2 and my coach said I needed to slow it down because my doubles partner wasn't there yet … she was taking her high school exams! So I "lost" the next three games as instructed. My partner finally arrived, I closed my singles out 7-5, and my partner and I won doubles. Ironically, at the end of the team competition, we were tied in singles and doubles. We then counted sets lost … tied again. We then counted games … tied again 178 to 178. A perfect tie. If only I could have closed out my second set as planned! There was a playoff and lucky for us, we won our doubles match again.

Later on in my Pro Team Tennis days, I had the chance to play on the same team as Amelie Mauresmo. She was number one and I played number five. It was a talented team, comprised of four grand slam players and me, the college graduate. I must say Amelie was a class act. She was the star, yet she remained friendly to everyone, including other teams. She was smooth, powerful and a fierce competitor. We all knew she was going to make it big. It was a thing of beauty to watch her shine in her craft. She also had a sense of humor and liked to have fun. One evening, we were all sitting around, and she suggested we dance to the *Men in Black* movie theme song, sung by Will Smith. I'm glad there had been no video cameras around because I'm about as good a dancer as I am a gymnast! However, looking back, it was quite fun and a memory for the ages. Another interesting occurrence? When I was playing with Amelie in Pro Team Tennis, there was a 15-year-old practicing on an adjacent court. Everyone was saying, "Hey come see this kid, she is the next big thing, you have to come watch this!" I was like, "Yeah, yeah, heard it before, the next big thing ... sure." As it turns out, the 15-year-old happened to be future number one and superstar, Justine Henin.

As far as nerves and pressure, that just comes with the territory. I do have a humorous story to share in that regard. I was playing doubles with my good friend, Vicky Maes, in a $10K WTA event in Reims, France. In the semifinals, we were down 5-0 in the third set and fought our way back to 5-4. I looked at Vicky and it was evident that the closer score had awakened her nerves—as well as mine. Not good! I uttered the following words in Flemish, *Ik moet eenjte caca doen,* the translation being, "I am so nervous I feel a number two coming!" We both smiled and relaxed instantly, and our comeback continued with a 7-5 third set win! We turned it around and won the title. In addition to our prize money, we won a huge bottle of Taittinger Champagne, which I proudly have on display to this day at my home in Anderson, South Carolina.

Ultimately, I feel as though I have had multiple tennis careers. Beginning as a junior, then followed by the pro tour, college tennis, and professional team tennis, each phase was uniquely interesting and challenging. Now I have the chance to play on the Senior Tour. I've won over ten National Women's Championships by age groups, including Intersectional National Team Championships with the Southern Team. I'm proud to say I played number one for Team USA and won bronze medals at the world championships in Turkey, Miami, and Croatia.

I also had the chance to further my studies. I went on to the University of Georgia, where I completed a Ph.D. in Sport Pedagogy under the leadership of Dr. Paul Schempp. I eventually built the Brookstone Tennis Club, beginning from scratch and supervising the construction of the 10-court facility, where I started the first junior camps and adult program. To include my parents, I gathered an incredible team of talent who helped me grow the club into a flourishing environment with over 200 members, a striving junior program, and 75 adult/senior league teams year-round. My experiences on the tour, and in the classroom, have opened incredible opportunities for myself and my family. It's been an incredible journey.

As you know from just reading his chapter, my 14-year-old son, Noah, is a nationally ranked junior player. Discussing my obligations as both mother and coach, where do I start? With Noah himself of course. He has the work ethic, talent, and desire to succeed playing tennis. However, maintaining a balance with him is very challenging and extremely important. He's my son and nothing will ever take precedence over that. The careful balancing act comes to the forefront when he loses a match. I don't get bothered by it because I'm looking at it from a long-term perspective. Noah, on the other hand, has to personally handle the loss. Thus my reaction involves the tricky combination of showing him that I care, disappointment for the loss, and having my wisdom and experience guide me to channel the loss into something positive for him. That being said, I'm okay with Noah having a bad day. As parents, we all have bad days and can find a way to fit in some decompression time. Junior tennis players don't really control their schedules and I find it important to give Noah space to regroup.

Thankfully, Noah has the work ethic, talent, and opportunities. I'm very satisfied with his progress thus far, and in my opinion, he is much better than I ever was at his age. So much so, he has a good chance of doing well in the long run, as long as he follows a road map. His goal as of this writing is to win a level one tournament. To do so, he needs to keep improving, get stronger, grow as a person—all while staying balanced. He doesn't expect things to happen overnight. We try to play tournaments that are difficult, as well as those that are confidence builders. Too hard of a schedule can hurt a player's confidence. He has an incredible support team, including myself, Andy, my parents, my husband, Colin, the Brookstone coaching team, as well as the necessary financial support. As long as he maintains the desire to play, he has the ability and opportunity to go places with tennis. It's a fun work in progress and time will tell!

WARD'S SKINNY ON SOPHIE

Sophie is one of the most confident people I have ever met—a great attribute to have to be a successful tennis player. She could have played longer on the tour, but she chose to pursue a higher education, to include her Ph.D. in Pedagogy, the science of teaching. She studied major league hitting coaches, golf coaches, volleyball coaches and tennis coaches, to name a few. She analyzed data and eventually studied what experts did in tennis. Doing so helped her to organize her thought process when it came to teaching, to include looking at the types of metaphors coaches use and what possibilities they might see in a player. Thus, she developed an expertise in coaching, making her a natural mentor for her son.

Sophie became a NCAA All-American playing just one year of college tennis. Her prowess on the court was limitless but she wanted to become a more scientific version of herself, certainly accomplishing that and more. Today, she owns Brookstone Tennis in Anderson, South Carolina, where she coaches numerous enthusiastic students, including one very special student named Noah. Thanks for your passion, Sophie! You are a credit to the sport of tennis, and more importantly, a fine role model and person for your son.

THE AUTHOR'S STORY

It's time to share my story. Why? Because I'm the author! No seriously, my story is relevant since most players vying for state, regional and ultimately national titles, fail as I did, their names never to be mentioned or lauded again. The victories, the failures, the mistakes, the regrets, the lessons learned—all part of my past and hopefully by sharing my own humble journey with you, it will add an integral voice to the contributions my peers just made.

My tennis journey began at the age of eight, when my parents gave me a Spaulding Pancho Gonzalez tennis racquet. Though I enjoyed playing several sports, including peewee football and baseball, tennis soon became my passion. It was an easy sport to embrace since all three of my sisters had taken up the game as well. Growing up in Silver Spring, Maryland, a modest suburb of Washington, D.C., we lived about a mile away from good tennis courts at the Indian Springs Country Club. Sadly, the club is no longer in existence, having been gobbled up by suburban sprawl. The vast land mass that once accommodated thirty-six golf holes, a dozen or so tennis courts, an Olympic sized swimming pool and club house, is now occupied by more than 700 homes.

After school each day, I fondly remember my sisters and I flipping the kick stands up on our gear-free bicycles, placing a racquet in the handlebar baskets, and riding the mile to Indian Springs. This was a daily ritual. My first tennis lesson came from an amazing human being, Dr. Mel Richter, an escapee from a Czechoslovakian concentration camp. Dr. Richter had his own unique teaching style, employing gadgets and using terms probably never used by anyone else at that time—or now. One of his teaching tools was a recycled car antenna with tennis balls shish-kabobbed up and down its length at various heights. I also remember the term "sticker" uttered by Dr. Richter in his thick European accent, imploring me to keep the racquet and arm closer to my body on the takeaway. Fifty-five years later, those words still resonate with me as a teaching pro myself.

Eventually, I found myself ranked number one in the 12 and Under, not only in D.C. but in Maryland and the Middle Atlantic region as well, known as M.A.L.T.A. (Middle Atlantic Lawn Tennis Association). I kept a scrapbook of several articles written in the Washington Post and Washington Star newspapers while simultaneously collecting silver trophies. In fact, my mother gave some of them back to the Greater Washington Tennis Association since they were becoming a dime a dozen and I ended up winning the same trophy twice! Being the best in the state and region qualified me to compete in the national championships at the Manker Patton Tennis Center in Chattanooga, Tennessee. This was the most important tournament of the year and only the best players from each state were eligible to play. However, there are times when putting your high ranking on the line can be absolutely demoralizing. After a shocking first round loss to Brad Nabors out of Texas, the worst headline imaginable was plastered on the next day's sports page. I remember it like it was yesterday. It read *Snyder, Only Seed to Lose.* I was seeded seventh and fully expected to live up to my seeding and maybe then some, but the moment and the opponent were just too much for me. Rudely awakened and humbled by Brad's good play, my entire year collapsed like a cheap tent! What an embarrassment. But as fortune would have it, there was someone staying in the same hotel that would come to the rescue of my battered pride. You see, I was good friends with future tennis prodigy, Harold Solomon, practicing with him often at Indian Springs. And my father was best friends with his father, Leonard "Lenny" Solomon. The families had traveled down together for the event, Lenny being in the stands to witness the breakdown of my one-handed backhand. He asked permission from my father if he could sit down and give me a much needed pep talk as there was still a consolation tournament remaining. He told me I had a chance to redeem myself and my ranking if I could just get my head out of my ass, even if it was via the back draw. He followed that with, "We're going out on the practice court and we're not going to leave until you hit 100 backhands in a row." So that's what I did. Lo and behold, I beat a very tough foe by the name of John Geraghty in the finals. The win salvaged an otherwise disastrous event and enabled me to attain a national ranking of 11 by the year's end. So, one would think being #11 in the country, I was heading toward something special in tennis and I honestly bought into that notion and dream. It was at that time, my parents decided to start wintering in Florida and thus, I continued to pursue winning titles by competing in the Sunshine State. My sisters and I attended school in Ft. Lauderdale, practicing daily at now legendary, Holiday Park, home of none other than Chris Evert.

The daily practice routine at Holiday Park became a habit and ritual. It was a training ground for numerous great players from the heyday of American tennis, including Chrissie, Harold Solomon, Brian Gottfried, Jimmy Connors, and the late Vitas Gerulaitis.

Maybe California had better junior development considering the state was vastly larger, but I would put up the world rankings from those mentioned above against anywhere else on the planet at that time.

Fast forward to 1969. My last year in the 14 and Under was significantly more important than my last year in the 12 and Under division, due to the larger field of players and the fact that one must improve to keep up with the ever-increasing talent. Playing daily after school or all day on the weekends helped to hone my skills, and upon reflection, I thought I was pretty good. My practice partners did not include the abovementioned names, although I did manage to hit with Chrissie a time or two. Nevertheless, they did include a very talented group of players that I still maintain friendships with to this day, many of them contributing to this book. Of course, when I faced them in an actual match, the rivalry took precedence over the friendship. Tournaments at Holiday Park, and Florida in general were intense, as bragging rights were a big thing at this tender young age.

Enter the Shamrock Invitational, a very prestigious tournament held in March at David Park in Hollywood, Florida during spring break. This event would attract the finest players in South Florida, along with others outside the region, including a great player named Trey Waltke. And wouldn't you know, the luck of the draw would pit me against him in the second round! An interesting story, so please hear me out.

My coach was an Australian player and one of the top teaching professionals in the world, Warren Woodcock. Unbeknownst to me, he decided to show up at my match. I was honored but also nervous that his presence might affect my performance. Would I go out there and hit the shots we had been working on or would I get tight and choke? The guy on the other side of the net was a much better player, possessed a one-handed backhand that was as elegant and efficient as any stroke in the country, and had touch and shots to compliment a repertoire that was quite impressive to say the least. Oh, don't get me wrong, my game could be very good at times when I got my head out of the way. But I knew I was not in Trey's league and figured that I had two chances—slim and none. To my surprise, the presence of Coach Woodcock standing tall on the sidelines inspired me to put on an improbable performance. Amazingly, I executed my shots without getting tight, and lo and behold, I beat Trey. That win would become indelibly tattooed in my mind for years to come. It has been fifty plus years since that victory. Back in touch with him recently, he claimed he had absolutely no recollection of the defeat. Obviously, my win over the stud was a bigger deal than his loss to a nobody. Eventually, he visited an online newspaper archive source and dug up the stats from our match. He reluctantly acquiesced, acknowledging the defeat. However, being the consummate competitor that he still is, he couldn't help but bring up his defeat of me in the Orange Bowl 10 and Under ... which humorously, I can't recall! I suppose turnabout is fair play among old rivals and I wouldn't expect anything less.

The victory over Trey was pivotal in my tennis journey as it gave me confidence and validation that I was pretty good. Just maybe my playing future was bright. I was intent on making it to the big stage and with the good win, it seemed I had a chance. My lessons continued with Coach Woodcock, the summer circuit just around the corner. My first stop was at the prestigious Western Open tournament held in Middletown, Ohio. The tournament had a limited field but atop the draw was one of the best junior players to ever play, Billy Martin. At the time, he was ranked as the nation's second best in the Under 12 Singles. He possessed the most solid game a player could ever have, with a two handed backhand and flat forehand that would find targets with consistency unlike any player that I had ever competed against. I played well in the earlier rounds, winning all my matches against higher seeded players, and ultimately found myself facing Billy in the final. I had my chances. He won the first set 6-4. I was up in the second set but could not close the deal. He won it 10-8. Looking back, he was the best competitor I ever faced in juniors and his record thereafter supports my assertion. An interesting tidbit. I served and volleyed against him. I wish there was a video of that match, but the VCR and Camcorder had not yet been invented. I still find it hard to believe that I could make it to the net behind my serve and volley against this titan of a player. I dislike the feeling of being satisfied with a loss, but the reality is, Billy was head and shoulders better than me, and to play him so close certainly exceeded most expectations. Bottom line, I departed Ohio a better player.

Next stop—Chattanooga for the National 14 and Under. I was seeded and projected to at least make it to the round of sixteen but ran into a formidable foe in Horace Reid. Horace had an unusual wardrobe accessory— about fifty rubber bands on his wrist! And man, did he have a huge forehand. Along with his quickness getting around my slice backhand, it would prove to be the big difference in the match. My ability to dominate at the net was thwarted by his speed and power. He crushed me and my teenage dreams! The loss knocked the wind out my sails since the Nationals was the showcase for the nation's talent and yet once again, I had failed. Playing Horace proved to me that to become a great player, one needed possession of a solid bread and butter shot. My game at that time was fairly solid, with a better volley than most. My choice of shots and strategy was to always pressure my opponent by taking the net at every opportunity, thus forcing him into hitting a passing shot. This strategy worked against most but on the big stage, and against a huge forehand like Horace's, it just wasn't good enough. I ended up being ranked number 20 in the country but that was way below my lofty goals and once again, the most important tournament of the year eluded me.

From that point on, my national ranking continued to plummet every year due to a string of defeats. I had a very harsh reality check and I'll never forget my father sitting down with me to face the music. My dream to make it on the big stage and the ATP Tour was never going to materialize, because at the end of the day, I just wasn't good enough. My goals then changed and though I knew the tour was most likely not in the cards, I felt my game was good enough to justify a college scholarship. And voila, I received one. Winning the very tough district championships in Ft. Lauderdale alongside my partner, Daniel Tauber, I was highly touted by Clemson University as a doubles specialist and recruited with Daniel to fill the void in their doubles line up. Both of us recruited by Coach Duane Bruley, we didn't do well together for some reason. We ended up playing with different partners and had mediocre results at Clemson. Once again, my game just wasn't good enough. Always painful to admit but necessary to make no excuses. At least I was able to repay my parents for their large financial sacrifice in the early junior days with a full ride through college.

So, the tough question. Why wasn't I more successful as a player? If I knew back then what I know now, would that have made a difference? Absolutely! Could I have made it on the tour with my accumulated knowledge and learned wisdom from over the years if I could have a do over? A good possibility. But could I have broken into the top 100? Highly unlikely—due to a little thing called DNA. I can thank my friend and rival, Trey, for his frank assessment of my compromised deoxyribonucleic acid. I told him about a recent, tightly contested loss to a very good player in the National Senior Tournament held in Atlanta in which I failed to close the deal. And he simply responded to me, "Ward, it's just part of your DNA." In other words, I learned how to compete and that's certainly one factor in being successful. But possessing a lethal backhand like Trey or that huge forehand like Horace, or the tenacity and heart of the great Harold Solomon, well, I must be realistic—I was not on their level. Top 200 maybe, but without a huge weapon, I could never have achieved greatness. That being said, and adding the adage, "Never say never", I would have spent a lot more time developing a big forehand. And I would have grooved an inside out forehand that would penetrate my opponent's backhand corner and then run around my backhand at every opportunity to use it. Growing up with the old technology of wooden racquets limited one's ability to hit with tremendous topspin but I can't disregard those pioneers of tennis who played outside the box and developed strokes to achieve loftier results. An example of one of the pioneers? Harold again. I witnessed his mental and physical tenacity firsthand. I faced him in the Maryland State High School championships. I got off to a good start, unnerving him with my pretty solid serve and volley, taking the very slim lead of 4-3 in the first set. But then he reeled off the next nine games, putting me emphatically in my place. He had a return of serve and two-handed backhand that put me on my heels, even after I hit my big serve. His game dominated the backcourt, and he took time away from his opponents by taking the ball on the rise. This was something higher level players were good at, putting relentless pressure on you at every given moment during a rally and in effect, taking you out of rhythm. I would have worked more myself taking the ball on the rise but hitting a two-handed backhand wasn't comfortable for me. No doubt the ability to hit this shot was an advantage.

How about practice? Did I fail there? I don't think so. My daily routine was good enough, especially in Florida, where practice would be with an array of very tough players, ranging from girls like Chris Evert and sister, Jeanne, Laurie and Carrie Fleming, and Carol and Judy Groever, to guys like Brad Milton, Chris Sylvan, Craig Campbell, Bill Tompkins, Drew Evert, Rick Quinby, Larry Gottfried, and Harold Solomon. What about when I was in college? Did I think that I still had a shot at making the tour even after my disappointing freshman year at Clemson? Not really but one could still hope. That was until I practiced with Harold during Christmas break of my sophomore year. It was at this point in his career that he had reached the world top ten. Had Harold and I not been lifelong friends, doubtful he would have taken the time as a top tenner to even step on the court with me. But then again, he loved to beat the crap out of anyone who dared to compete against him. Well, it was a big mistake on my part asking him for the court time. Long story short, he basically thrashed me with his amazing serve returns and ground strokes. He took whatever confidence I had left and sent it off into oblivion. The scars of battling him put the final nail in my coffin. However, looking back, I realize my college kid hothead assessment of "that's it, I'm toast, no tennis future for me!" was probably a bit of rush to judgment. I regret that I marked the loss so significantly. I didn't give myself a chance to learn from the defeat even though he was on a whole other level. Did I take into consideration the advantage he had playing on his private home court and on his favorite surface, Hartru? No, not at the time. Did I take into consideration he might have just been on fire that day? What if we'd played on a different surface and he'd had a bad day? Maybe the outcome would have been more encouraging. If I'd been a little more objective at the time, it's possible my tennis future could have turned out differently. I put the ceiling up so high, it blocked the stars! The lesson learned here is never base your tennis future on one practice match—even if it is with a tennis legend.

So, there you have it. I'd finally given up the last vestiges of my dream for good and life moved onto finding real income producing opportunities. My post Clemson years consisted of various entrepreneurial ventures (several quite entertaining, which I expound upon in my other book, *Shark Life, A Memoir*). After 40 some odd years of successes, failures, and general burn out, I found myself tired and frustrated. The real estate debacle in 2007 and 2008 was the final straw. It caught me like quicksand and nearly buried me alive. It was time for a major change. At the time, my son was attending Clemson. So, his mother and I decided to make the move from Florida to South Carolina to be closer to him. We found the amenity rich gated community of Keowee Key, located on beautiful Lake Keowee and just a 20-minute drive to Clemson. The main amenity drawing me in? Tennis of course. Before I knew it, the perfect opportunity presented itself—I found myself hired along with Brad Huff, as one of two head tennis pros, a job-sharing arrangement that gives us alternating weeks off. I'd come full circle—back to my first love. And that's what I've been doing for the last six years. To see the club members progress in the sport is incredibly gratifying. The rewards go far deeper than anything I ever could have imagined. At the end of the day, I hope they will remember me for being a tennis pro that sincerely cared about making them better tennis players. I can't stress how wonderful it feels when a member sends me an email saying that I helped them achieve a breakthrough in their game. It gives me a sense of joy that is seldom experienced in the dog-eat-dog business world.

I believe that I've come into my own as a tennis professional since that first day on the Keowee Key courts. For the most part, my teaching philosophy has evolved due to what I learned from teaching professionals and players alike. I learned the game from some of the best, including Jimmy Evert, Warren Woodcock, Nick Bollettieri, William Riordan, Lenny Solomon, Dr. Richter, Mike Sprengelmeyer and the Clemson Hall of Fame coach, Chuck Kriese. My methodology combines not only the key elements these greats espoused, but my own experience in competitive matches, both in college and satellite pro events. It's my personal belief that a tennis professional with a background playing at least at the college level, offers much more wisdom and expertise for obvious reasons, than someone without it. My methodology combines several of the following fundamentals taught by the previously mentioned instructors, along with my own interpretation:

- Jimmy Evert would reiterate, "Racquet back, watch the ball, okay ... racquet back, watch the ball, okay ...." Suffice to say tennis is not nearly as simple as Mr. Evert made it sound, but I can tell you without a doubt that if you were ever lucky enough to observe this wonderful man teaching a student at Holiday Park, those key words were repeated over and over and over ... until the lesson was over.

- Warren Woodcock—This Australian great was an incredible teacher and player alike. Some of his students included Harold Solomon, Chris Sylvan, Vitas Gerulaitis, Peter Fleming, Ricky Meyer and probably numerous others that were not familiar to me. Warren was a big believer of a pre-shot routine on the serve (evidenced by Peter Fleming and Vitas Gerulaitis), as well as a distinct take back on the ground strokes. Among the many fine points this maestro ingrained in my psyche was the need for good footwork, and by the end of the lesson trust me, you were breathing very hard!

- Nick Bollettieri—Nick was a brilliant promoter of the game and such a selfless man. He had a big heart and passion for his players. He emphasized important fundamentals among his top students. He attracted the nation's best juniors to his academy, his skills in communicating his vast knowledge and expertise to his students, legendary. Suffice to say, the emphasis on possessing a big shot was a critical and necessary component of graduating successfully from his academy.

- William Riordan—This man was an incredible tactician and knew the game better than anyone I had ever been around. To sit and hear him tell stories about a fictitious player he conjured up named Stanley "Stan" Pinzack was priceless. One would swear this might have been the greatest player ever to walk on the court. Mr. Riordan would entertain his students with stories about Stanley's mighty serve, which could rip the racquet out of some opponent's hand, and that his uniform included a war helmet! I can't ever thank this man enough for coaching me to a victory over a player much better than I, in the Eastern Shore tournament in his hometown of Salisbury, Maryland. It was a match against Jonathon Gross from New York. He had defeated the very tough Tim Delaney in the quarterfinals, and there I stood figuring to have two chances for an improbably victory in the semis—slim and none. But the great Mr. Riordan calmly asked me, "Do you want to win the match"? "Of course," I replied. The wise one then said, "Okay, you must do what I tell you to do." He told me when playing a two hander, go to the other side. He said don't hit any balls to his backhand—no matter what. He forecasted that if I could withstand Gross's forehand, it would no doubt break down by the end of the match and he would be beside himself. Fast forward to my victory since the first set did not go my way and the guy hit ended up hitting many good forehands. I looked over at Mr. Riordan and he gave me a positive and reassuring gesture that it would be okay. By the third set, Gross could not find the court with his forehand! I won a match that I never would have without the wise guidance of the great Mr. Riordan. May he rest in peace.

- Mike Sprengelmeyer—Mike played on the tour in the late 1960's making it to the U.S. Open and tangling with many of the tour greats along the way. Mike has an innate knowledge of the game and when I can't solve one of my member's shot issues, I simply show him the video from my iPhone and voila—he renders the solution! Not only is Mike a great human being, but he has a passion for the game and gives his time to anyone interested in improving. His son, Mitch, a former All-American at Clemson, has a great stat in that he never lost a match to the Bryan Brothers. Mitch learned from his dad and that speaks volumes.

- Chuck Kriese—I had issues with my low volley, and vividly recall Chuck hitting a basket full of balls directly at my feet, forcing me to get down to hit those tough low volleys. In an ensuing match versus our rival, the University of South Carolina, I remember hitting a deft low volley winner while Coach was watching in the stands and hearing his enthusiastic shout of approval. The passion from this great coach is unmatched.

- Lenny Solomon—aka "The Fox". Lenny, father of Harold had wisdom beyond his years in most anything he touched—except for running the boat he co-owned with my father! I won't get into those entertaining stories, but he didn't come by the nickname of "Fox" by accident. Remember how he advised Steve Krulevitz to a great win at Kalamazoo over Mac Claflin? Well, Lenny did the same for me in the 12 and Under nationals in Chattanooga, Tennessee. I was in the finals of the feed-in consolation versus a future All-American and tour player, John Geraghty. Lenny had observed my backhand failure upon losing earlier in the main draw, and he politely asked my dad if he could spend some time with me before the feed-in draw began. My dad gave him the green light and before I knew it, he was standing on the opposite side of the net hitting balls to my backhand, insisting that I hit one hundred in a row! I am proud to say I followed his direction successfully and won the event.

All these great teachers, coaches and passionate lovers of the game helped to mold me into the teaching pro that I am today and I'm grateful to each and every one of them. There is no one size fits all when it comes to teaching but there is a root cause to many issues and that is precisely what I endeavor to do with my students—identify the cause rather than the effect. In other words, by solving the cause, the effect becomes a non-issue. For example, one of the most common swing ailments is late ball contact. The effect of this is a lack of follow through, power loss, no weight transfer, and inconsistency. My goal is to keep the solution simple. Prepare earlier—the opposite arm pointed at the incoming ball and then meeting it out in front. This process will eliminate many of the effects as described above.

Another tip I'd like to pass on comes from good friend and *Tennis Life* contributor, Rob Castorri. He says to "Hit the six and cover the twelve." Rob learned this from Ivan Lendl and shared it with me. I find this tip to be extremely helpful for most of my students and use it with tremendous success. Imagine the ball as a clock with the bottom of it being six and the top being twelve. Try and hit the bottom of the ball (position 6) and then cover the 12 (top position) with your finish. This eliminates the net initially and by covering the 12, it brings the ball into the court. This might be the single best tip that I've ever heard.

One more thing I incorporate when teaching has to do with the serve. The idea was given to me by my good friend and former doubles partner at Clemson, Pike Rowley. It comes by way of British player, Mark Cox, and Pike's wife, Laurie Fleming (a contributor to *Tennis Life*). Mark and Laurie played World Team Tennis and were teammates for the Florida Flamingos. Mark simply said, to hit a serve, one should begin by imagining a fence directly in front of you. You shouldn't hit the ball until it's above the fence. Then follow through to bring it into the service box. That being said, you must start out with a proper ball toss as many serving errors originate with an improper one. I tell my students to toss the ball approximately one foot out in front and at the 1:00 position on the clock. Add Mark's suggestion and your serving woes go away. Of course, not as simple as I make it sound, but I guarantee you will have more success. One caveat though: unless you're the height of John Isner or Reilly Opelka, you must hit up on the ball. These fortunate giants only hit down into the box and as luck or genes would have it, being close to seven feet tall makes the serve a natural weapon.

I hope these simple tips will help you to improve and become a more complete tennis player. It's never too late to get better in and I've now made it my mission as a tennis professional to preach one's ability to learn, regardless of age, and refute the adage of "can't teach an old dog new tricks". Tennis will always be there for me as my first love—in the form of recreational, teaching and tournament opportunities. It truly is the sport of a lifetime. And speaking of a lifetime, I stumbled across something on the internet that took me completely by surprise, my pride most pleased after all these years and of course, I feel the need to share. It was an online reader commentary from the May 28, 2020, Baltimore Sun newspaper, the writer of the commentary an absolute stranger to me. He talks about my tennis playing ability ... along with Baltimore Colts quarterback, Johnny Unitas, all taking place back in 1970! You're thinking, huh? It will make sense once you read it:

A FOND TENNIS MEMORY OF BALTIMORE'S JOHNNY U/READER COMMENTARY

For the Baltimore Sun, May 28, 2020, at 12:29

It has been about 50 years since I played in a Baltimore City tennis tournament and lost 6-1, 6-3 to a kid named Timmy Rimpo. At that time, I lived on the VA Hospital base at Fort Howard and had learned tennis the previous year from an old security guard named Ray, who was a champion boxer in his own day. Well, after teaching me all that he knew about tennis that year, Ray decided that it would serve me well to sign up for the 12-and-under tournament being held at some fancy golf course and tennis club in Baltimore. With my parents' permission, I signed up for the tournament and was beaten soundly in the first round. Still, it was fun to come back the next day and watch Ward Snyder, a highly ranked tennis player in the 14-and-under mid-Atlantic region, dispatch a number of very good tennis players. According to the newspaper article I read, his father was an attorney in Baltimore, and they lived there part of the year and in Florida the remaining months. And no doubt, he was a talented tennis player — he moved his opponents around the court and then took advantage of any short balls with crisp volleys at the net. Like dozens of other spectators, I enjoyed watching the tennis matches.

But then during a break in one of the matches, an older guy in his 30s asked me if I wanted to hit with him on the adjacent tennis court. He said his name was John Smith and he had two tennis rackets, so why not hit a few tennis balls with him. Mr. Smith was just learning the game and could run down any shot I hit. I like to think we were fairly evenly matched, but I suspect that is a memory that has grown with the years. After rallying for a while, we started a match — until one of the strings broke on my racket. Without hesitation, Mr. Smith switched rackets with me, and we finished our set with him playing with a broken string. He was a competitor in chasing down every one of my shots, but he was more than fair and gave me a close call or two. He was a class act, a hell of a nice guy to hit some tennis balls with a 12-year-old kid who had just lost his first tennis match, and he left me feeling good about myself and playing tennis. That said, he didn't quite fit into the country club atmosphere there.

After Mr. Smith thanked me for hitting with him and encouraged me to continue playing tennis, my older brother approached me and asked me if I knew who I had been hitting tennis balls with, and I answered, "John Smith." He promptly told me I that I was an idiot and that I had just played tennis with Johnny Unitas.

Submitted by John Ryan, Potomac Falls, VA.

John Ryan, wherever you are now, I'm incredibly honored that you remembered my "crisp volleying" after all these years and that you thought enough about my playing ability as a teen to write about it for the Baltimore Sun—50 years later! Me and Johnny U sharing the spotlight, who would have thunk? Ah, those were my glory days ...

TENNIS LIFE IN PICTURES

Rob Castorri

Ferocious Taylor Dent!

Ward and Taylor at a USPTA Conference
Serve Demonstration

Jenny Dent, Taylor, and father, Phil Dent, at their academy

John McEnroe and Larry Gottfried

Ilie Nastase, his girlfriend, Steve Krulevitz and wife, Ann

Billy Martin and Trey Waltke

Legendary UCLA Coach Glenn Bassett and Billy Martin

Living the dream in Rome! Trey, Billy, Ruta (Vitas's sister), Vitas Gerulaitis

Martina Navratilova, Trey, and Chris Evert

Ivan Lendl and Trey at Wimbledon

Brad Huff and ex Clemson Tigers—Ward Snyder, Fernando Maynetto, Chris Brown, Steve Vaughn, Pike Rowley, Dewey Stroud, and Andy Johnston, reuniting for bragging-rights tennis and a Clemson home football game in 2014.

Ricky Meyer back in the day

Ricky Meyer playing John McEnroe at U.S. Open

Bjorn Borg and Ricky Meyer

Keith and his wife, Marilyn

Keith winning a Penn Circuit Event

Harold Solomon and Adriano Panatta

Harold and Ward in 2020

Chris Sylvan, Ward Snyder, John Geraghty, Bill Tompkins at the Sarasota Bath and Racquet Club event

Chris Sylvan and Trey Waltke catching up

Robbie Weiss after beating world #2 Stefan Edberg in the 1992 Miami Open

Bunner Smith, Nick Bollettieri Mid-Atlantic Tennis Camp Brochure

Bunner Smith and Nick Bollettieri with Team Success Tennis

Noah Johnston with mom/coach Sophie looking on

Noah (left) receiving the gold ball at the 2022 Easter Bowl with runner-up, Evan Sharygin

Noah, father/coach Andy, and mother/coach Sophie

Lawson Duncan at Clemson

Noppawan Lertcheewakarn and her coach, Chuck Kriese, at the 2009 Wimbledon Ball

Noppawan Lertcheewakarn, Roger Federer, and Chuck Kriese chatting it up at the Wimbledon Ball

Chris Sylvan, top left, coming in at #2 in the Fastest Serve Contest during the 1976 Pacific Southwest Open

PROFESSIONAL SATELLITE TENNIS
Growth-Entertainment-Rewards

GROWTH

Just a few years ago the younger, up-and-coming players in the world had few places to play to improve their game. With the advent of satellite tennis, these men and women were offered an opportunity to play on circuits specifically designed for players ranked below 100 in the world. W.A.T.CH. (now USTA/PENN) started the satellites off and was followed by the Southern and Missouri Valley circuits, the Futures and the American Express circuit. Satellite prize money has increased dramatically—from less than $75,000 in 1973 to more than $250,000 this year.

Player participation has also grown substantially. The USTA/PENN circuit qualifying draws have 256 players from twenty-five or more countries playing for the eight slots in the main draw. Interest is so keen that we even have "mini satellites" of these tournaments each week. The unsuccessful qualifiers play at another site from Thursday through Saturday.

ENTERTAINMENT

Satellite tournaments are enjoyable social events. Players stay in private housing, parties with club members are common and Pro-Am tournaments and clinics are normal. The players are vying for prize money and those "all-important points" so the tennis is competitive and entertaining. The international flavor of the circuit adds a unique touch which few other sports can offer.

REWARDS

The rewards are numerous! The players gain experience, money and points to help their world ranking. The clubs benefit from the publicity and the local community from the fine tennis. The media has a major event to cover,

By **Dave Grant**
USTA/Penn
Circuit
Administrator

club members can socialize with the players, and sponsors gain from exposure of the circuit. All in all everyone benefits.

We sincerely thank all tournament committees for their efforts, all local sponsors for their support, and the USTA and Penn for their financial backing of the circuit.

As satellites continue to grow, enjoy them and participate in the rewards of helping build tomorrow's champions.

Dave Grant
Circuit Administrator

Acknowledgements

Suzanne Grant	John Smith
CIRCUIT SECRETARY	DIRECTOR USTA PRO TENNIS
John Kunnen	Mimo Sullivan
CIRCUIT ADVANCE MAN	PAUL SULLIVAN TENNIS APPAREL

CIRCUIT SITES

DATE	CLUB ADDRESS	SURFACE	QUAL. SIZE	QUAL. START	TOUR. DIR.	PRIZE MONEY
Feb. 11-19	West Side Racquet Club, P.O. Box 279A, Vero Beach, FL 32960, (305) 562-7690	Har-Tru	128	Feb. 11	Dale Talbert	$10,000
	SPONSOR—Jim Wood—Superior Fertilizer & Chemical Co.					
Feb. 18-26	Bath & Racquet Club of Lakeland, 400 Imperial Blvd., Lakeland, FL 33803, (813) 646-0639, 646-2644	Hard	Open	Feb. 18	Jack Hamelryck	$10,000
	SPONSOR—Michelob—Bernie Little Distributors					
Feb. 25-March 5	Beach & Tennis Club, 1070 Hickory Blvd., Bonita Beach, FL 33923, (813) 992-1121	Har-Tru	Open	Feb. 25	Gene Nolan	$8,500
	SPONSOR—George Freeland—Southgate & Naples Datsun					
March 4-12	Hialeah Recreation Department, City Hall P.O. Box 40, Hialeah, FL 35011, (305) 822-4521	Hard	Open	March 4	Mike Jula	$10,000
	SPONSOR—City of Hialeah—Dale Bennett (Mayor)					
March 11-19	Oceanside Country Club, Box 367, Ormond Beach, FL 32074, (904) 672-1921	Har-Tru	Open	March 11	Fred Clouser	$10,000
	SPONSOR—Birthplace of Speed Patrons					
March 18-26	Pensacola Racquet Club, Box 1183, Pensacola, FL 32503, (904) 434-2434	Har-Tru	Open	March 18	Bob Balink	$7,500
	SPONSOR—William E. Pernewell—First American Bank					
March 31-April 2 GRAN PRIX	Sweetwater Oaks R.C., 1000 Wekiva Springs Rd., Longwood, FL 32750, (305) 869-1910	Har-Tru	—	—	Bill Treise	$12,000
	SPONSOR—E. Everette Huskey—The Huskey Co.					

W.A.T.CH./Penn USTA Circuit Flyer

ONE MORE THING

My sincere gratitude and thanks to each person in *Tennis Life,* for participating in my endeavor and taking time out of their busy schedules to do so.

Before I reached out to the first contributor, I drafted a general questionnaire with subject matter I thought relevant to a player's or coach's experience. They incorporated their answers into the individual stories you just read. The remarkable fortitude shown from these men and women throughout their tennis journeys is nothing short of admirable. Unfortunately, the room at the top is small. They were knocking on that small room, but the men and women at the top were stingy. A very fine line indeed, but upon hearing their firsthand accounts, I consider the contributors in *Tennis Life* to be great in their own right. I hope you the reader feel the same.

Speaking of the *Tennis Life* readers, if you would ever like a lesson or advice from the handful of players-turned-teaching pro's represented within these pages, here is what they offer and how you can contact them:

Evan Phillips
Online coaching only. Can be reached at
evphil50@comcast.net.

Rob Castorri
General Manager at the Chapel Hill Tennis Club, in Chapel Hill, North Carolina. Stop by and ask him for a game.

Taylor Dent
The Birch Racquet and Lawn Club, home of the Dent Tennis Academy
660 Keller-Smithfield Road
Keller, TX 76248
817-431-2000
info@thebirch.com

Steve Krulevitz
Steve will answer any of your junior, college, or pro tour tennis related questions. Just email him at **Krulevitztennis@gmail.com or** Vitz19@aol.com.

Bunner Smith
You can find him online at Bunner Smith Tennis or social media via Facebook.

ACKNOWLEDGEMENTS

My parents, Myrta and Leonard Snyder, and siblings, Liz, Louise and Kathy. If my parents hadn't introduced me to tennis, and if my sisters hadn't taken the time to hit with their kid brother, this book wouldn't exist.

Lenny (The Fox) Solomon—My dad's close friend and role model. Lenny was the light in a dark room. His energy and enthusiasm for life, and his love for tennis can never be forgotten. Never a bystander in life, he helped me win a national junior title by inspiring me to employ grit, determination, and hard work. I wouldn't have won the trophy without him.

Harold Solomon—Harold is a chip off the old block of Lenny. No matter the competition, he is the best fighter I have ever known. But always the gentleman, displaying a kind and generous smile after he beat you. We share many wonderful childhood memories, and I grew up watching him on the sidelines, as he attained records, trophies, and awards around the globe.

Dr. Mel Richter—He gave me my first tennis lesson at Indian Springs Country Club in 1965. I like to use a few of his unique terms when giving lessons.

William (Bill) Riordan—This tennis legend inspired me to the most amazing win in my junior career. His tactical brilliance was special and his storytelling unmatched. As mentioned in my chapter, the mythical character he created, Stanley "Stan" Pinzack captivated his students. I spent numerous hours practicing with his son, Billy, and together, they inspired me to become a better player.

Warren Woodcock—This Australian tennis professional taught me concepts that I like to pass on to my students. One of the best instructors I have ever known, he inspired me to defeat one of the top juniors in the U.S., the victory forever embedded in my memory.

Coach Chuck Kriese—This pioneer in coaching taught me so much about the true meaning of competing. One of the greatest warriors I've ever known, he defied conventional wisdom and took the Clemson tennis program to another level. So grateful to have Chuck in my life.

Robin Elder—This Keowee Key tennis player and all-in-one editor/cover designer/self-publisher/author produced my memoir, *Shark Life*. Her tenacious resourcefulness, creativity, and desire to create the same professional product with *Tennis Life* has been invaluable. And having to deal with yours truly during the process and my constant "multitasking"? Well, I'd say that makes her a saint!

Keowee Key members. First and foremost, thanks to Kevin McCracken for having faith in Brad Huff and myself to turn the tennis program around. Teaching the members, seeing them improve, and receiving their positive feedback and appreciation, is just another reason I wanted to write *Tennis Life*. The warm reception I've been given the last five years at this country club community has been incredibly special to me. And a special thanks to my hitting buddy, Scott "The Professor" Irwin!

Last but not least, I'd like to give a shout out to a group of very special players who left an indelible mark on my tennis, during both my junior and college playing days. Thanks for the fond memories and sharing the court with me! The Middle Atlantic contingent: Billy Riordan, John Foote, Gary Addie, and Randy Kennedy; The South Florida contingent: Chris Evert, Brad Milton, John Geraghty, Frank Froehling, Andy Guerke and Rick Quinby; The Clemson University contingent: Steve Vaughn, Ali Akbar, Asif Hussain, Bhanu Nunna, Herb Cooper, Howie Orlin, Pike Rowley, Stefan LaPorte, Dewey Stroud, Chris Brown, Dick Milford, Mike Gandolfo, Mark Buechler, John Anderson, and Dave (Cacti) Loder.

ABOUT THE AUTHOR

If you want to know more about me and my wild ride through life, please check out my first book, *Shark Life, A Memoir*. I can't think of a better way to tell you more about myself. I've had some truly crazy fishing and business adventures that I think you will find most entertaining. Scanning the QR code will send you to my Amazon page for more details and a link to purchase.

Printed in Great Britain
by Amazon